A Brush with the Borders

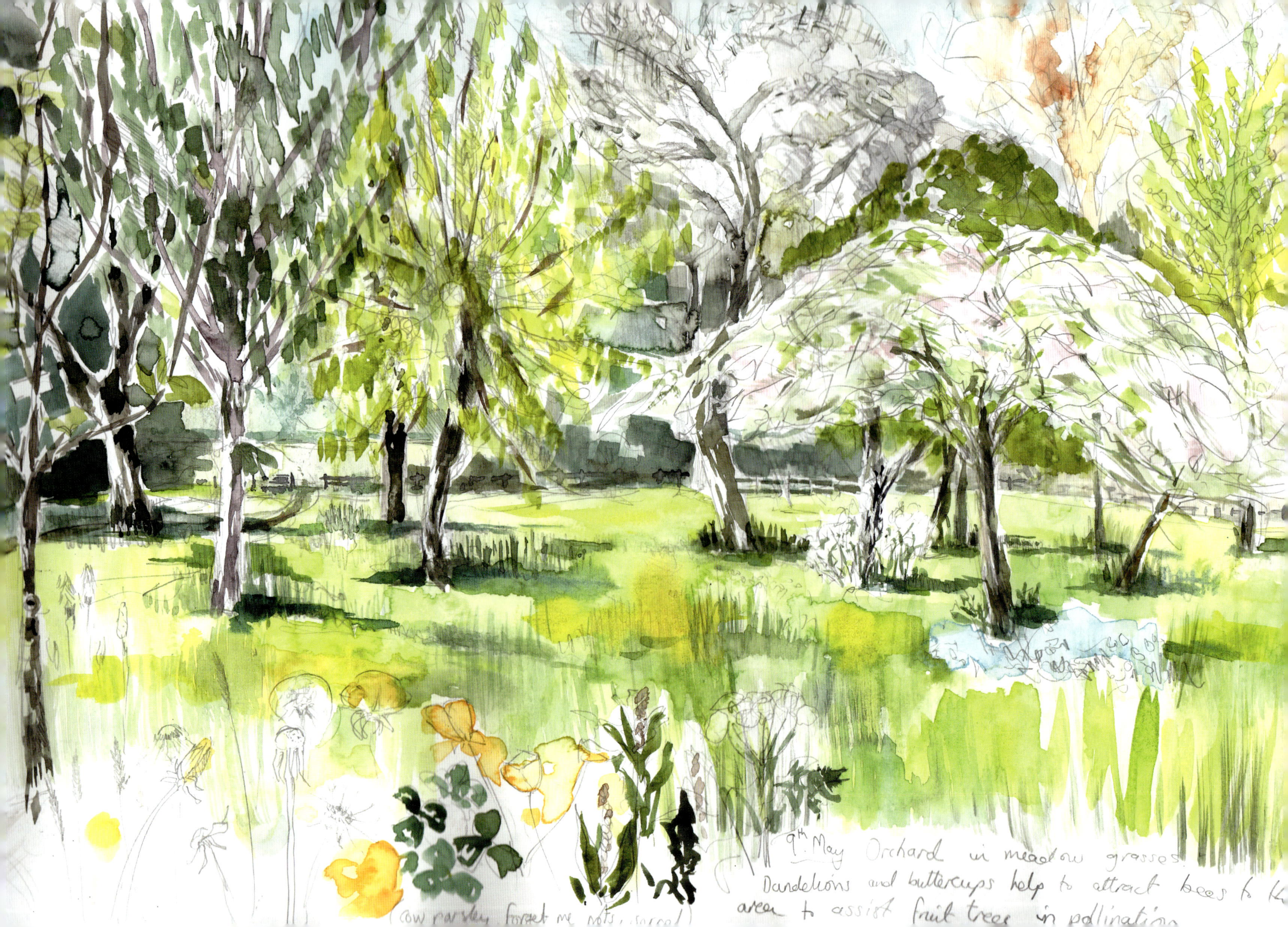
9th May Orchard in meadow grasses.
Dandelions and buttercups help to attract bees to
area to assist fruit trees in pollination
(cow parsley forget me nots, sorrel)

A Brush with the Borders

An Artist's Year

K̲athryn M̲oore

LOGASTON PRESS

First published April 2024 by Logaston Press, The Holme, Church Road, Eardisley HR3 6NJ. www.logastonpress.co.uk. An imprint of Fircone Books Ltd.

ISBN 978-1-910839-73-7

Designed and typeset by Richard Wheeler in 11 on 17 Garamond. Cover design by Richard Wheeler.

Printed and bound in the Czech Republic.

Logaston Press is committed to a sustainable future for our business, our readers and our planet. The book in your hands is made from paper certified by the Forest Stewardship Council.

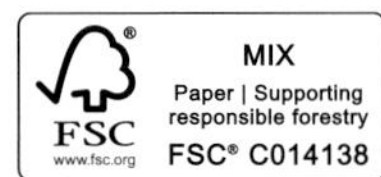

British Library Catalogue in Publishing Data. A CIP catalogue record for this book is available from the British Library.

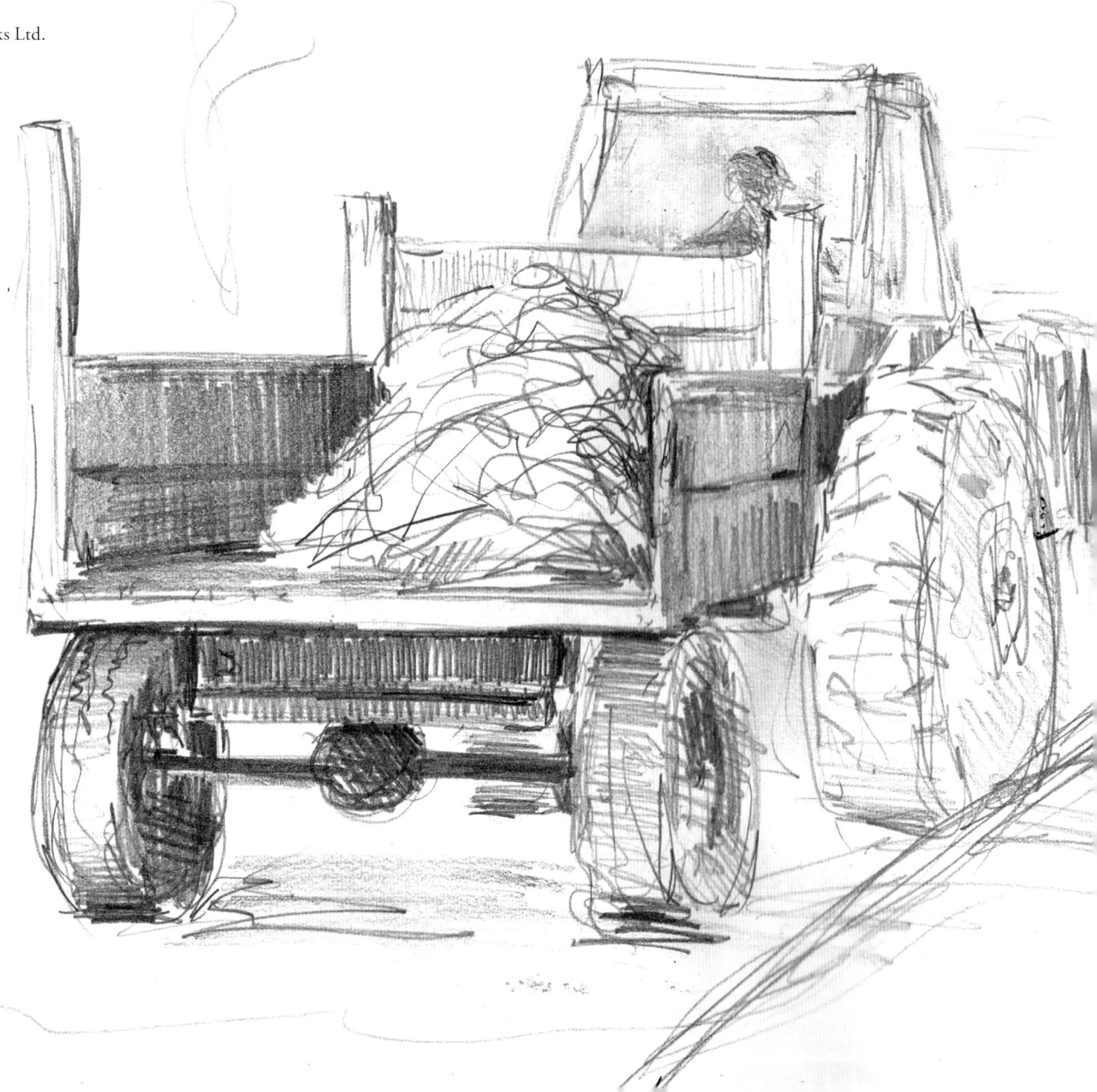

CONTENTS

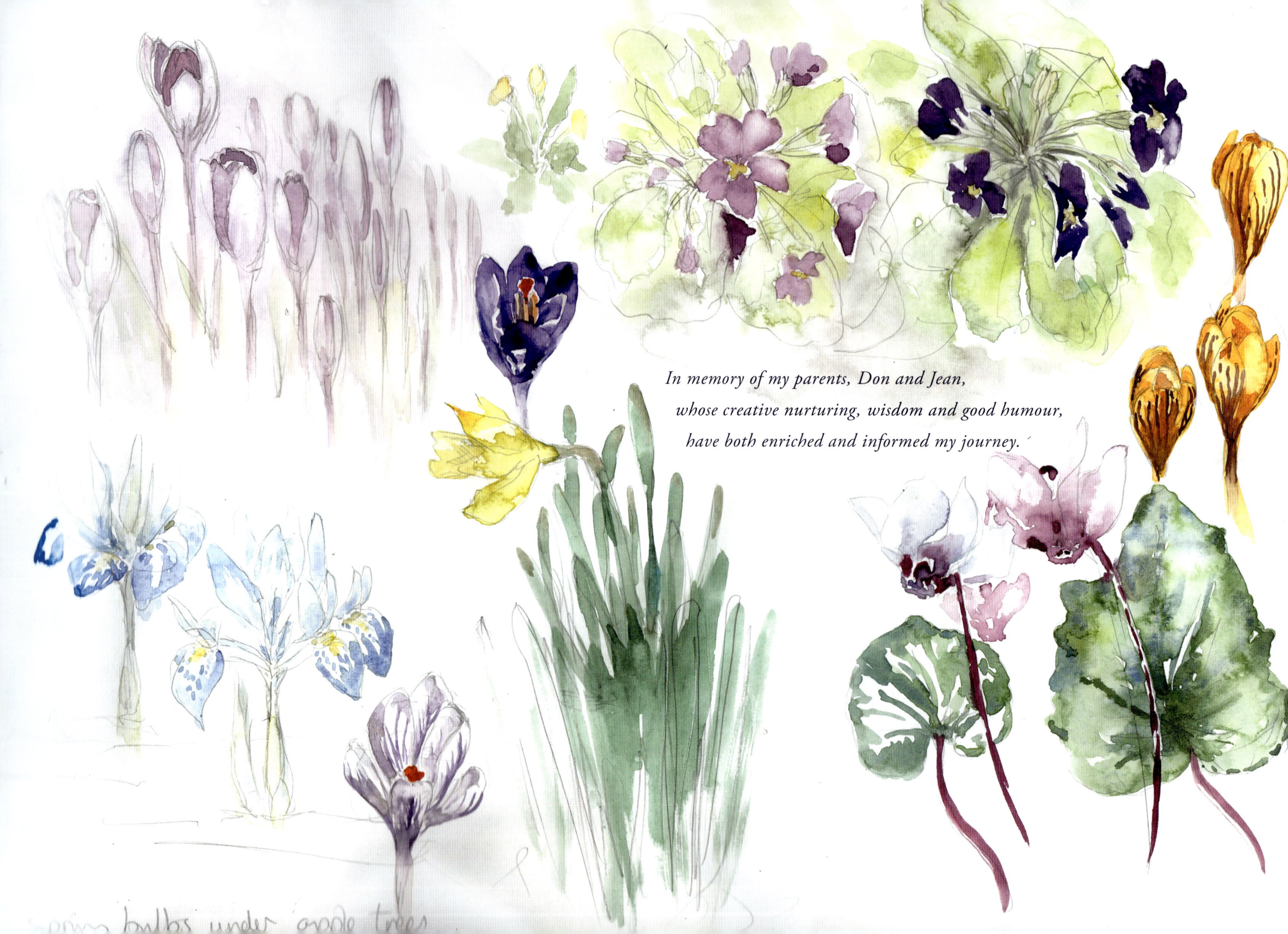
In memory of my parents, Don and Jean,
whose creative nurturing, wisdom and good humour,
have both enriched and informed my journey.

It gives me great pleasure to write the foreword for this book of sketches and paintings by an artist who has captured every detail of Hergest Croft Gardens during 2023. Starting with the cold, clear winter days of January, through the blossoming of spring, the intense heat of summer, the cooling and bright colour of autumn and finally back to the clarity of winter. Kathryn has portrayed her powerful impression of the gardens from sketches to paintings, to written details on each page. These provide a stunning snapshot of a year in the gardens.

Kathryn strode around the garden at all times of the day. I often met her early in the morning as I walked my dogs, carrying a stool and all her equipment on her back. Weather did not disturb her. She was out in all conditions. Her fluency of style and the speed at which she was able to capture the spirit of the place in her drawings is remarkable (and that she managed to keep them dry is staggering!)

All the Banks' family are entranced by the pages, the beauty, fun and range of drawings shown on each entry. I can imagine the creators of Hergest Croft Gardens, Dorothy and Willie Banks, appreciating Kathryn's skill and enjoying the sketchbooks. In fact, all five generations of the family would have done so.

Although the garden is internationally recognised as having a significant collection of trees and shrubs, the planting is not all woody. As you can see from these extracts of Kathryn's sketchbooks, the gardens also contain an attractive Kitchen Garden with startlingly colourful spring herbaceous borders and a rose garden, as well as vegetable plots which Kathryn has brilliantly captured.

This is a record of the seasons, the effect they have on the gardens and how it looked some 128 years after it was created. How delighted the family are at this amazing book.

Elizabeth Banks, CBE DL *President Emeritus* RHS

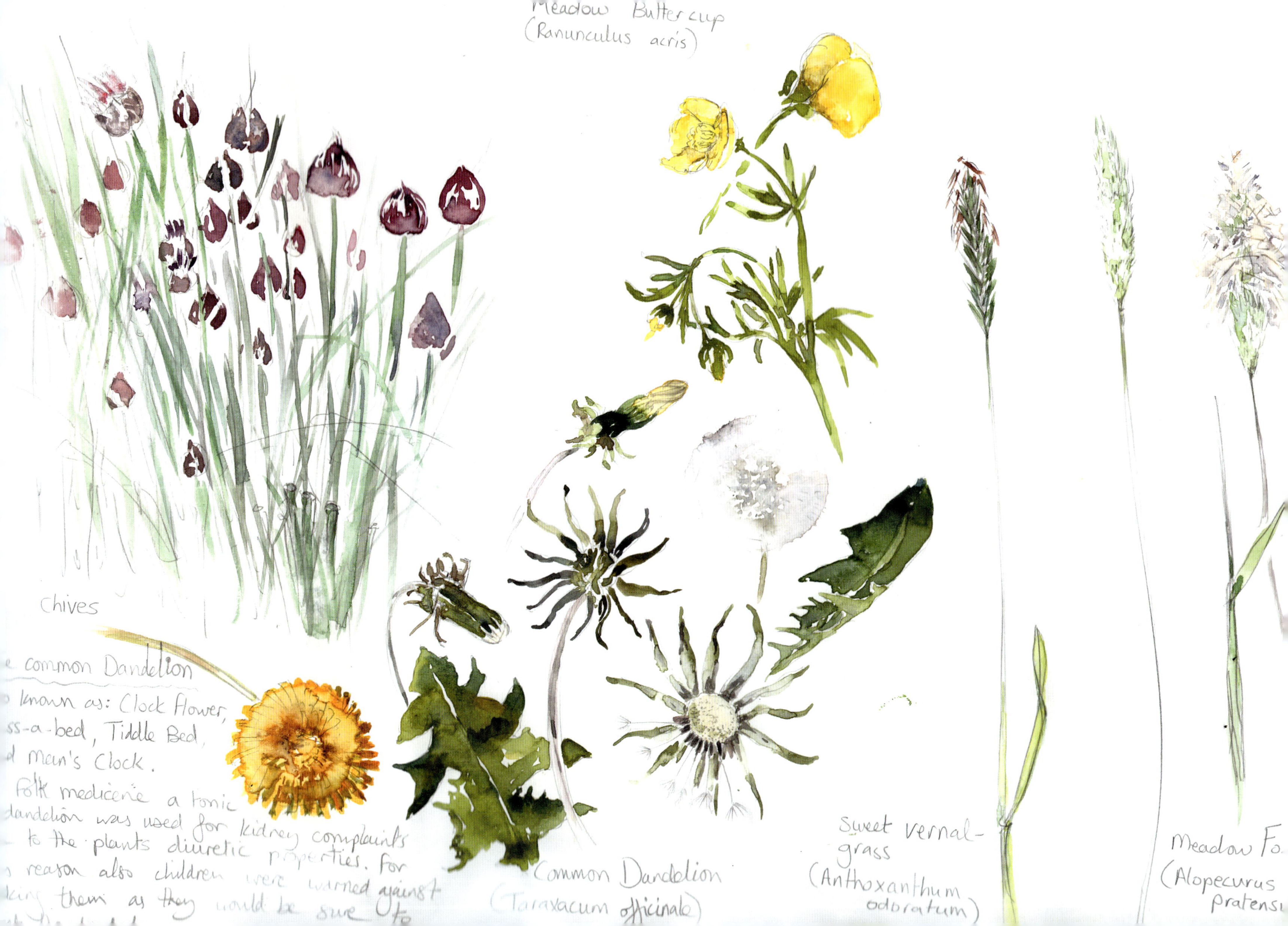

Meadow Buttercup
(Ranunculus acris)
Chives
e common Dandelion
known as: Clock Flower,
ss-a-bed, Tiddle Bed,
d Man's Clock.
Folk medicine a tonic
dandelion was used for kidney complaints
to the plants diuretic properties. For
reason also children were warned against
ing them as they would be sure to
Common Dandelion
(Taraxacum officinale)
Sweet vernal-
grass
(Anthoxanthum
odoratum)
Meadow Fo
(Alopecurus
pratens

ACKNOWLEDGEMENTS

Robert Pearson, Project Design Architects Limited — *digital scanning*

Ros Horner — *information technology support*

Paul Harris/ Leslie Jarrett — *photography*

Richard and Su Wheeler — *Logaston Press*

Steve Lloyd, Rowan Griffiths, Kristie Legg, Rob Price — *gardening team*

Heather Pegg — *archivist, Hergest Trust Archive*

Estate office staff — *Hergest Croft Gardens*

Mel Lloyd and team — *Maples Tearoom*

All have contributed with their invaluable support, experience and knowledge, for which I am indebted.

Special thanks to Mrs Elizabeth Banks and the Banks family for granting me access
to roam freely during my year as Artist in Residence at Hergest Croft Gardens.

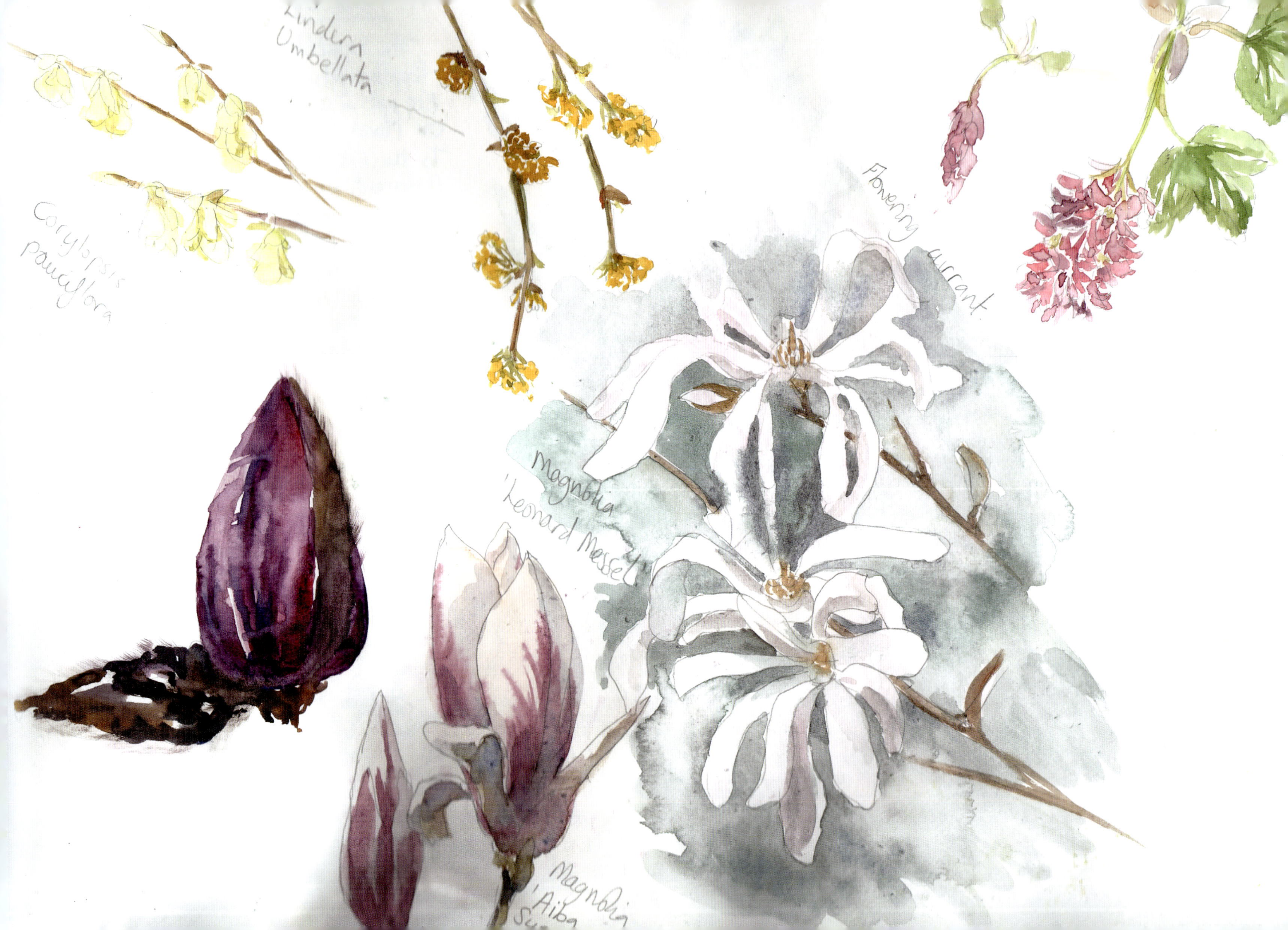

Lindera
Umbellata
Corylopsis
pauciflora
Flowering currant
Magnolia
'Leonard Messel'
Magnolia
'Alba
Superba

Introduction

*Art ... must do something more than give us pleasure:
it must relate to our own life so as to increase our energy
of spirit.* **Sir Kenneth Clark – *Looking at Pictures***

'Sitting silently, secretly beneath the overhanging bows of a *Prunus sogdiana*, I am encased in an emerald jewel – a cave of dappled greens, studded with stars of sunlight, etched angular twigs and branches forming the framework surrounding me. Drops of last night's rain fall upon my sketchbook, whilst all around birds, thrilled, take advantage of the damp, rejuvenated ground. At my feet a hole for a small mammal.'

The sensation of opening a new page of blank paper, pencil in hand, having been stopped in my tracks by a subject, and proceeding to draw, never ceases to thrill. The act of being arrested mid-gait by something seen – a vista through trees at sunset; a minuscule insect feeding from a flower; the effect of wind interacting with grasses across a meadow; a repeat pattern of leaves in an overhead canopy – becomes the essential identification required in my work as an artist. That fundamental, primeval awareness of one's surroundings informs me of the natural world – of geology and meteorology; of the physical and psychological effects of light and subsequent colour – even before the more personal 'emotional' response is considered.

The sketchbook is an extension of the artist's being, an appendage without which one feels bereft. However, with inventive tendencies there is always some scrap or surface and mark-making tool available swiftly in desperation if needs be – eye-liner pencil and a tissue come to mind on my travels in the past, along with twigs dipped in mud onto an old till receipt! In this age of instant imaging with phone technology, it becomes easy to rely on this form of documentation. Old fashioned as I may be, the process of pausing to sketch, and of extracting exactly the aspect that did indeed 'stop me in my tracks' is an invaluable one. The act of halting either briefly or longer, perching on my trusty camping seat, not only allows me time to look deeply but also to use other senses. What are the surrounding sounds? What 'sensations' am I feeling by being in that particular place at that particular time? Besides which, when sat quietly in the environment, all kinds of unexpected occurrences happen – a pair of bullfinches shyly moving amongst the tall shrubs; a vole scurrying through the ground cover; the sun momentarily casting rays across the clouds – these useful snippets ultimately influence my work, and could be unnoticed, fleetingly traversing the landscape, phone in hand.

The notion of artist in residence at Hergest Croft Gardens occurred to me while walking through Park Wood one late October afternoon. Observing the richly-carpeted woodland floor beneath my feet, I retrieved a bunch of ash keys. I mused over the wonder of nature and the English language; I placed the keys in my pocket. The woods in the dingle above the lagoon (pond) remind me of travelling through Southeast Asia (the squawking jays could almost be parrots!) The continual delight these sizeable grounds possess is ultimately down to the vision with which they were conceived and planted in the late 1890s. Rather than the *Pterocarya macroptera* from China, or the rhododendron tree from Nepal sitting incongruously in the Herefordshire landscape, these exotic, rare species from around the globe are complimentary to their habitat. The amalgamation of imported and native plants is harmonious rather than at odds.

The seed of thought was planted firmly that the gardens needed recording through the eyes of an artist. My enquiries to the estate owners duly proved successful, and my role as resident artist began in January 2023 for the duration of that year. My contributions included providing a regular commentary through diaries of pencil sketches, watercolours, written notes and poems, two paintings from the diaries each month, weekly drop-in sessions and guided walks. With any diary, retaining momentum for a year can prove a challenging, arduous task. Documenting the changing seasons daily, however, proved a wondrous journey of discoveries. Having access to explore the gardens at all times provided opportunities to investigate the natural history of insects, wild flowers, native trees, mammals and birds; cultivated plants, shrubs and trees; the history of the estate, with invitations to view the archives; and of garden design. Dialogue with the gardeners assisted my knowledge, their weekly duties reflecting and impacting the evolving grounds. It was important for me to include the Latin names of flora and fauna, from which I personally learnt a great deal. In addition, my jottings stirred the poetic within; inclusion of relevant poems enriched each month. Research into local geology, history, horticulture, agriculture, plus re-educating myself in biology and ornithology added to my existing specialist knowledge of art and art history. The residency was truly a journey of discovery, enriching and productive, and a great privilege.

As the months progressed, the idea of an illustrated book began to take shape. Reproduced in these pages are extracts from the diaries, providing a glimpse into the gardens, and giving a comprehensive overview of the year. Accompanying the pencil drawings and watercolours, hand-written extracts are included to give the viewer an insight into the context. The Gallery pages in the latter section of the book show the monthly paintings that resulted.

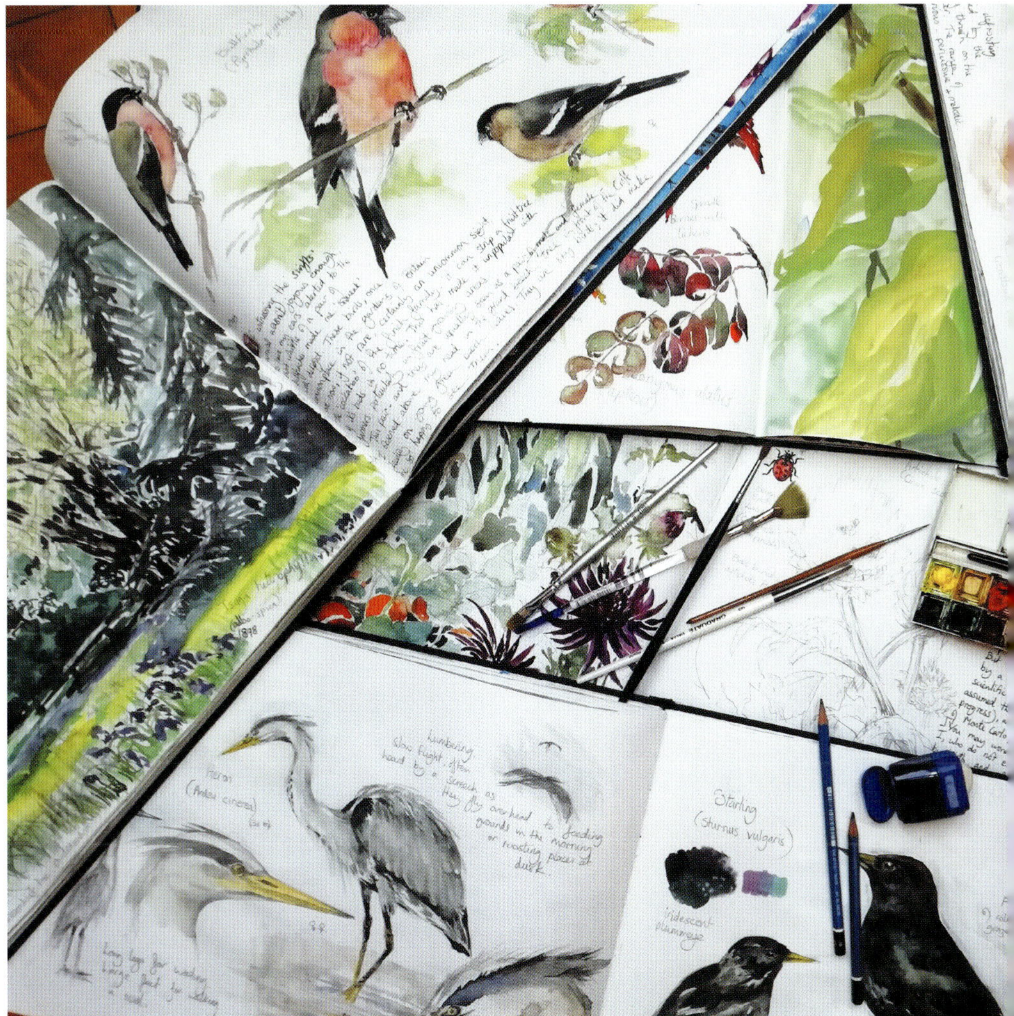

JANUARY

The aim of the year's Artist in Residency post is to document, through drawings, paintings and notations, the evolving seasons from January to December. These 'painted diaries' will provide information from which to create mixed media paintings. The subject matter will predominantly be of Flora, owing to the wealth of species within Hergest Croft Gardens, but will also include the settings in which these specimens thrive, and the ecosystems essential for their existence — birds, mammals, Fungii. References will be made to the landscaping designs of the gardens — the role that colour, texture and structure plays in these designs throughout the year. Research into the history of the gardens, and how, if the case, the designs and planting has changed over the decades. Architectural features will be an aspect too

Natural history has always been a significant interest and played a part increasingly as my artistic career has developed; (my first painted natural history diary I completed at the age of seven!) Though my interest is keen I am in no way a scholar when it comes to many specimens, though I do like to include Latin names where possible as informative. My research will extend to art and literature — paintings, prints and poems by artists and writers inspired by nature. By the end of the year's term I anticipate having achieved a substantial body of sketchbook references, and hopefully a dozen paintings, for display. I feel most privileged to have this opportunity, and to be able to share this with the visiting public through talks and exhibitions.

Walking through the grounds on a chill January eve, the last plays of light catching the droplets of rain clinging to every barren twig, blackbirds chucking as they upturn the leaf mould in the twilight, there is a great sense of excitement and expectation mixed. What discoveries lay ahead? The variety of tree barks alone could form the basis of a year's study!

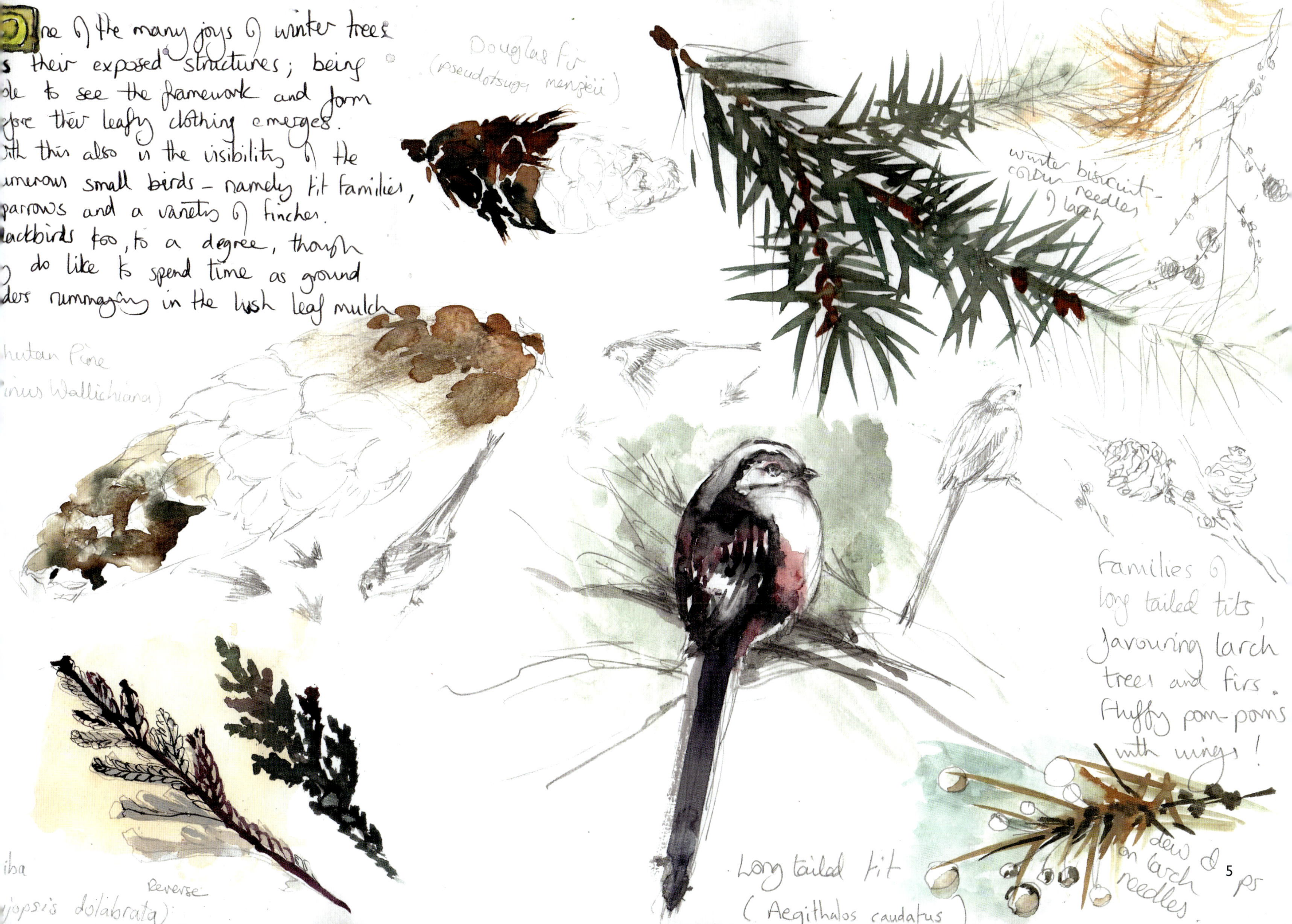
One of the many joys of winter trees
is their exposed structures; being
able to see the framework and form
before their leafy clothing emerges.
With this also in the visibility of the
numerous small birds - namely tit families,
sparrows and a variety of finches.
Blackbirds too, to a degree, though
they do like to spend time as ground
feeders rummaging in the lush leaf mulch
Douglas Fir
(pseudotsuga menziesii)
Bhutan Pine
(Pinus Wallichiana)
winter biscuit-
colour needles
of larch
families of
long tailed tits,
favouring larch
trees and firs.
Fluffy pom-poms
with wings!
Long tailed tit
(Aegithalos caudatus)
dew
on larch
needles
Hiba
(Thujopsis dolabrata)
Reverse
5

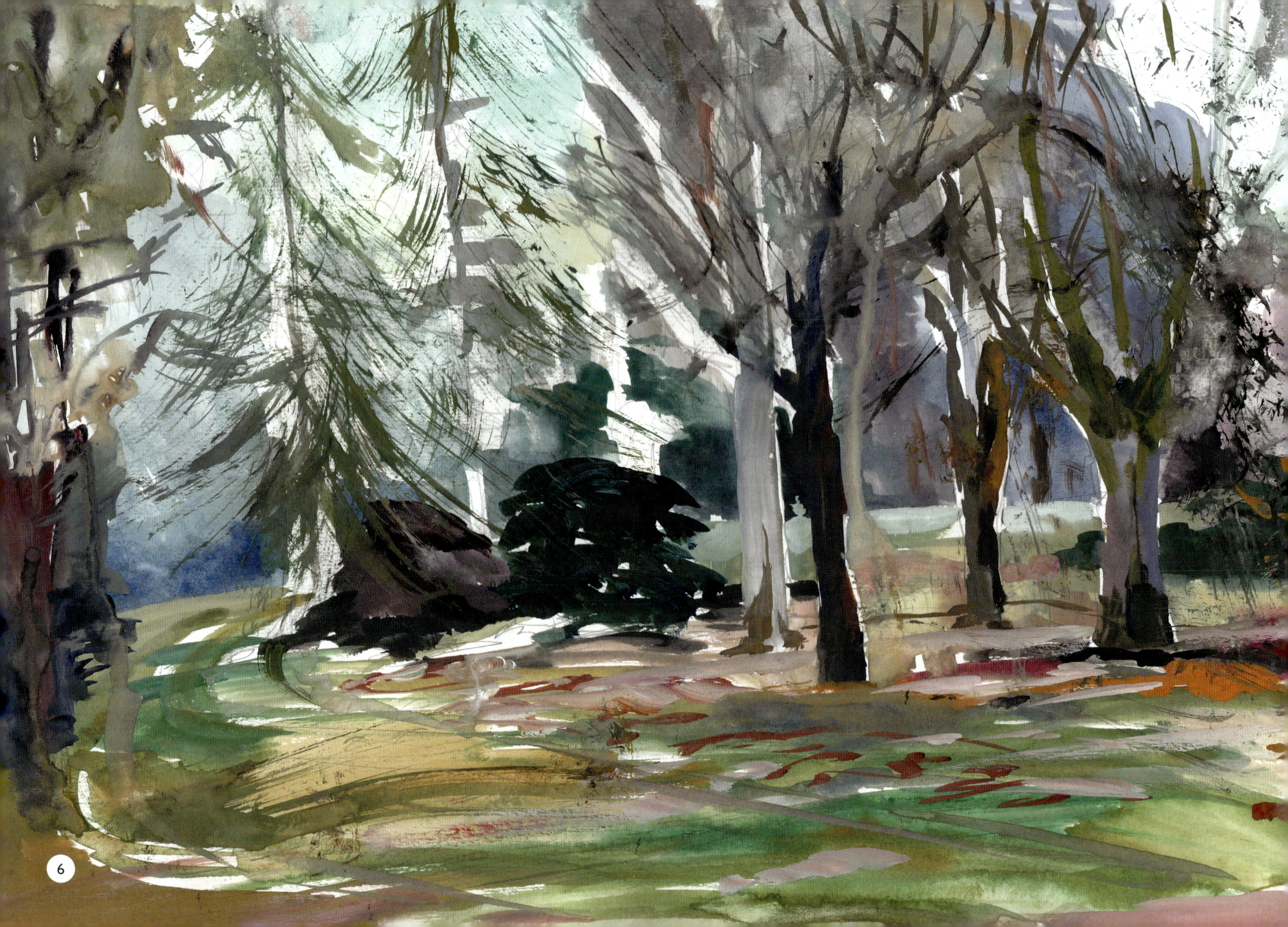

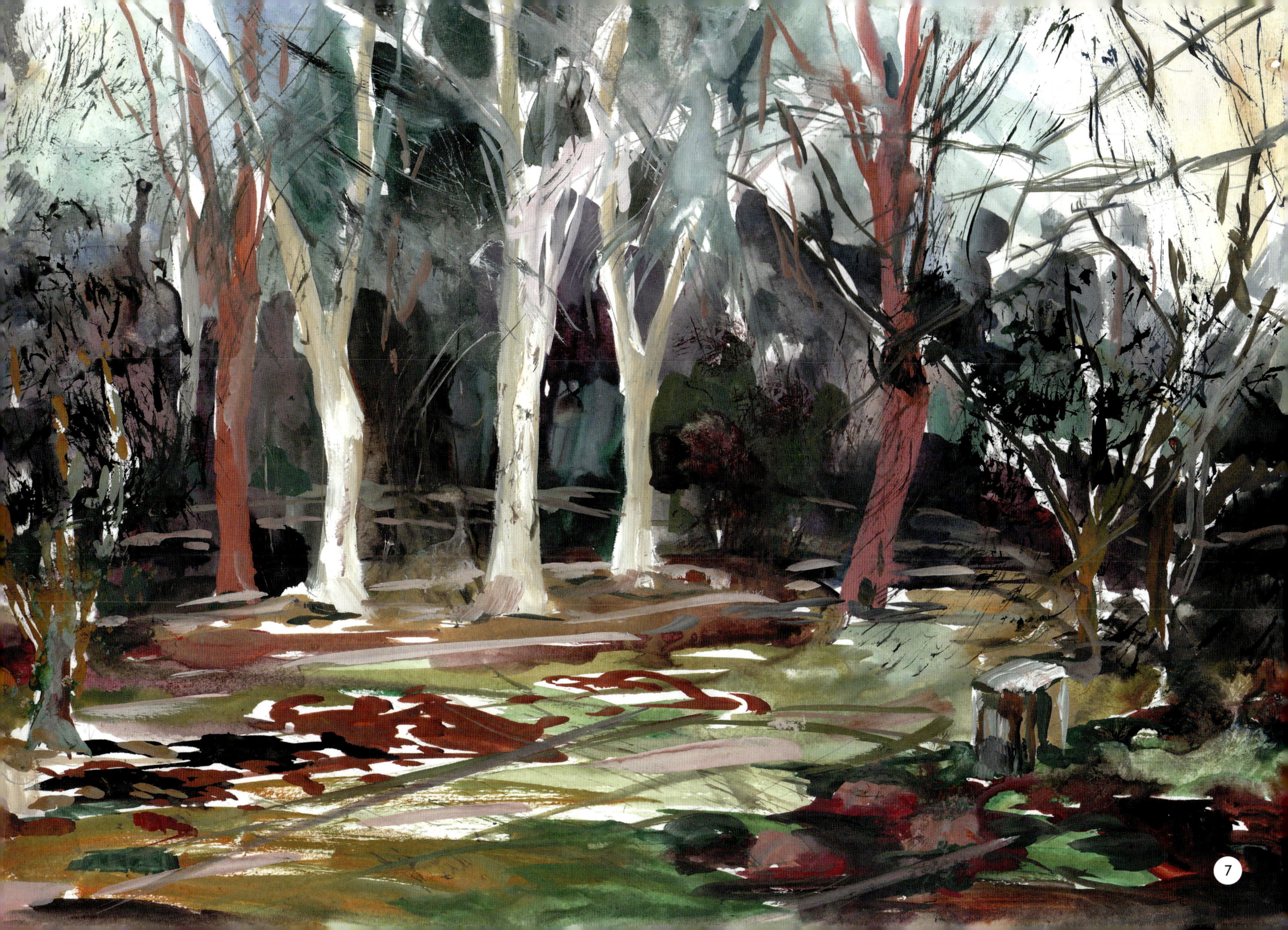

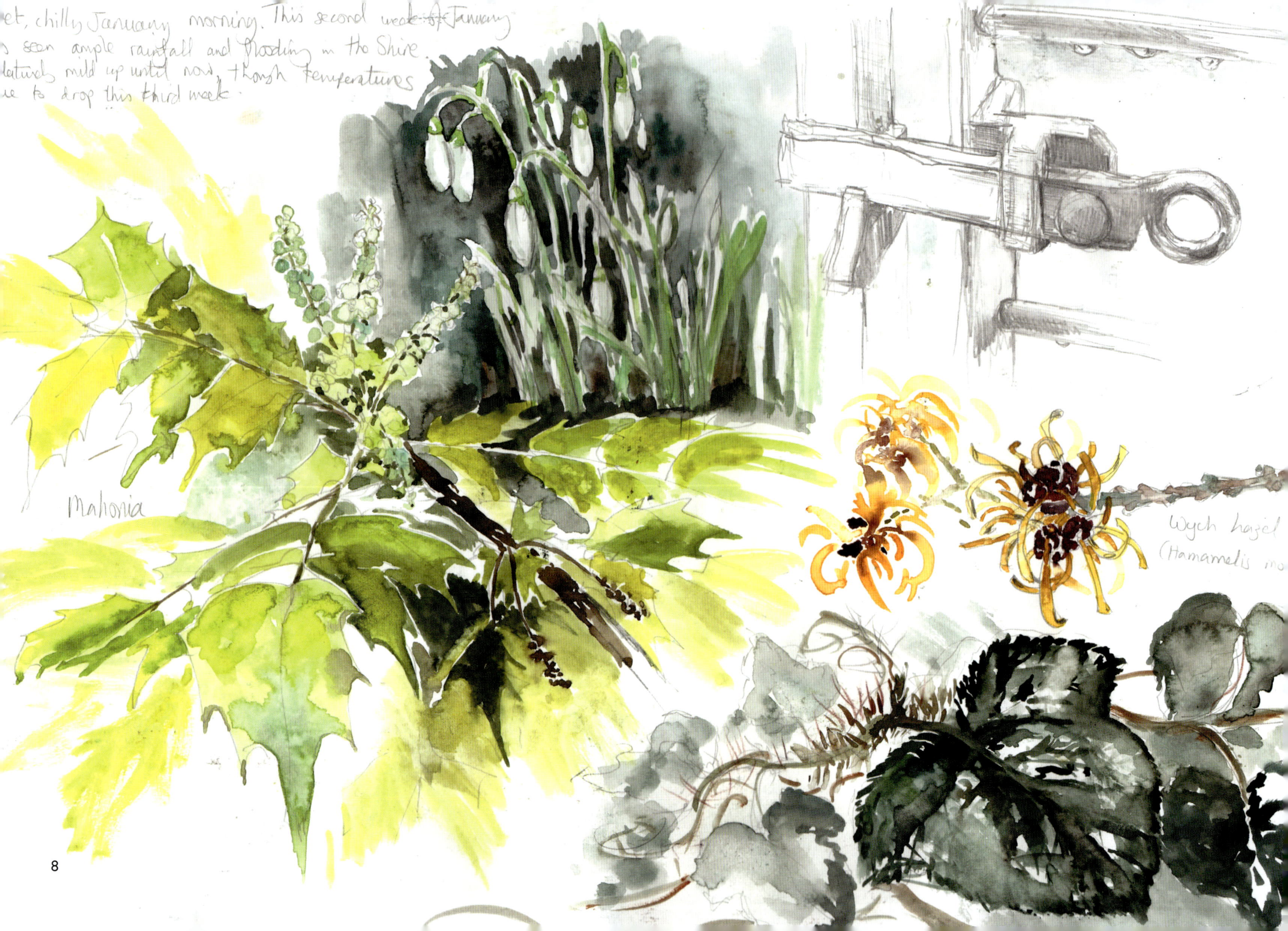
et, chilly January morning. This second week of January
s seen ample rainfall and flooding in the Shire.
aturally mild up until now, though temperatures
e to drop this third week.
Mahonia
Wych hazel
(Hamamelis mo
8

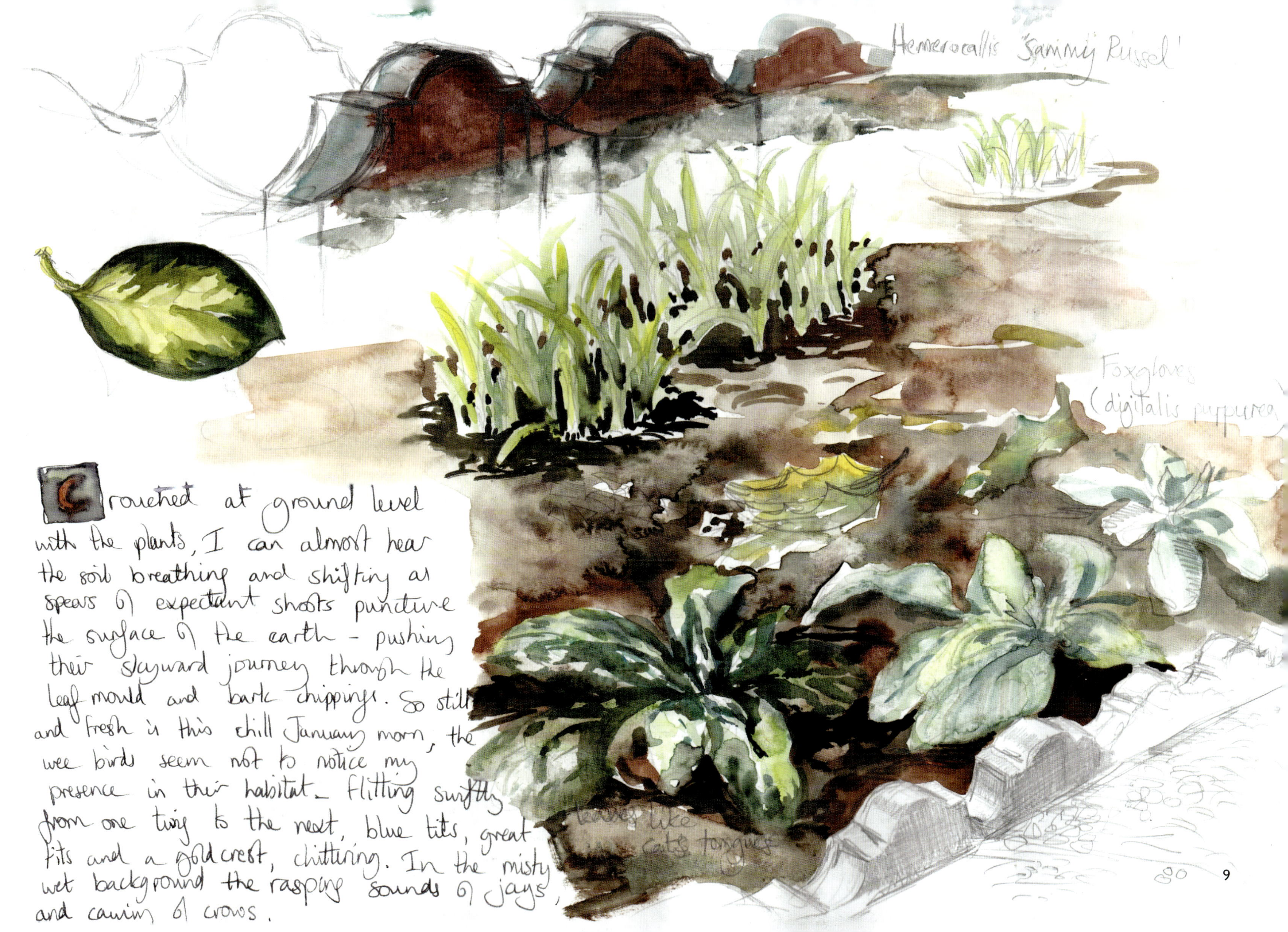

Crouched at ground level with the plants, I can almost hear the soil breathing and shifting as spears of expectant shoots puncture the surface of the earth – pushing their skyward journey through the leaf mould and bark chippings. So still and fresh is this chill January morn, the wee birds seem not to notice my presence in their habitat– flitting swiftly from one twig to the next, blue tits, great tits and a goldcrest, chittering. In the misty wet background the rasping sounds of jays, and cawing of crows.

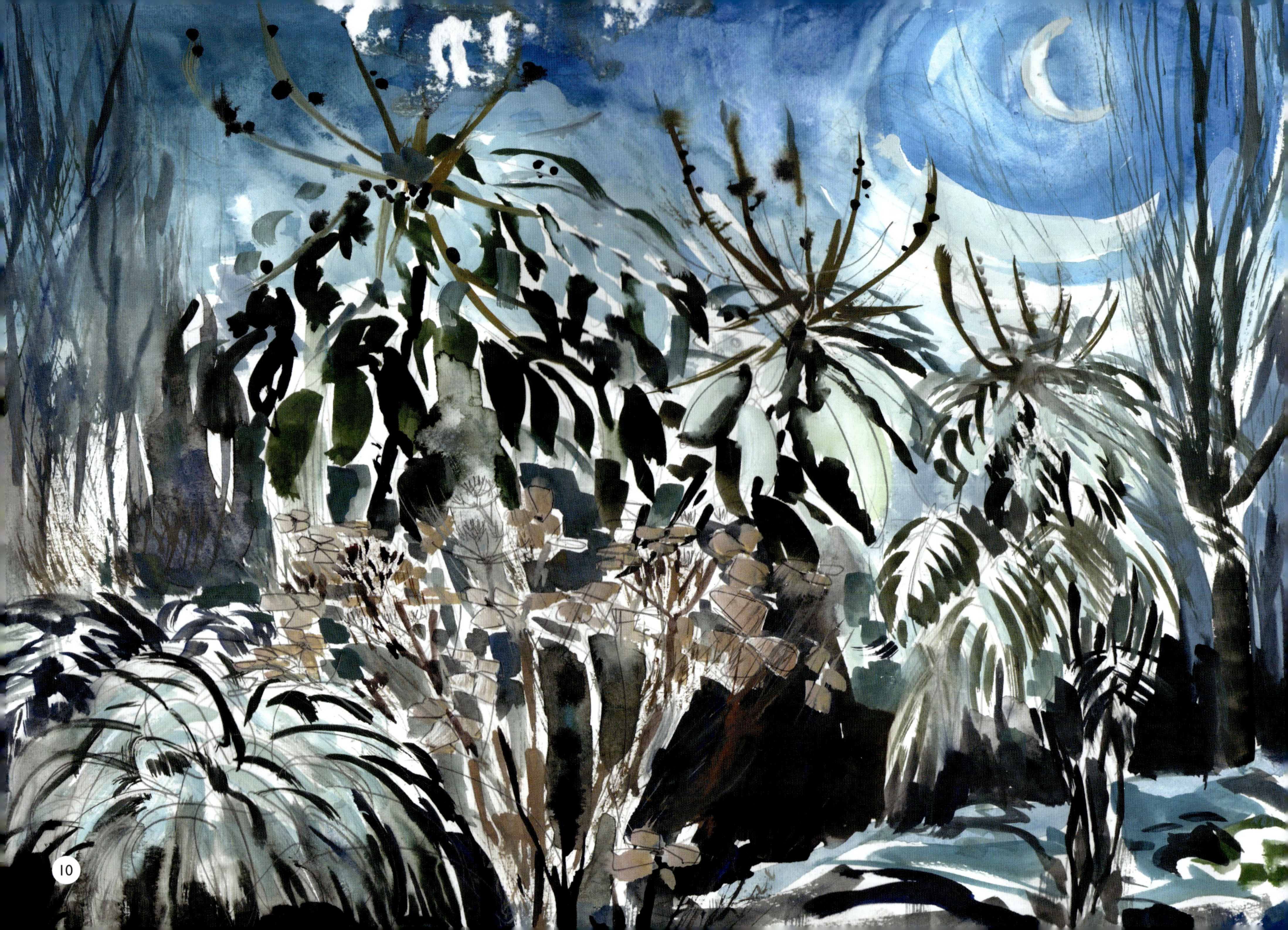

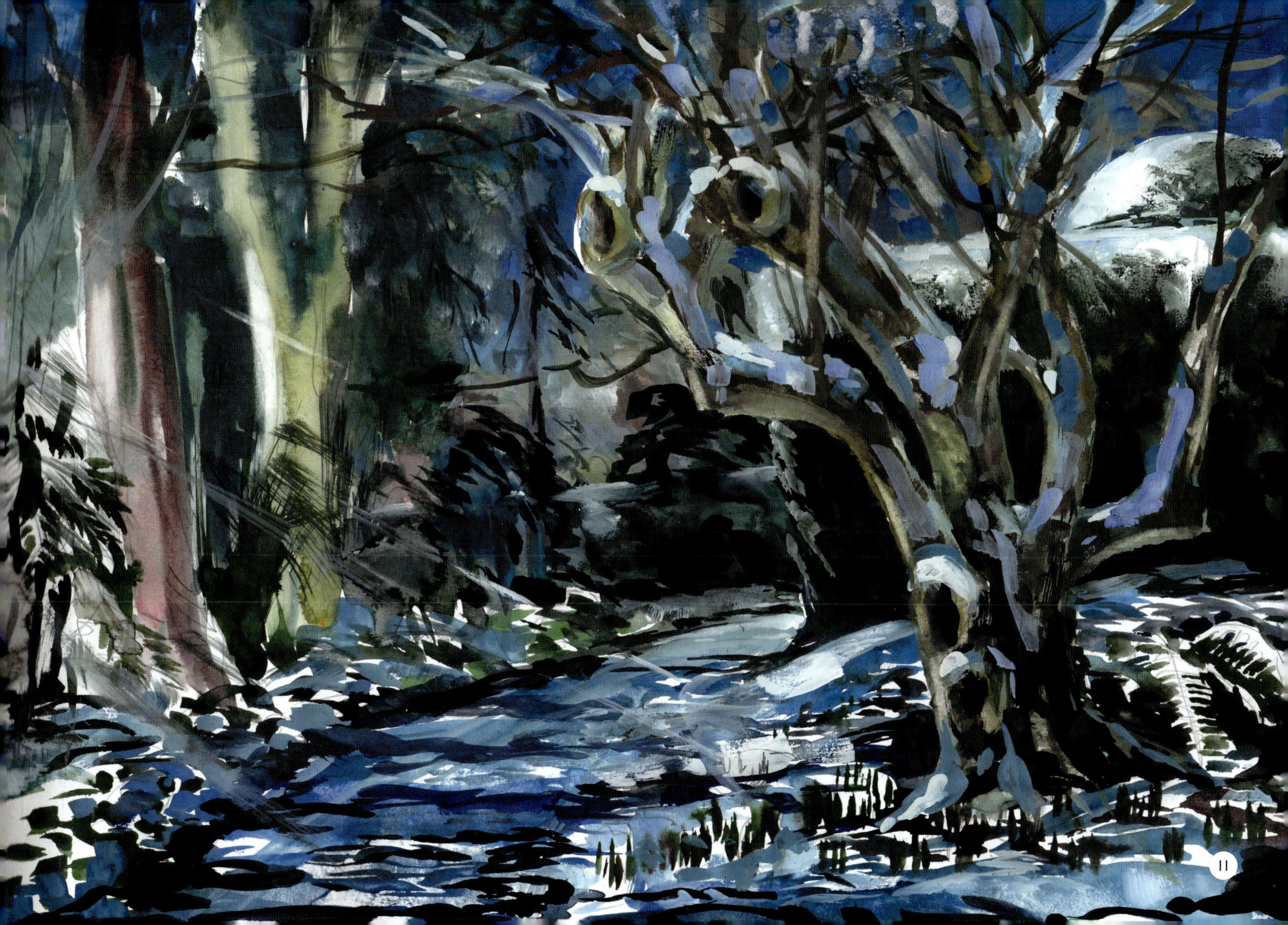

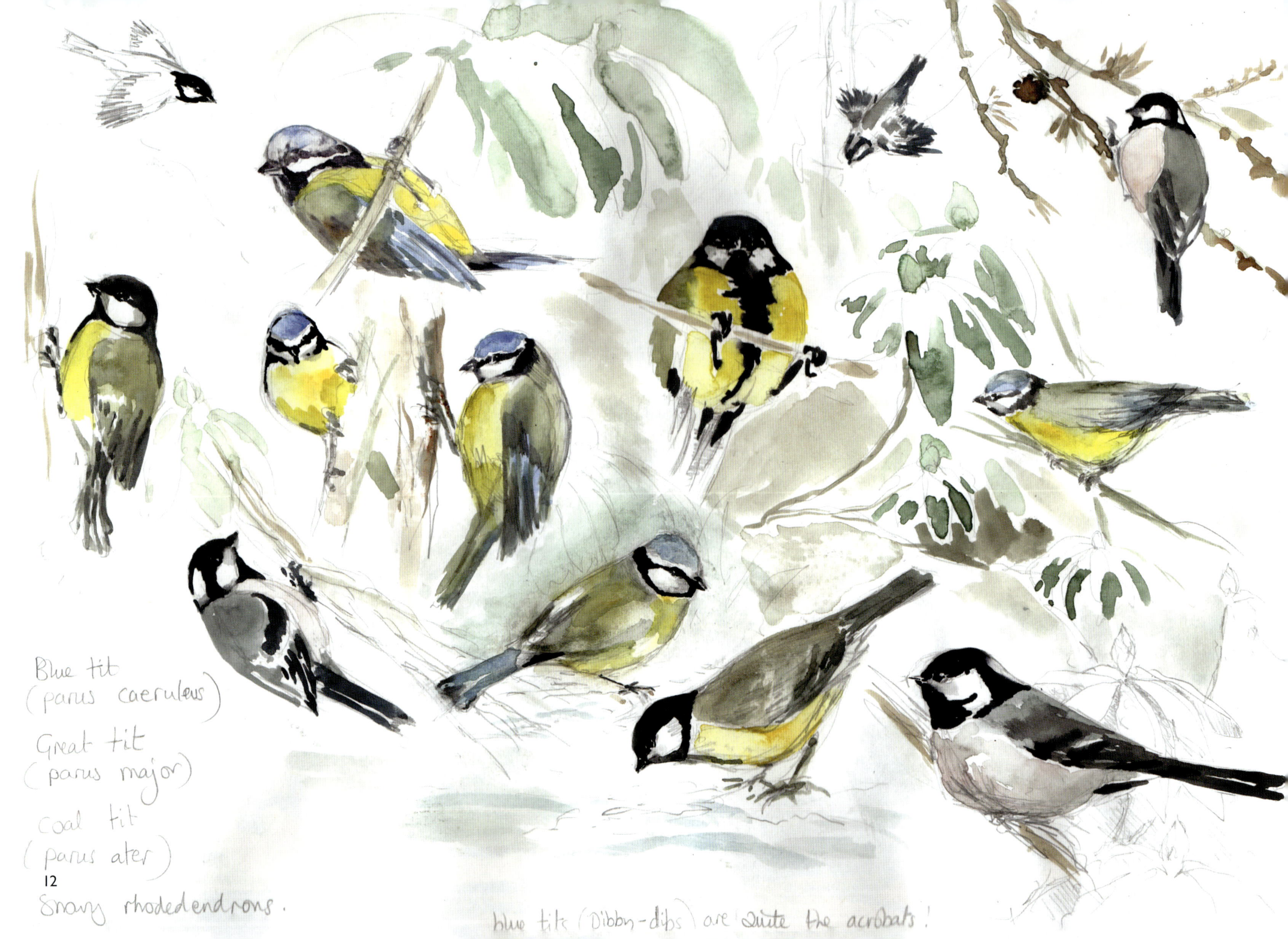

Blue tit
(parus caeruleus)
Great tit
(parus major)
Coal tit
(parus ater)
12
Snowy rhododendrons.
blue tits (Dibby-dibs) are quite the acrobats!

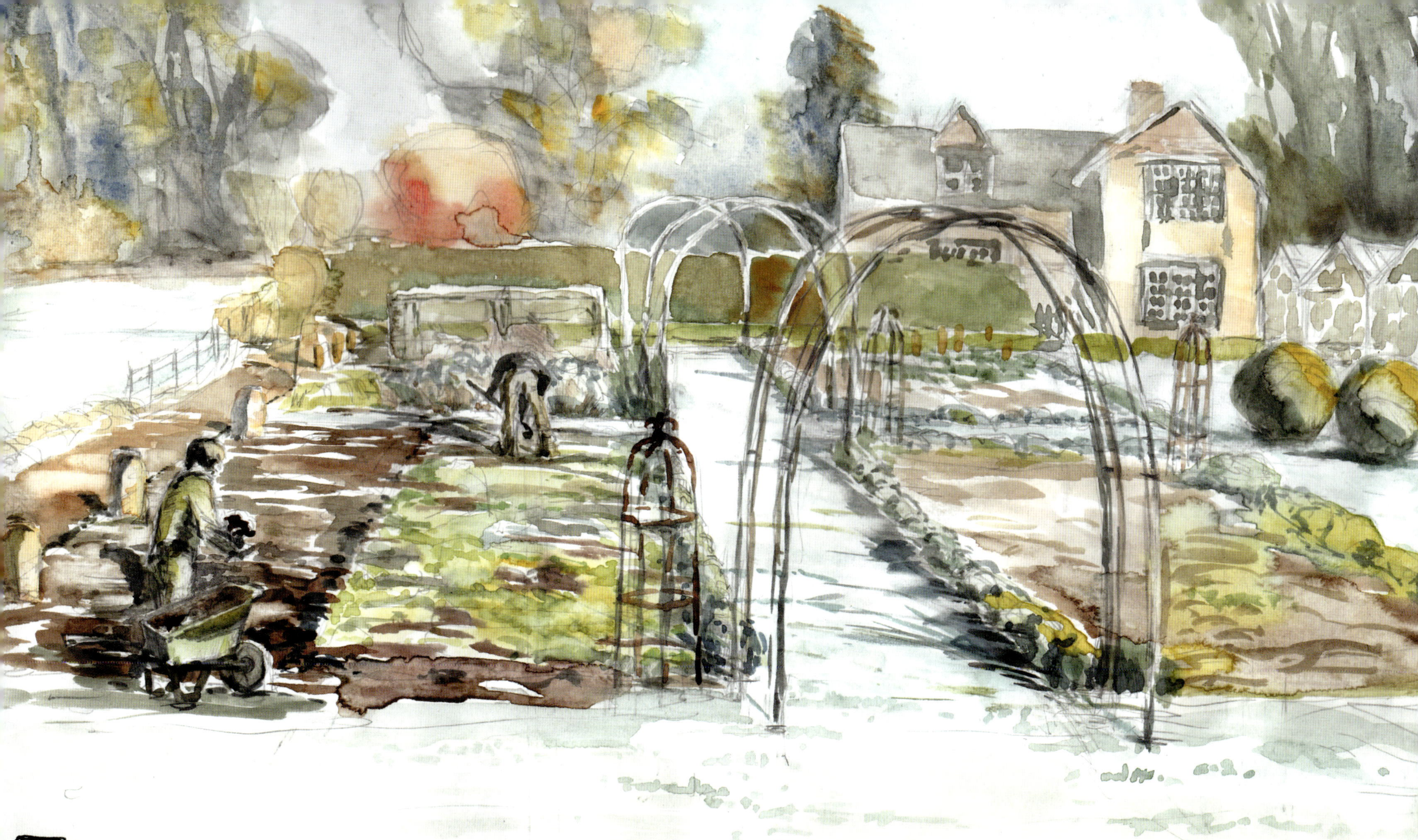

Clearing winter weeds in the vegetable beds,
and digging in well rotted horse manure compost.
Frosty morning in the kitchen garden.

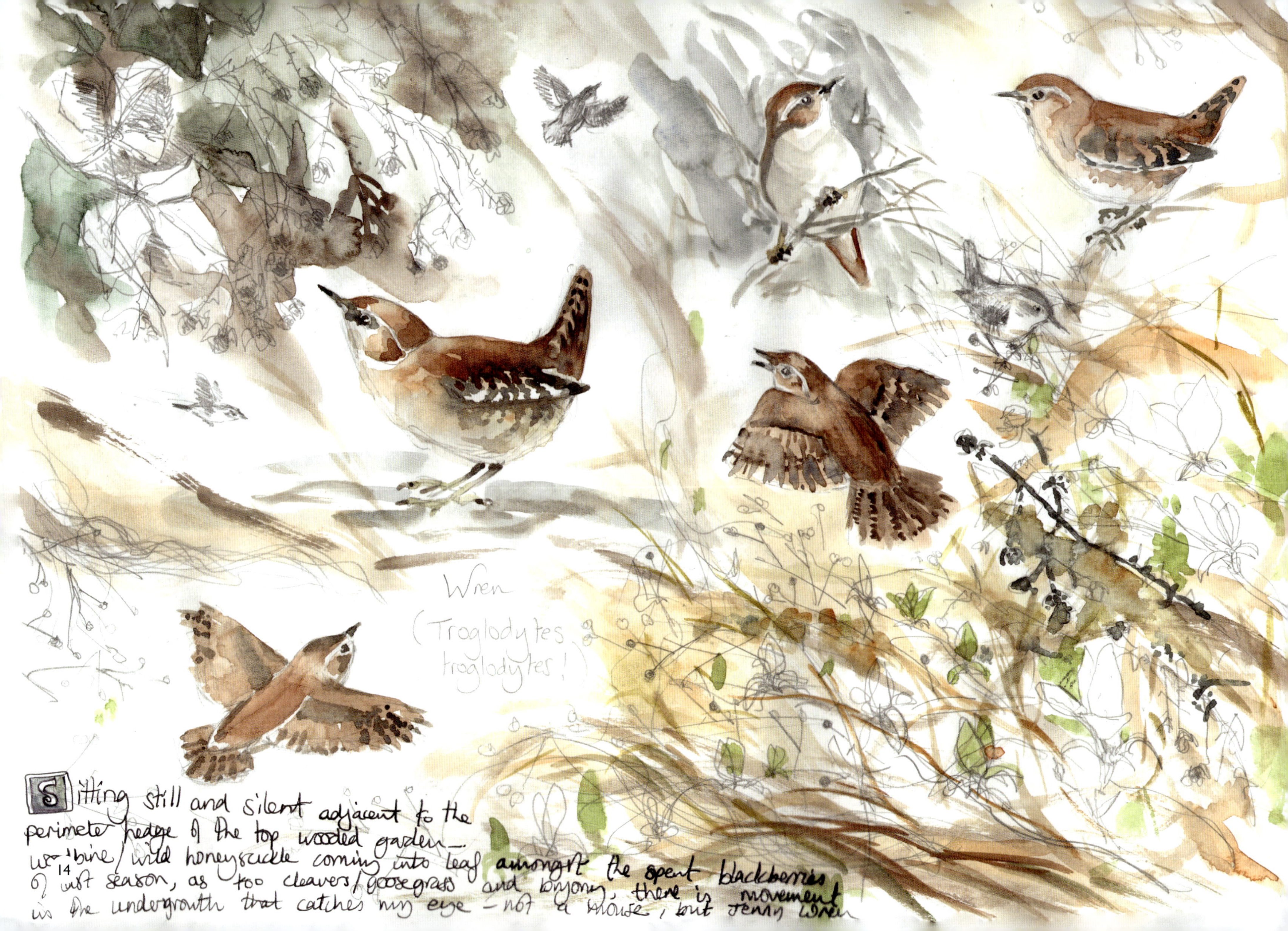
Wren
(Troglodytes
troglodytes!)
S itting still and silent adjacent to the
perimeter hedge of the top wooded garden —
woodbine/wild honeysuckle coming into leaf amongst the spent blackberries
of last season, as too cleavers/goosegrass and bryony, there is movement
in the undergrowth that catches my eye — not a mouse, but Jenny Wren
14

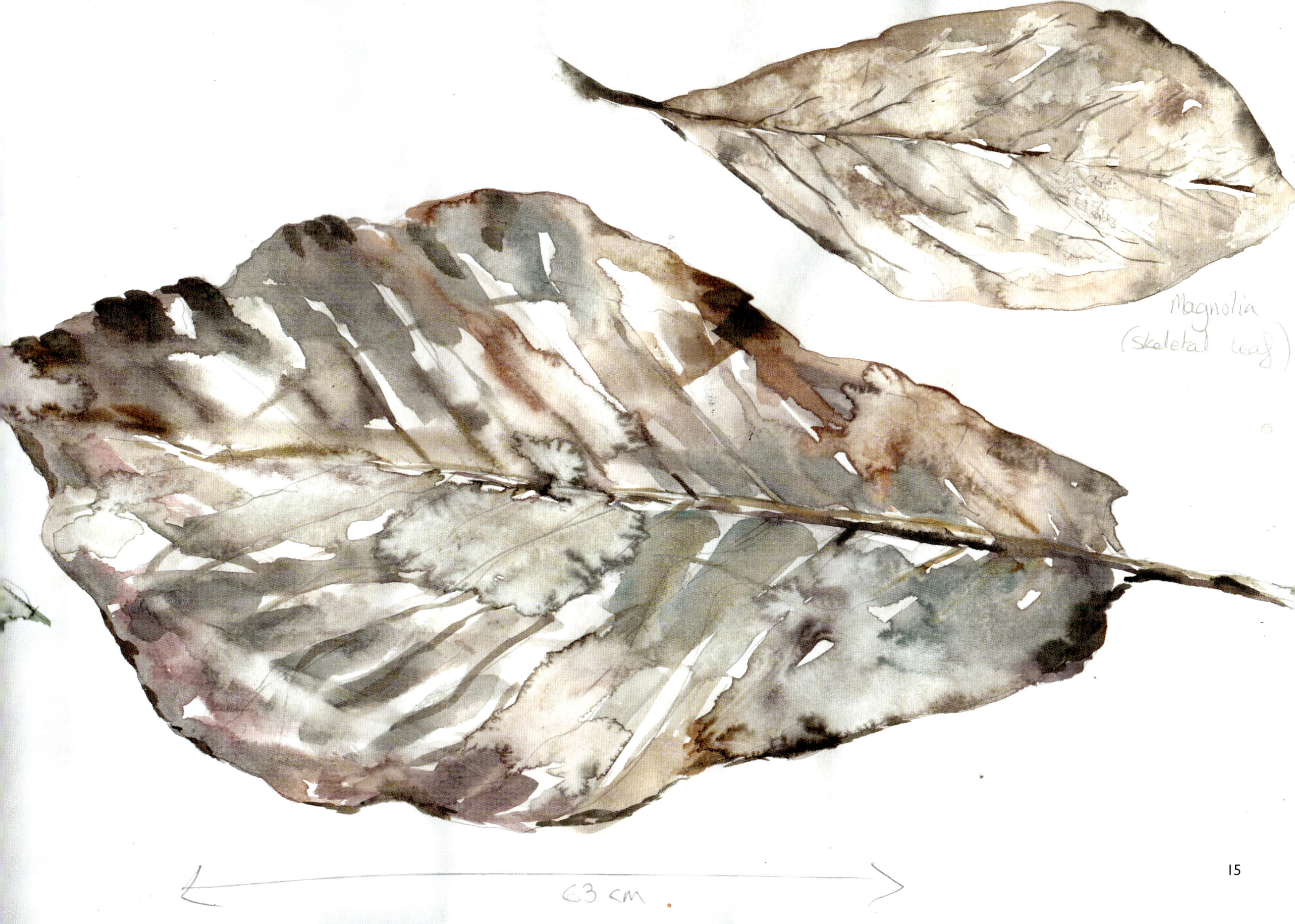

Magnolia
(skeletal leaf)
63 cm.
15

FEBRUARY

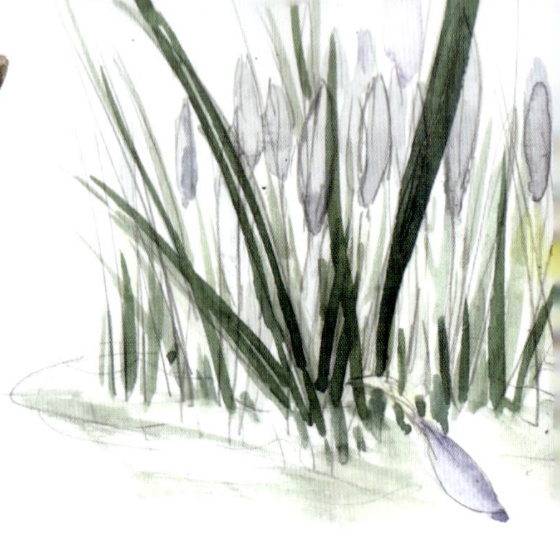

Since the snows and frosts have subsided there has been a residing quietness, stillness and dormancy in the landscap[e]. It seeps into your being without notice. The rising moon at the start of this month has brought clear night sk[ies] and vibrant sunrises, as cloud-cover is pulled over like a blanket from the west, clothing the gardens in muted tones. Despite this, nature is busy. There is so much to capture in pencil and paints; the changes are swift. Gardeners too, are busy. The activities have included hedge cutting along the perimeter hedges; raking mulched leaves allowing spring bulbs to be seen; cutting down last season's dried stems and seed heads; and tractor loads of rotted manu[re] leaf mulch compost being transported from the composting area on the lane to the kitchen garden for digging into the vegetable beds. (The latter activity to much excitement from the tame, eager robins.)

Amidst the undergrowth blackbirds busy themselves upturning decaying leaves; the leafless dense shrubs host familie[s] of tits, finches and dunnocks; and high on it's perch in the uppermost twigs of a birch sings the song thrush – [a] glorious accompaniment to my sketching.

The frosty frozen nights' clear starry skies bring forth days of sunshine; with that in turn nature is unfurl[ing] itself. Not yet the strong fresh colours of spring instead a slightly subdued colouration – primroses not qui[te] as bright, and even a red admiral butterfly emerging into the sunshine looking a little dull and tardy.

« Through primrose tufts, in that green bower,
The periwinkle trailed 'its wreaths;
And 'tis my faith that every flower
Enjoys the air it breathes »

(extract) Lines written in early Spring
William Wordsworth.

« The birds around me hopped and played
Their thoughts I cannot measure :–
But the least motion which they made
It seemed a thrill of pleasure. »

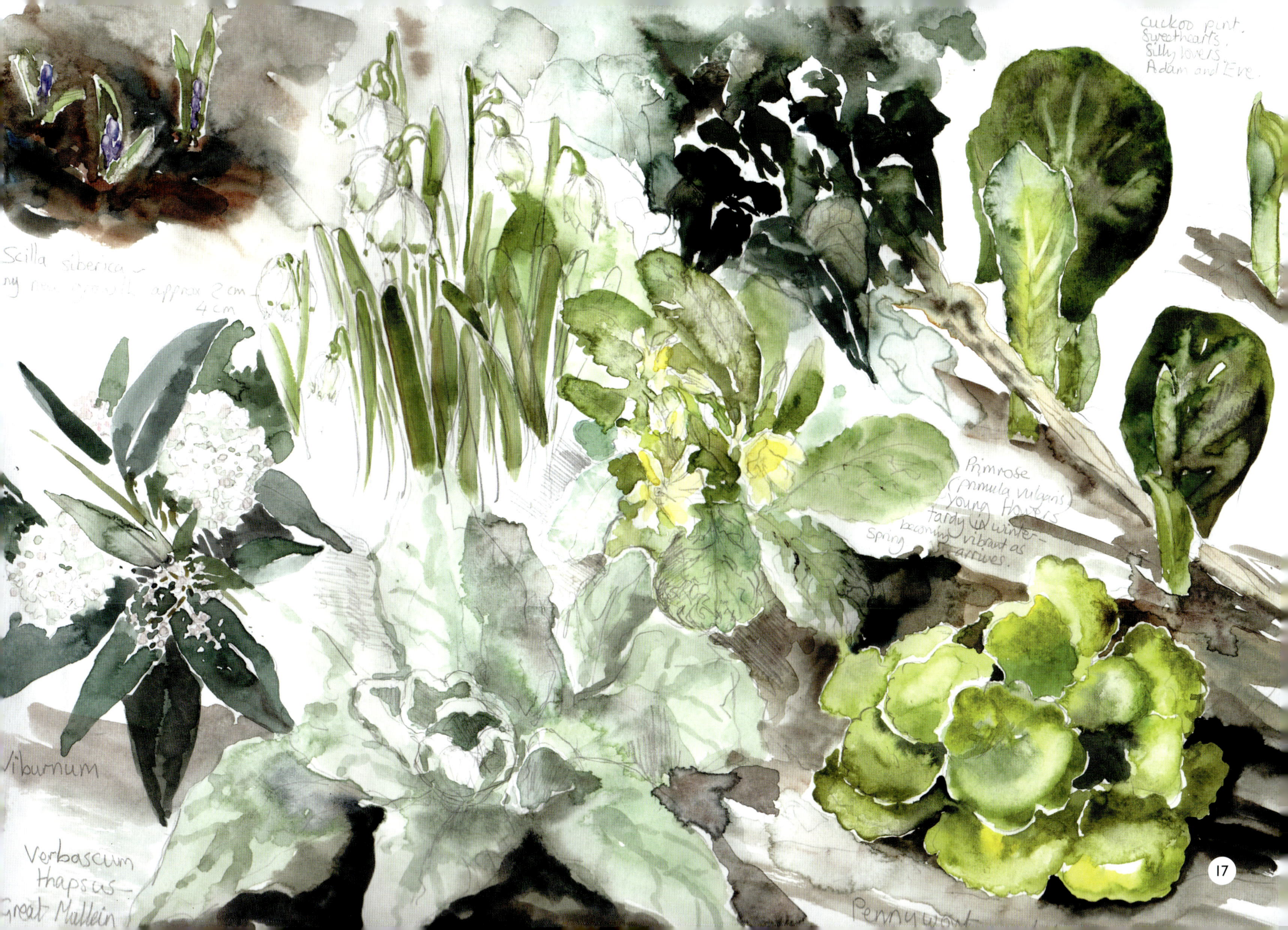

Cuckoo pint.
Sweethearts.
Silly lovers.
Adam and Eve.
Scilla siberica —
my new growth, approx 2 cm —
4 cm
Primrose
(Primula vulgaris)
young flowers
tardy in winter —
becoming vibrant as
spring arrives.
Viburnum
Verbascum
thapsus —
Great Mullein
Pennywort

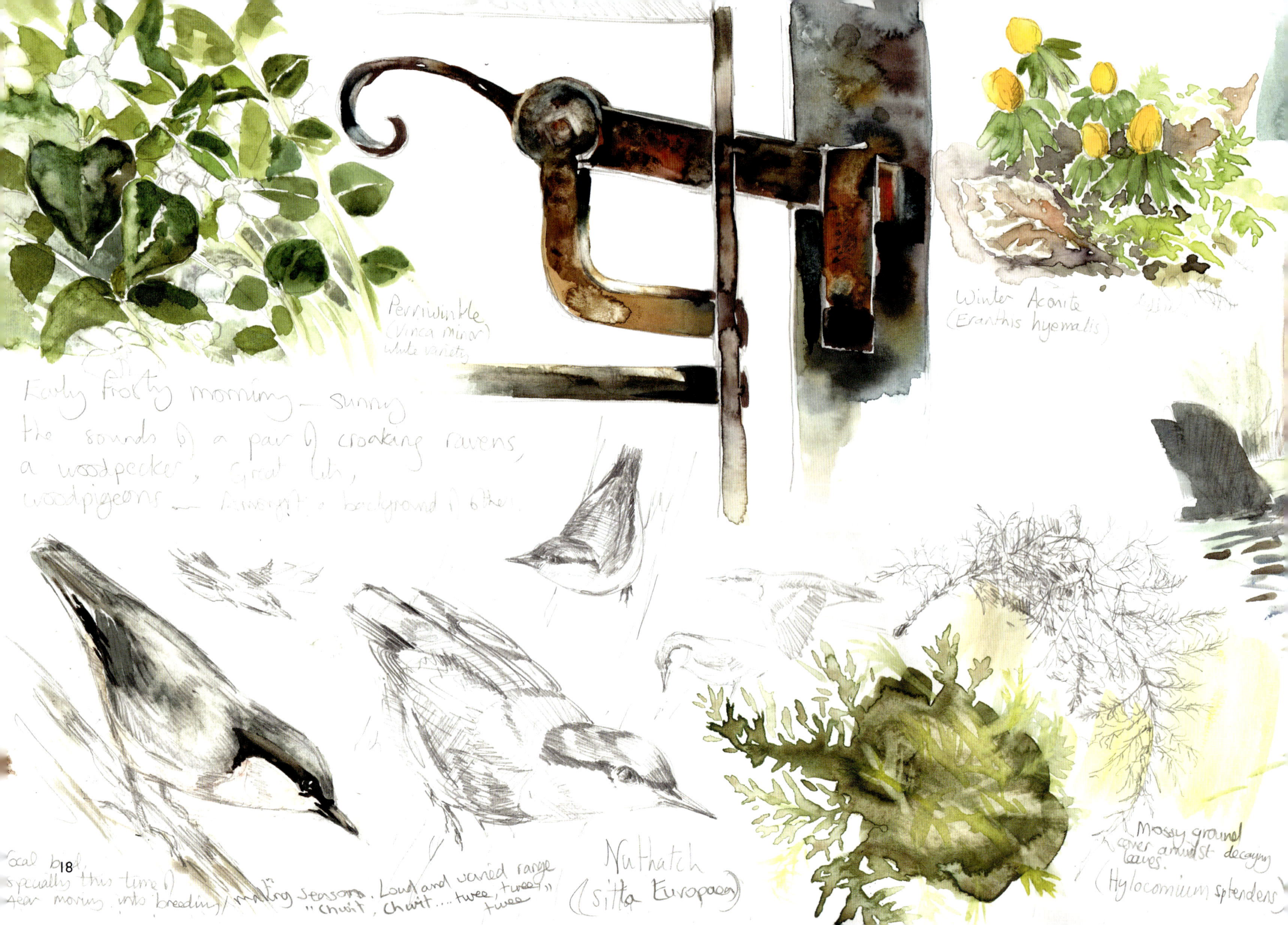

Perriwinkle
(Vinca minor)
White variety
Winter Aconite
(Eranthis hyemalis)
Early frosty morning — sunny
the sounds of a pair of croaking ravens,
a woodpecker, great tits,
woodpigeons — Amongst a background of other
18
Vocal bird especially this time of
year moving into breeding/ mating seasons. Loud and varied range
"chwit, chwit....twee, twee" twee
Nuthatch
(Sitta Europaea)
Mossy ground
cover amongst decaying
leaves.
(Hylocomium splendens)

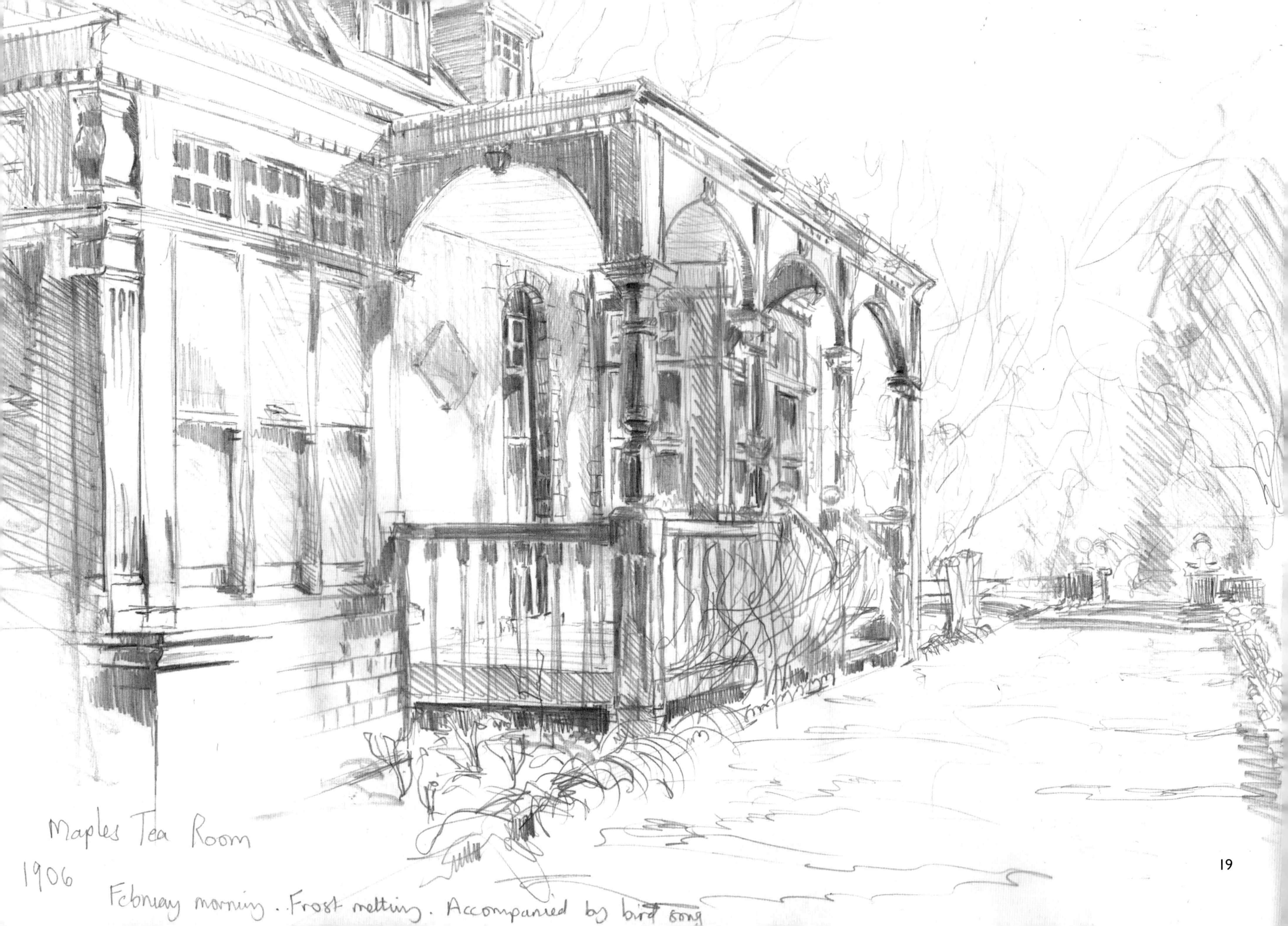

Maples Tea Room
1906
February morning . Frost melting . Accompanied by bird song
19

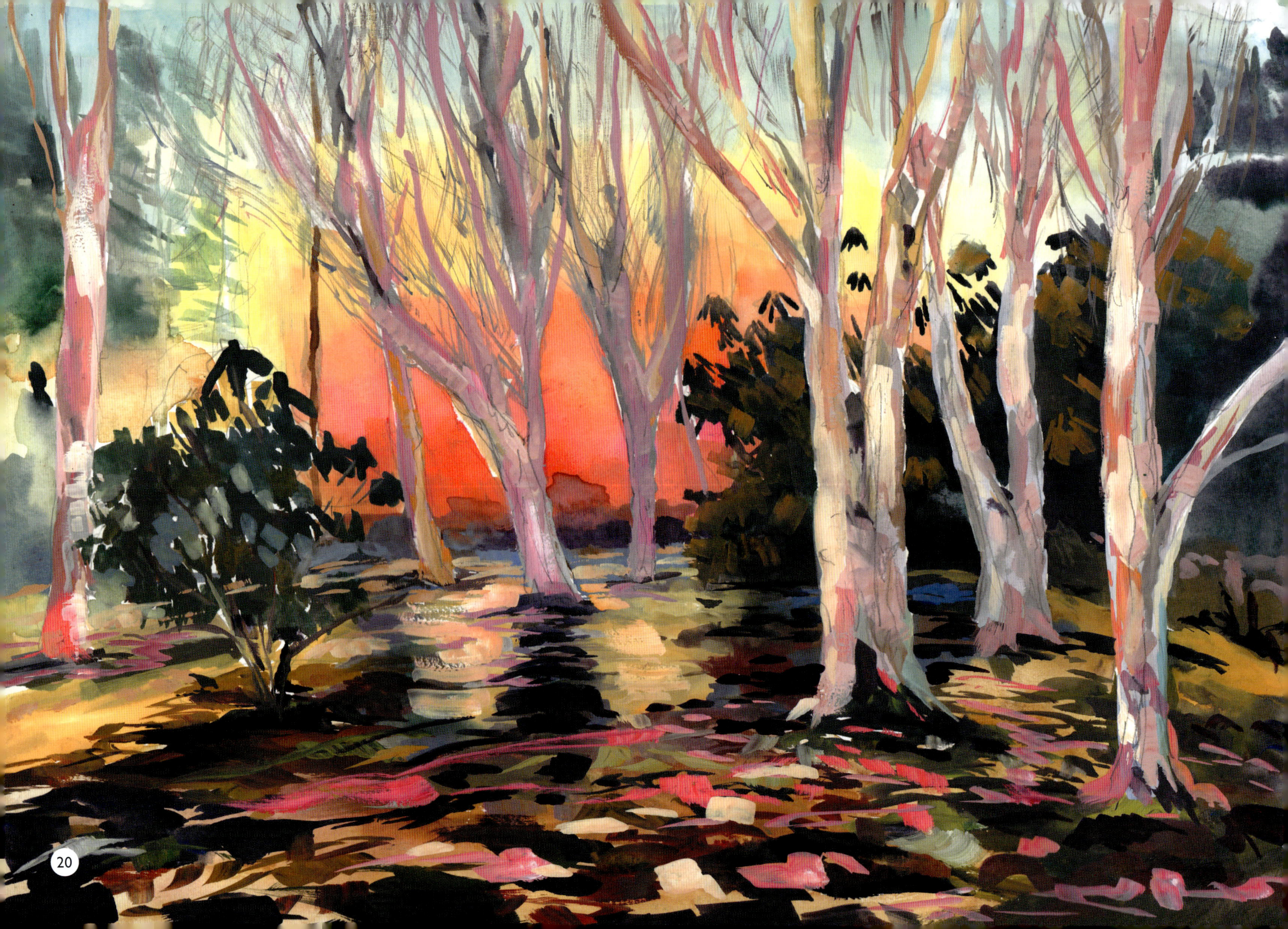

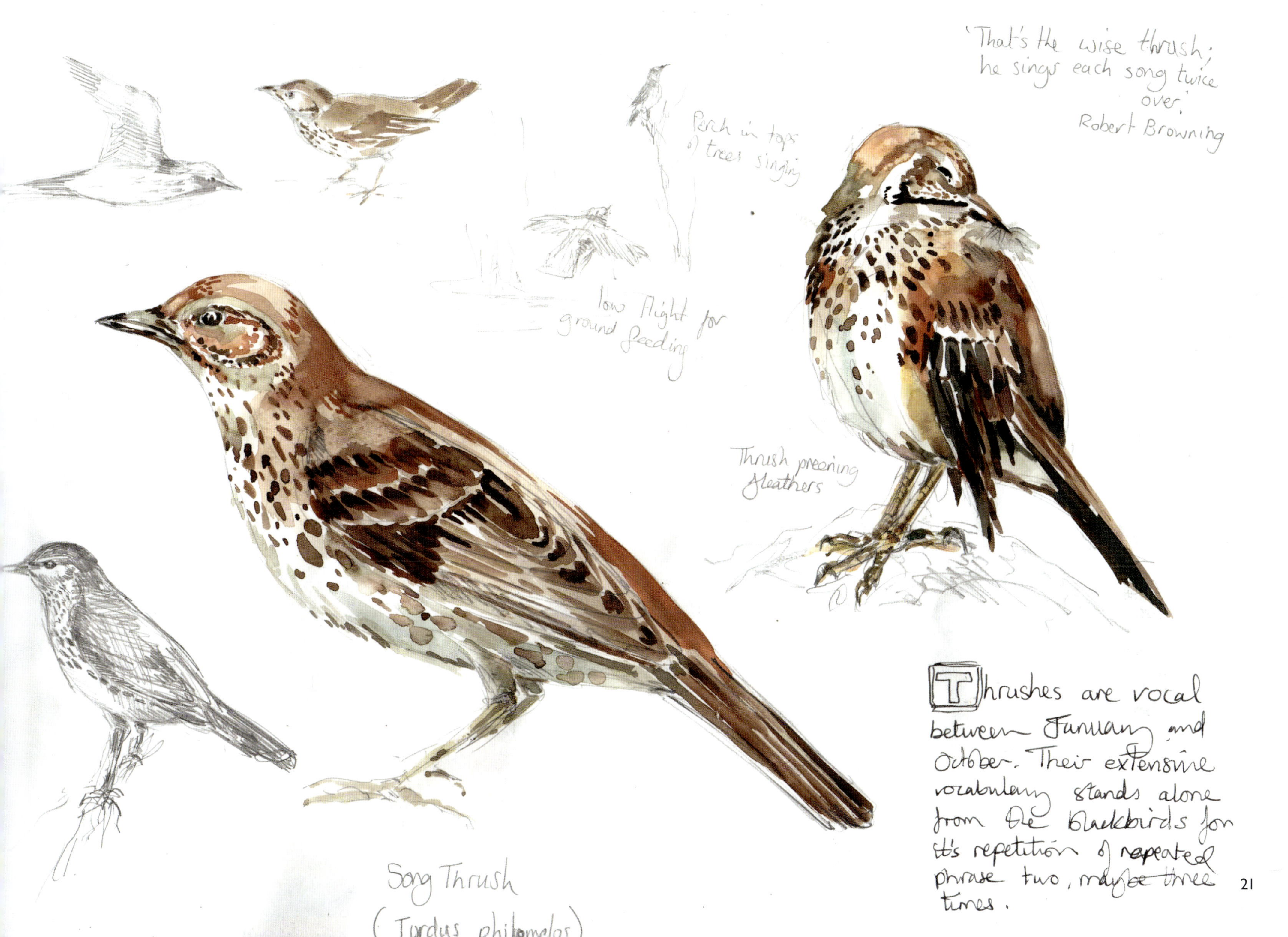
'That's the wise thrush;
he sings each song twice
over.'
Robert Browning

Perch in tops
of trees singing

low flight for
ground feeding

Thrush preening
feathers

Song Thrush
(Turdus philomelos)

Thrushes are vocal
between January and
October. Their extensive
vocabulary stands alone
from the blackbirds for
it's repetition of repeated
phrase two, maybe three
times.

21

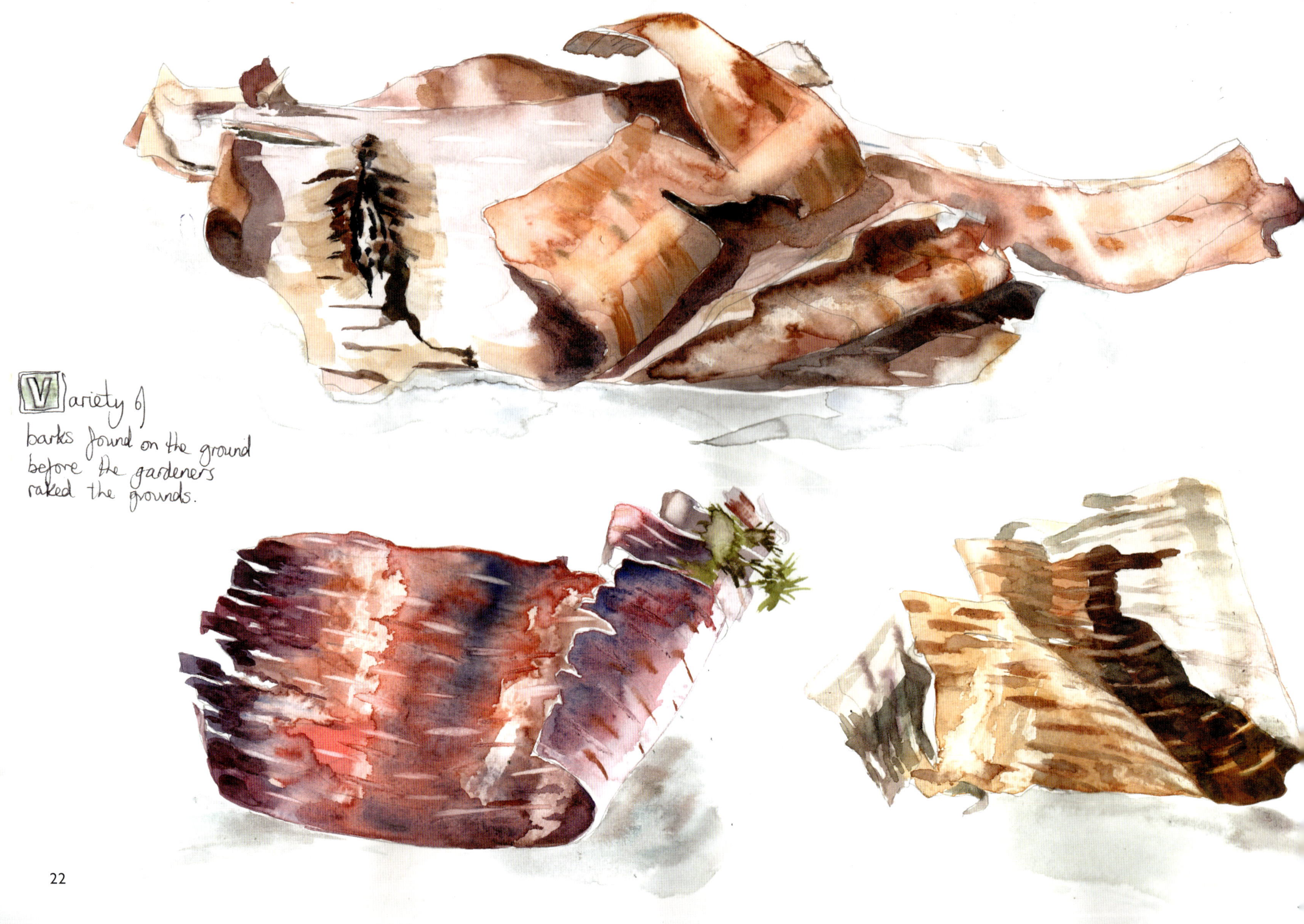

Variety of
barks found on the ground
before the gardeners
raked the grounds.

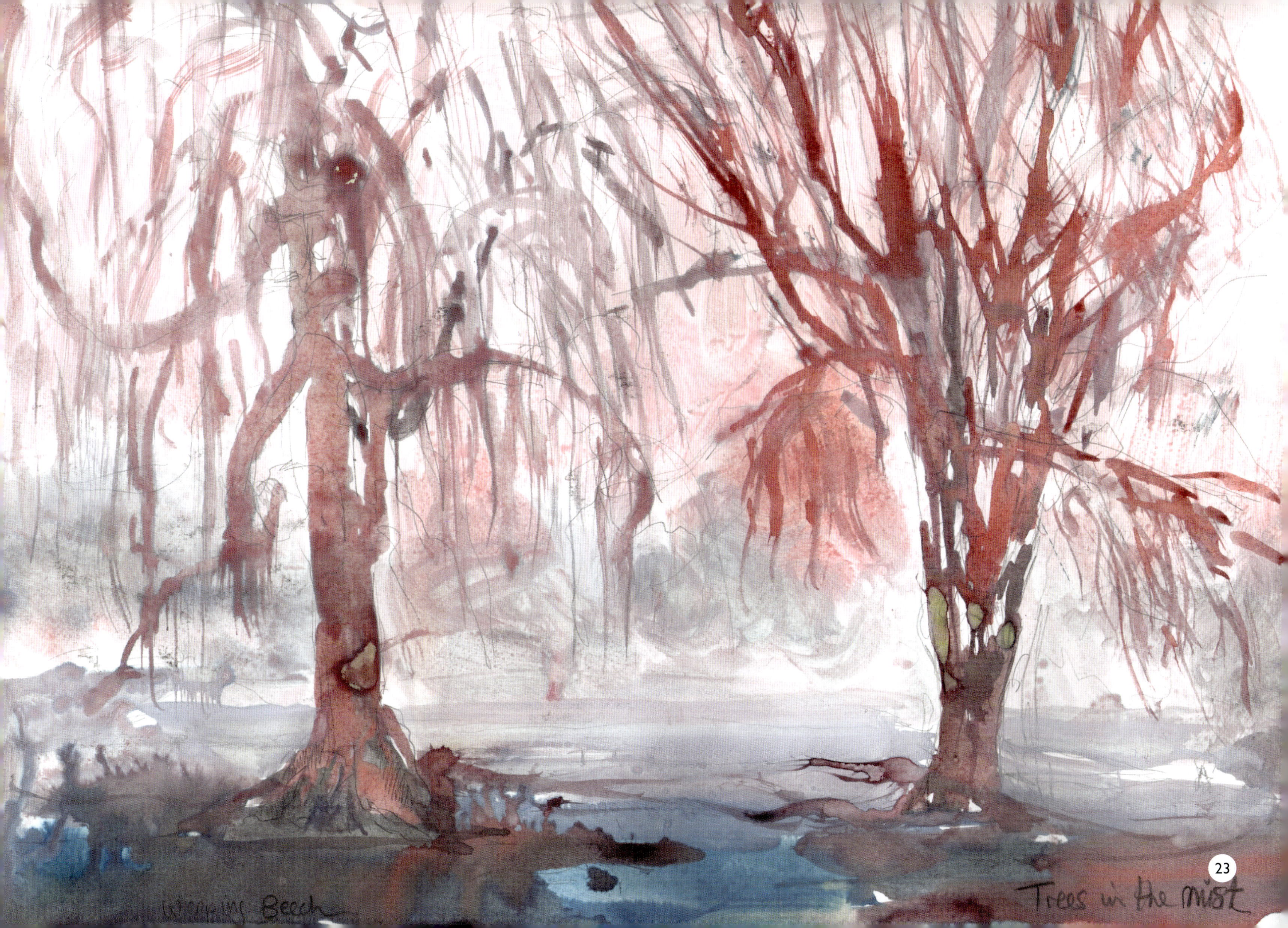

Weeping Beech
Trees in the mist
23

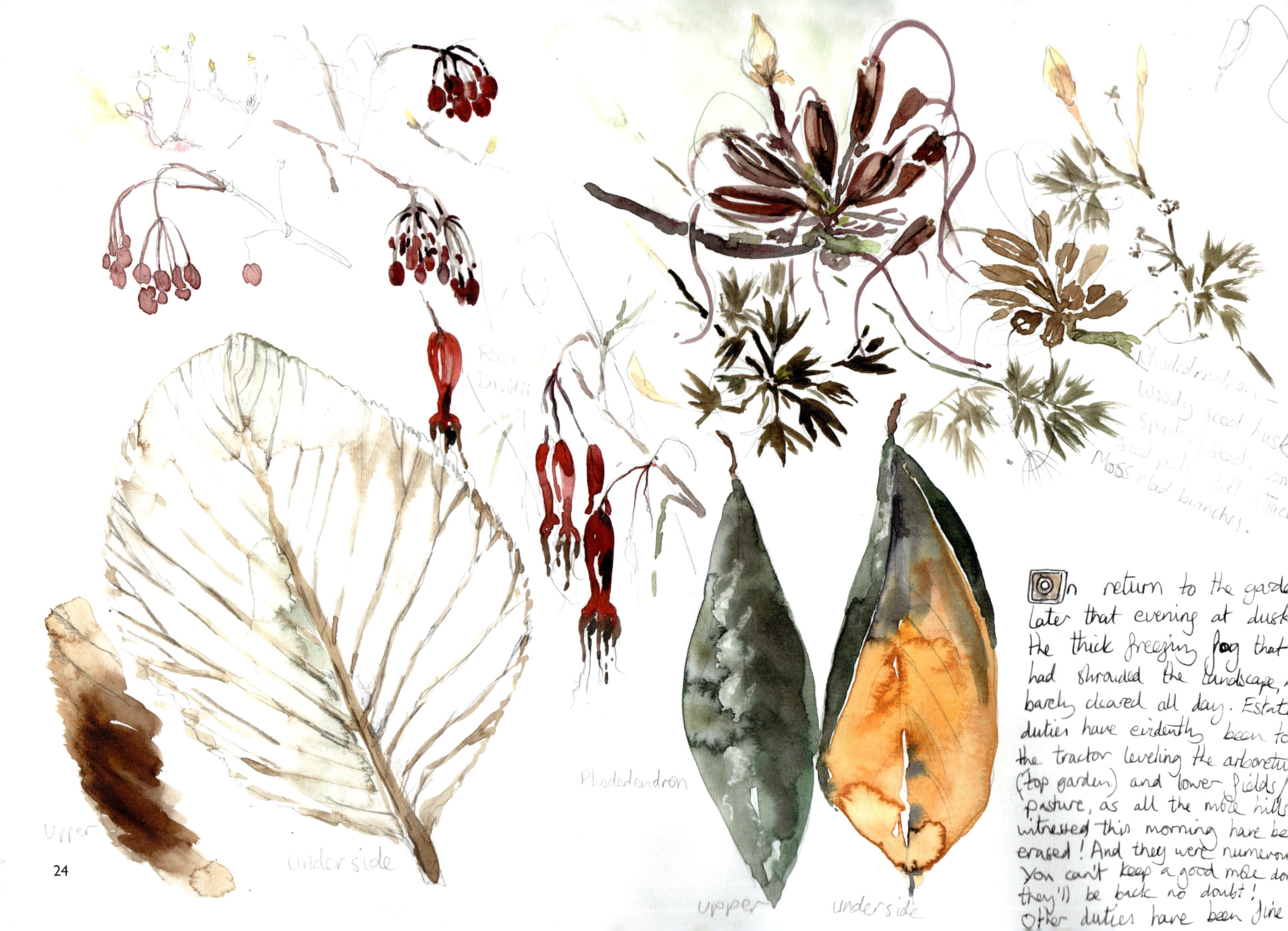

Rosa Davidii

Rhododendron

Upper

Underside

upper   underside

Rhododendron —
Woody seed husk
Spent seed
Moss clad branches.

On return to the garden
later that evening at dusk
the thick freezing fog that
had shrouded the landscape,
barely cleared all day. Estate
duties have evidently been to
the tractor leveling the arboretum
(top garden) and lower fields/
pasture, as all the mole hills
witnessed this morning have been
erased! And they were numerous
You can't keep a good mole down
they'll be back no doubt!
Other duties have been fine

24

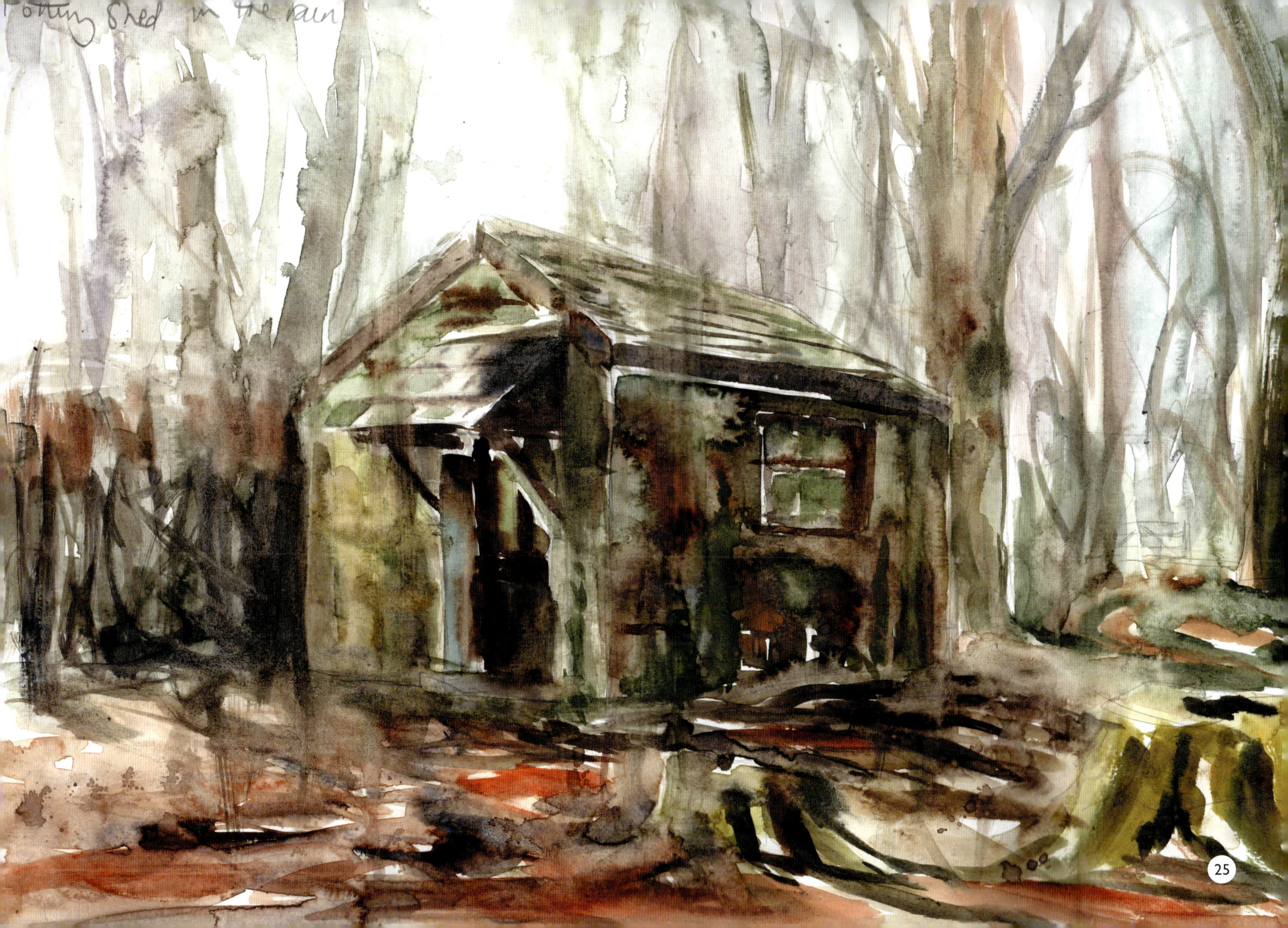

25

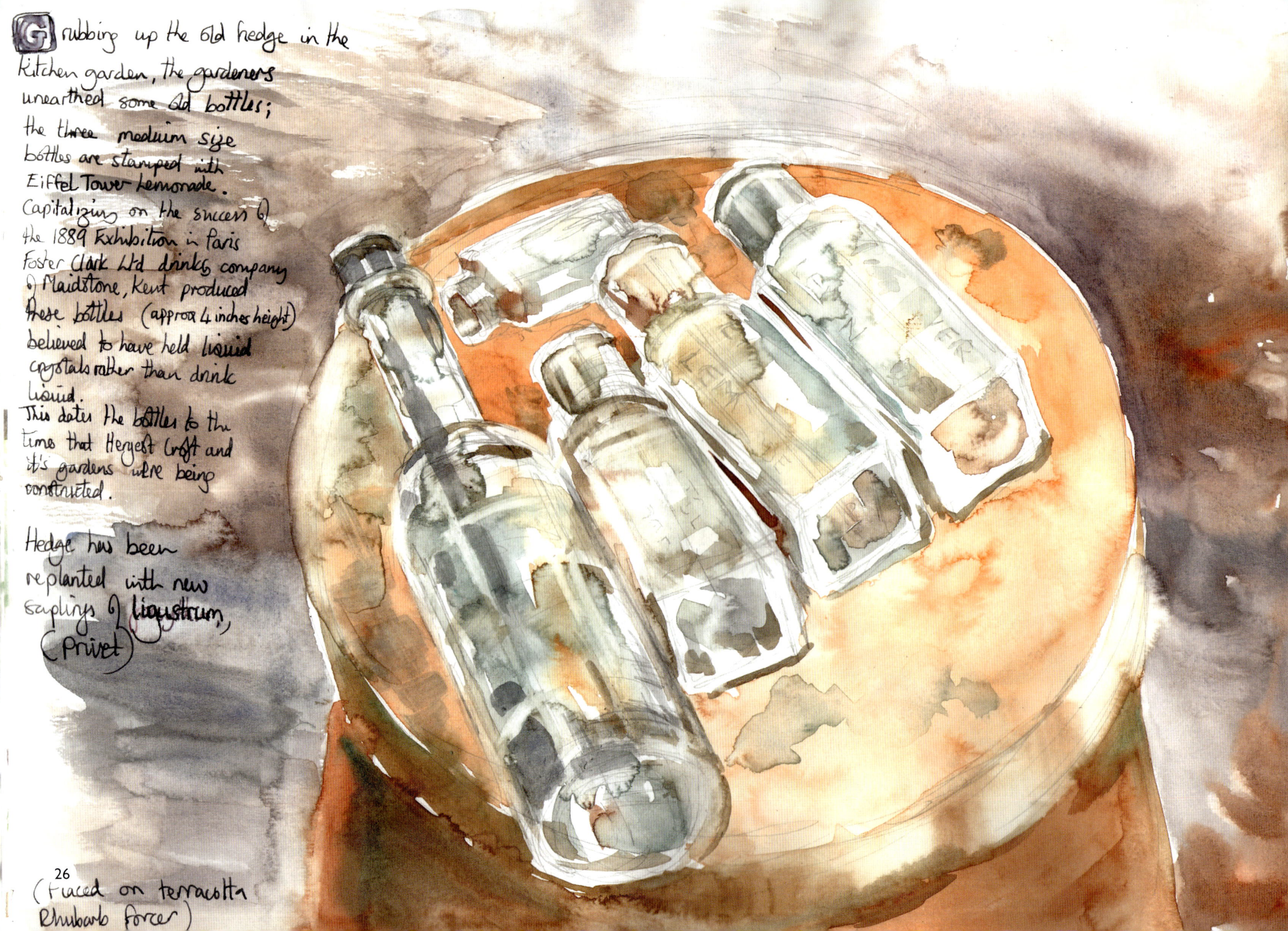

Grubbing up the old hedge in the
Kitchen garden, the gardeners
unearthed some old bottles;
the three medium size
bottles are stamped with
Eiffel Tower Lemonade.
Capitalizing on the success of
the 1889 Exhibition in Paris
Foster Clark Ltd drinks company
of Maidstone, Kent produced
these bottles (approx 4 inches height)
believed to have held liquid
crystals rather than drink
liquid.
This dates the bottles to the
time that Hergest Croft and
it's gardens were being
constructed.

Hedge has been
replanted with new
saplings of ligustrum,
(privet)

(Placed on terracotta
Rhubarb forcer)

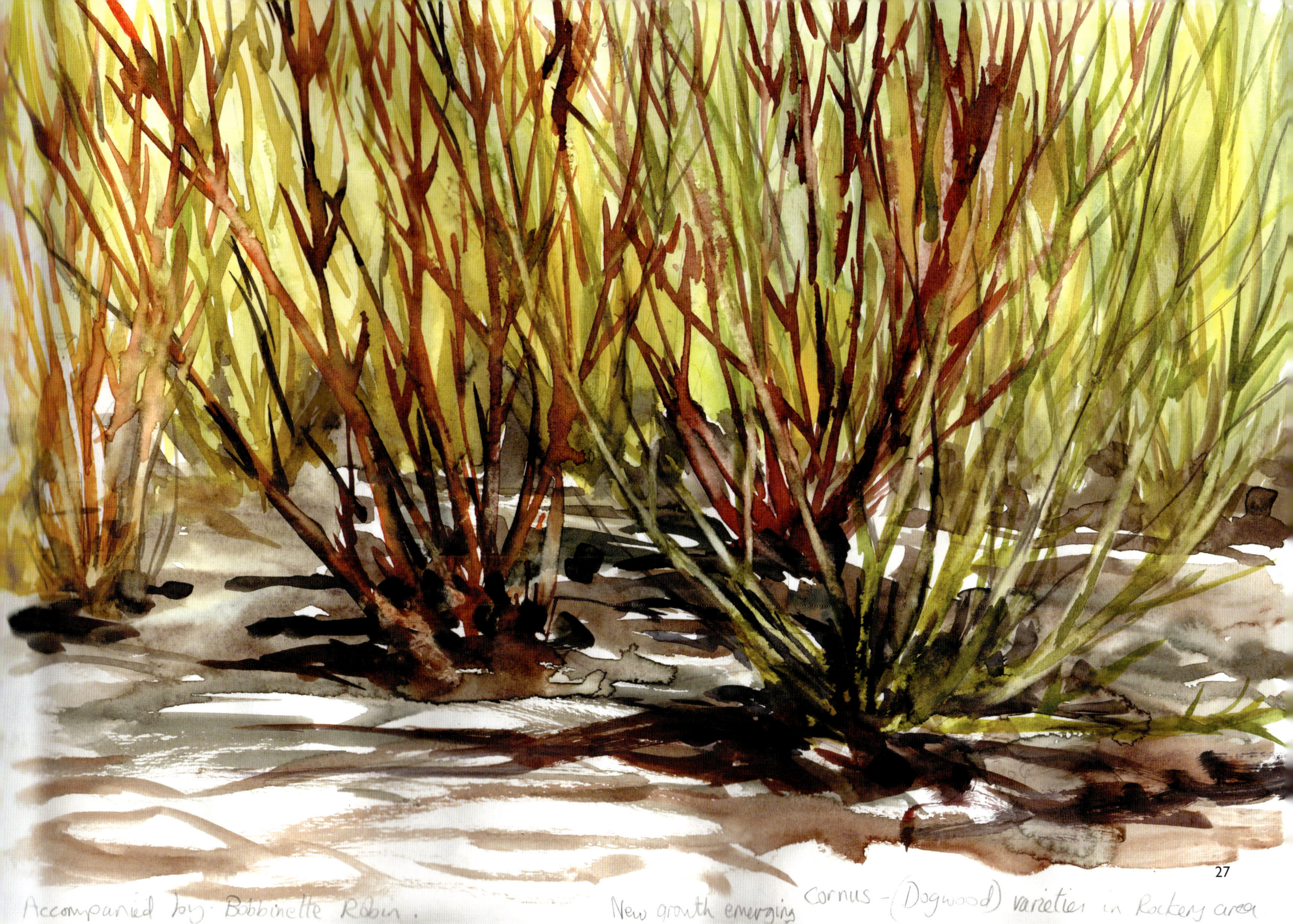

Accompanied by: Bobbinette Robin.
New growth emerging
Cornus - (Dogwood) varieties in Rockery area

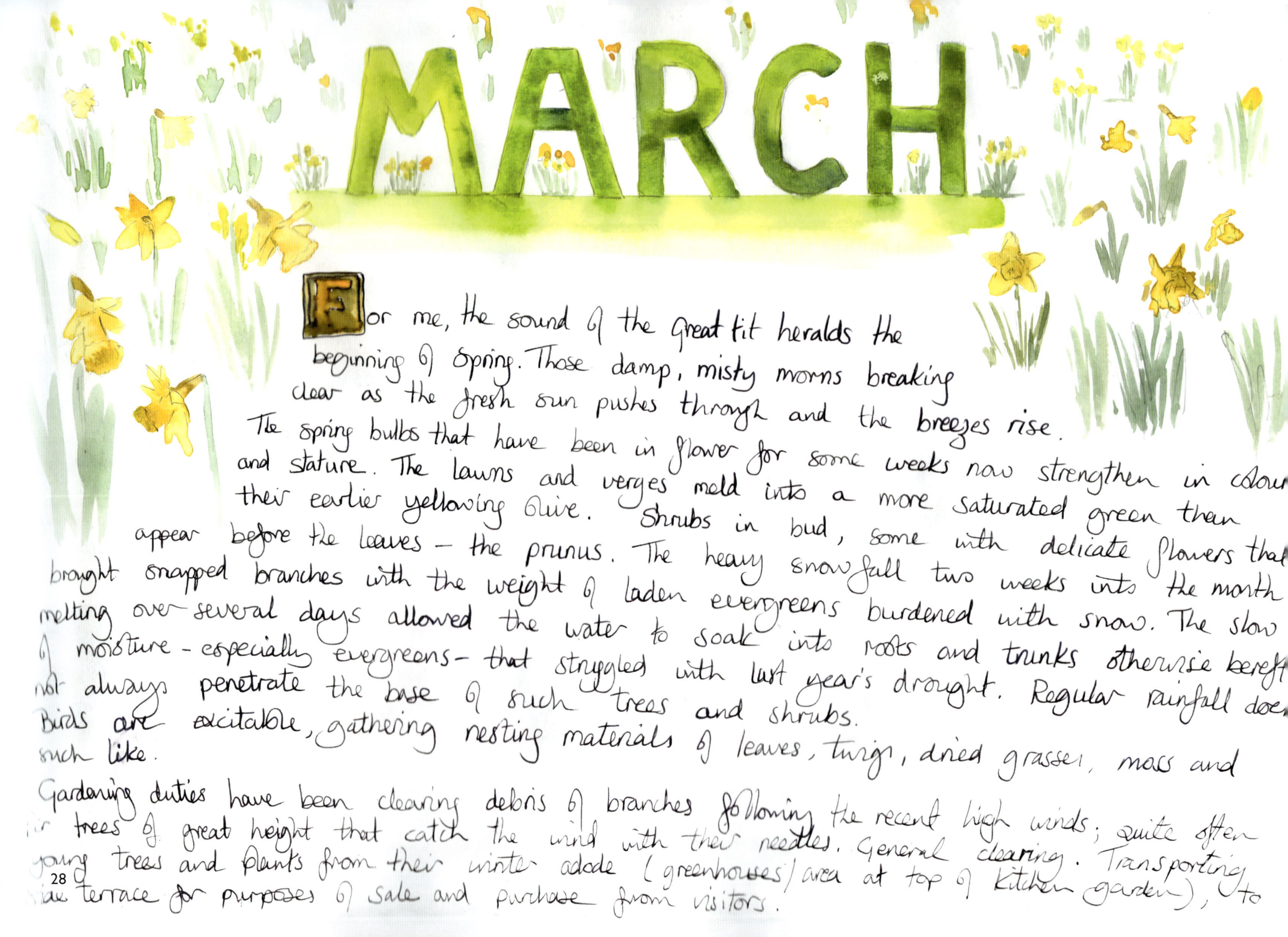

MARCH

For me, the sound of the great tit heralds the beginning of spring. Those damp, misty morns breaking clear as the fresh sun pushes through and the breezes rise.

The spring bulbs that have been in flower for some weeks now strengthen in colour and stature. The lawns and verges meld into a more saturated green than their earlier yellowing olive. Shrubs in bud, some with delicate flowers that appear before the leaves – the prunus. The heavy snowfall two weeks into the month brought snapped branches with the weight of laden evergreens burdened with snow. The slow melting over several days allowed the water to soak into roots and trunks otherwise bereft of moisture – especially evergreens – that struggled with last year's drought. Regular rainfall does not always penetrate the base of such trees and shrubs.

Birds are excitable, gathering nesting materials of leaves, twigs, dried grasses, moss and such like.

Gardening duties have been clearing debris of branches following the recent high winds; quite often fir trees of great height that catch the wind with their needles. General clearing. Transporting young trees and plants from their winter abode (greenhouses/area at top of kitchen garden), to the terrace for purposes of sale and purchase from visitors.

28

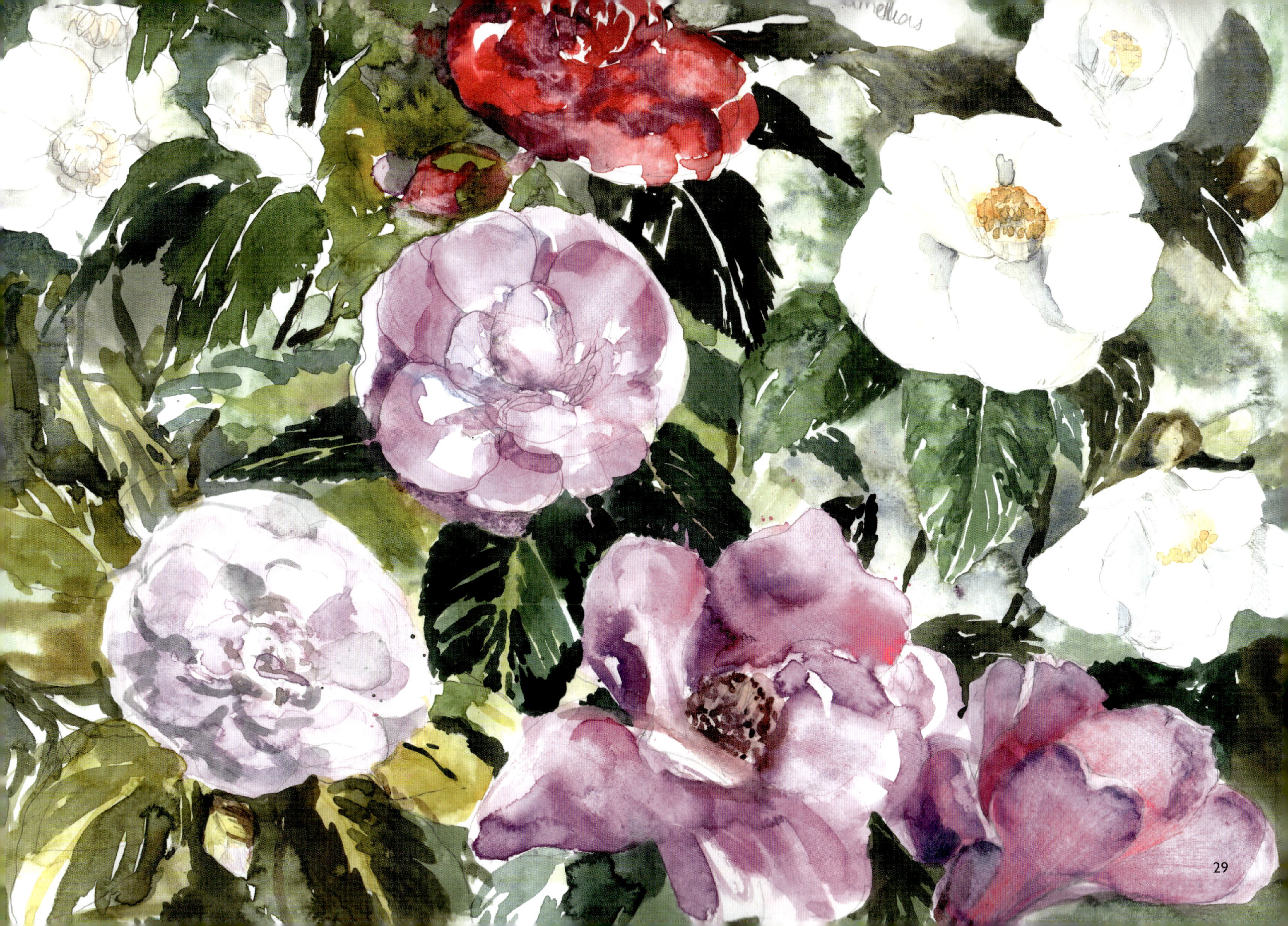
Camellias

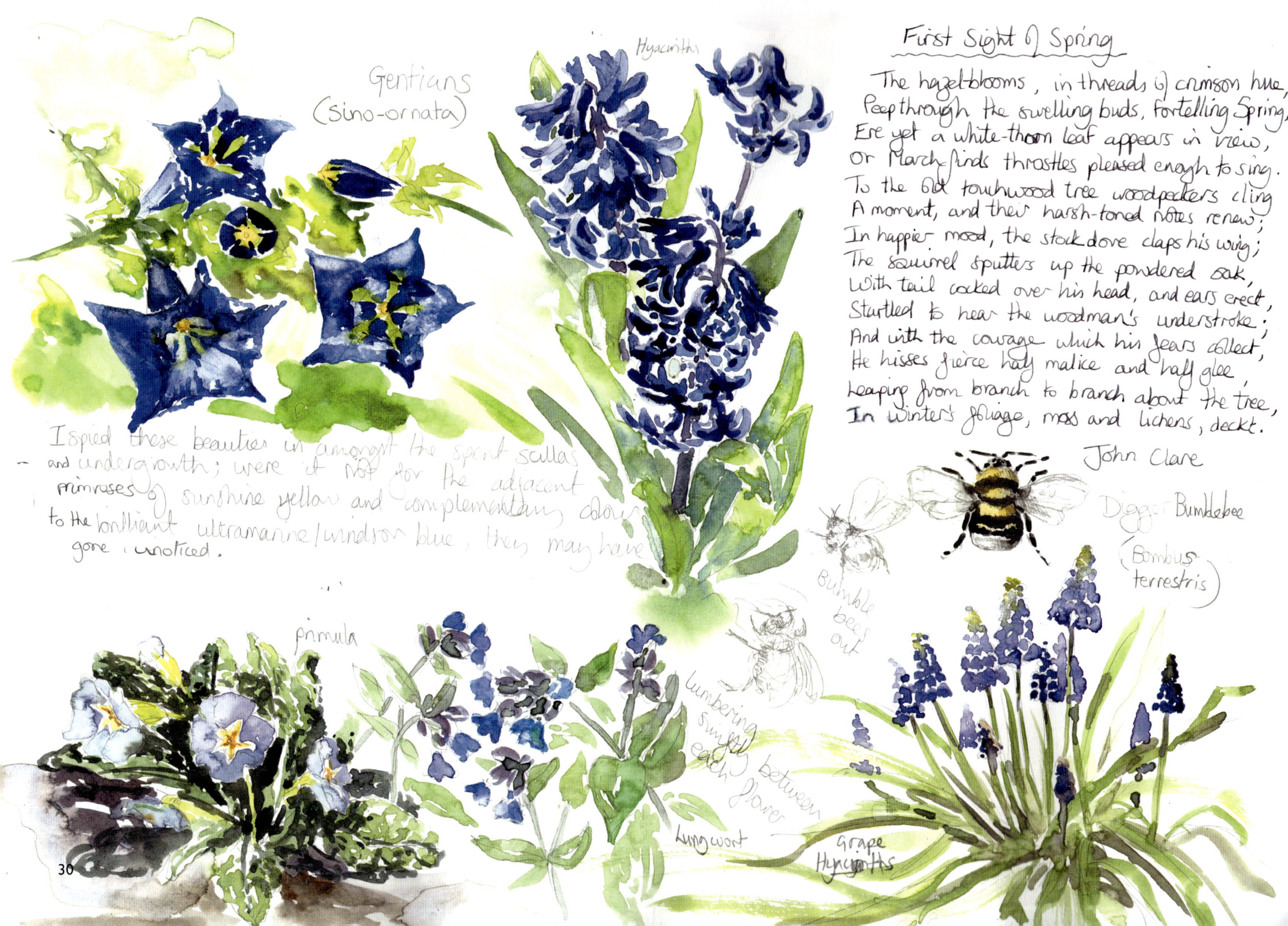

Gentians (Sino-ornata)

Hyacinths

First Sight of Spring
The hazel-blooms, in threads of crimson hue,
Peep through the swelling buds, foretelling Spring,
Ere yet a white-thorn leaf appears in view,
Or March finds throstles pleased enough to sing.
To the old touchwood tree woodpeckers cling
A moment, and their harsh-toned notes renew;
In happier mood, the stock dove claps his wing;
The squirrel sputters up the powdered oak,
With tail cocked over his head, and ears erect,
Startled to hear the woodman's understroke;
And with the courage which his fears collect,
He hisses fierce half malice and half glee,
Leaping from branch to branch about the tree,
In winter's foliage, moss and lichens, deckt.
John Clare

Digger Bumblebee (Bombus terrestris)

Bumble bees out

I spied these beauties in amongst the spent scillas and undergrowth; were it not for the adjacent primroses of sunshine yellow and complementary colour to the brilliant ultramarine/windsor blue, they may have gone unnoticed.

Primula

Lumbering swiftly between each flower

Lungwort

Grape Hyacinths

30

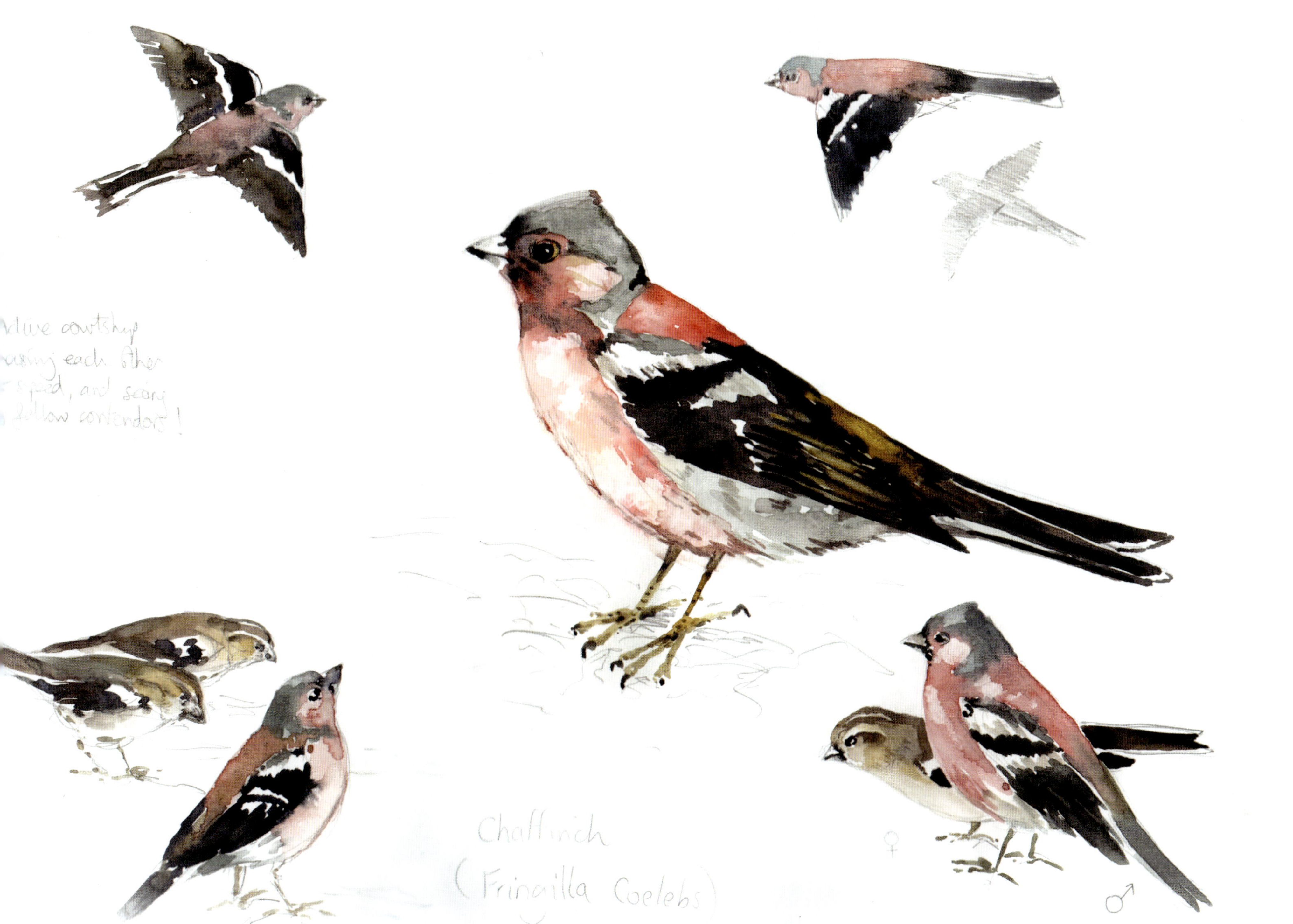

...tive courtship
...asing each other
...speed, and scare
...fellow contenders !
Chaffinch
(Fringilla Coelebs)
♀
♂

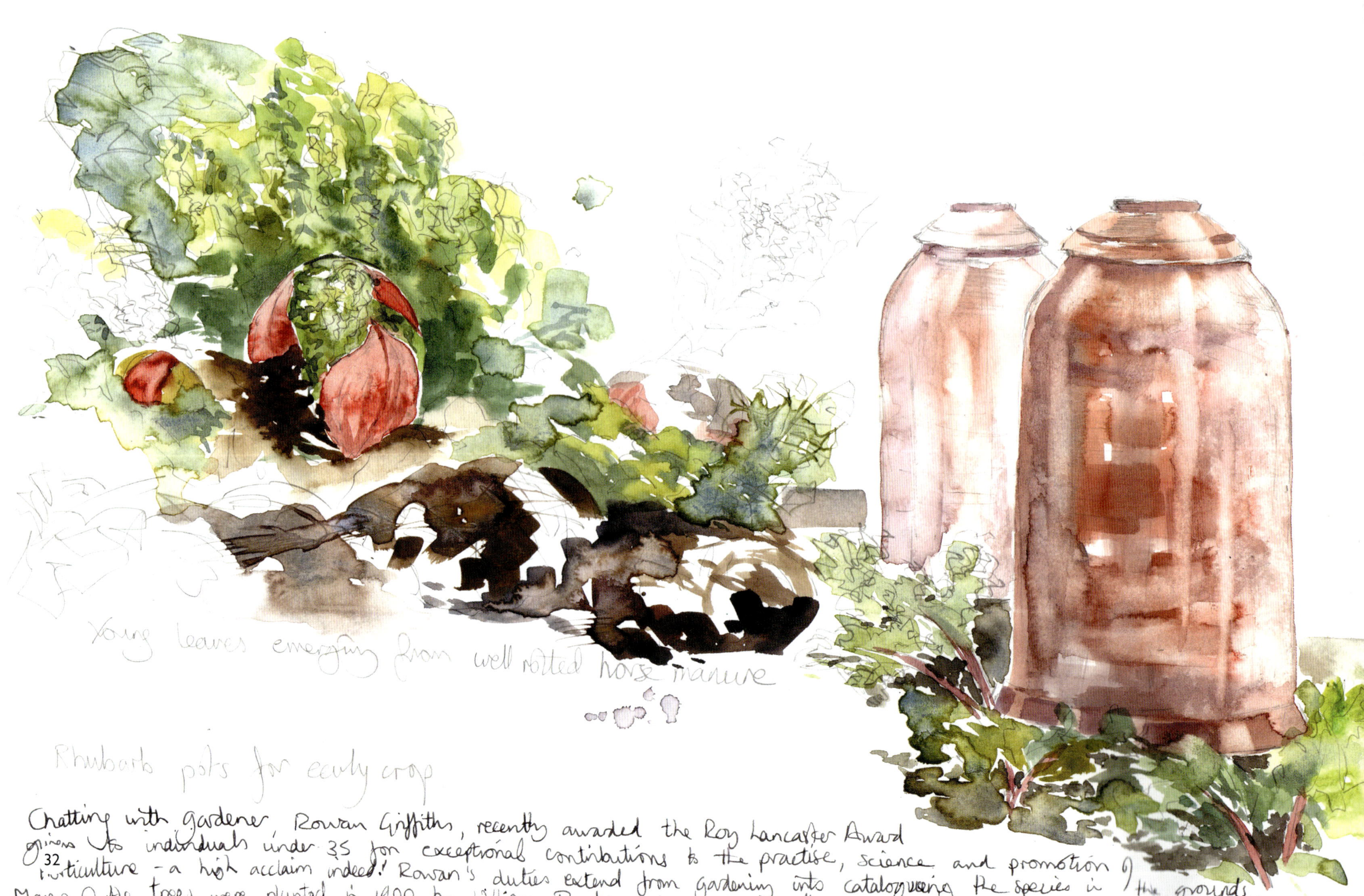

Chatting with gardener, Rowan Griffiths, recently awarded the Roy Lancaster Award given to individuals under 35 for exceptional contributions to the practise, science and promotion of horticulture - a high acclaim indeed! Rowan's duties extend from gardening into cataloguing the species in the grounds. Many of the trees were planted in 1900 by Williams Banks and subsequently in the 1980's by Lawrence Banks.

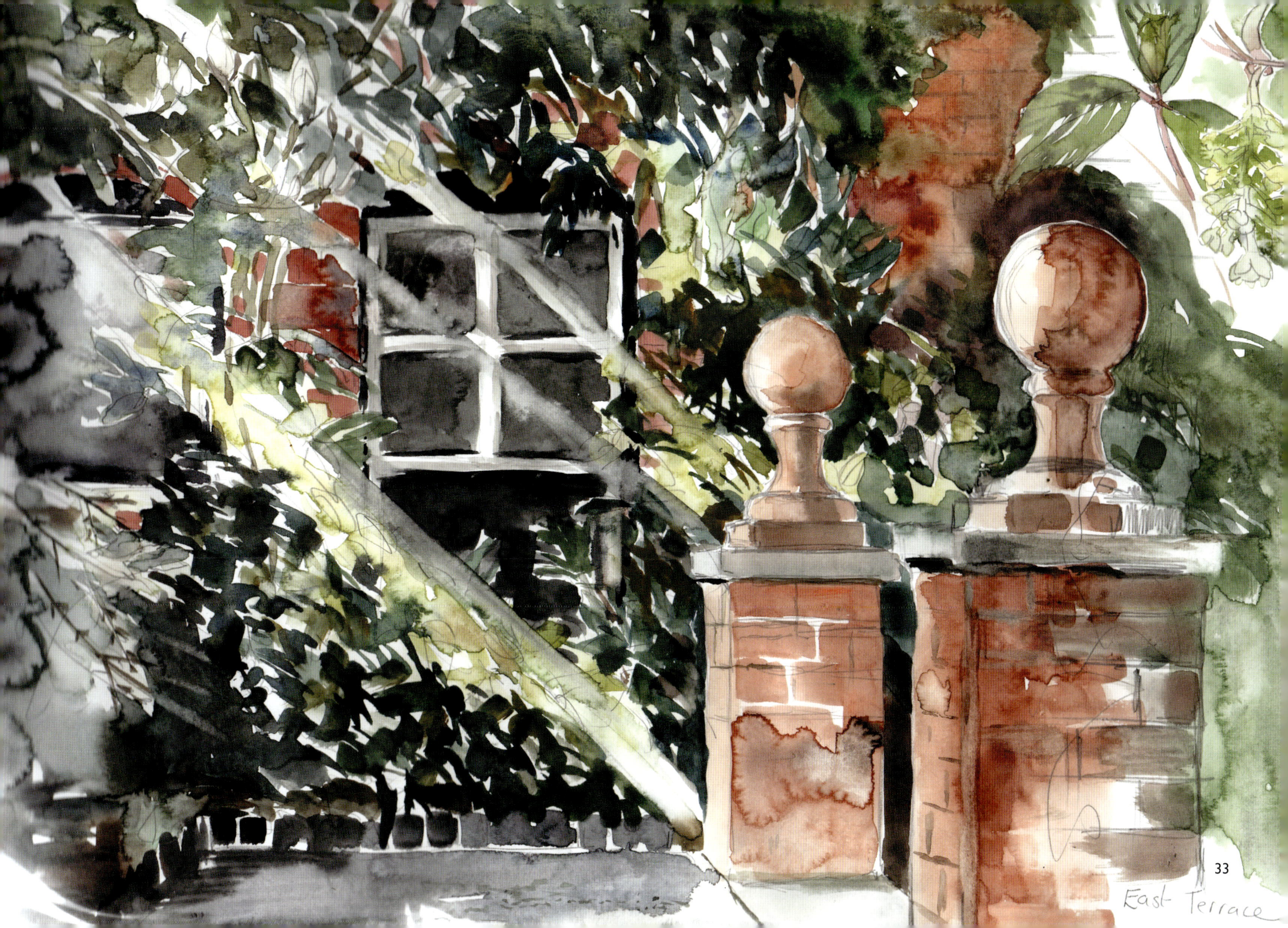

33

East Terrace

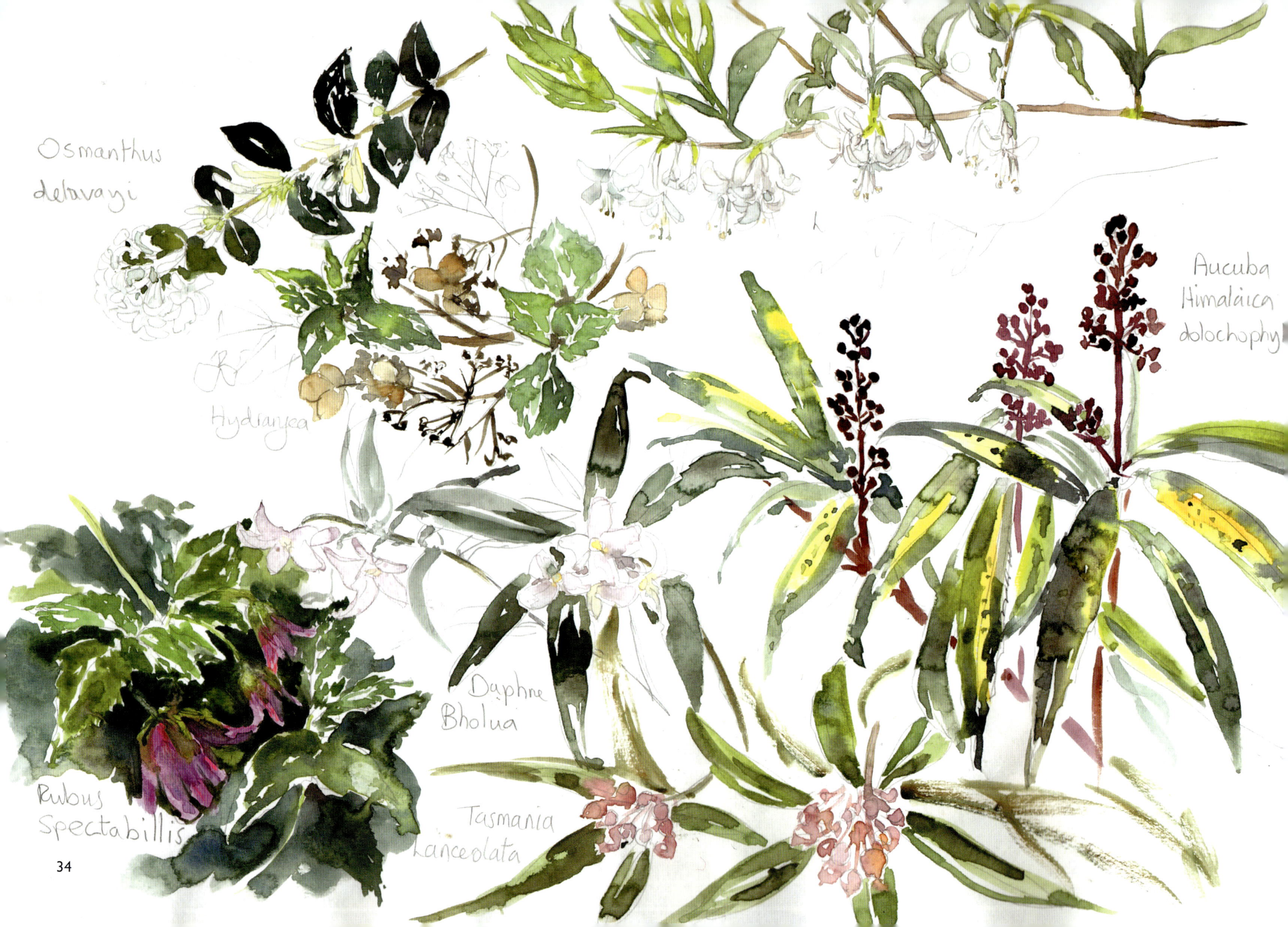

Osmanthus
delavayi
Hydrangea
Aucuba
Himalaica
dolochophy
Rubus
Spectabillis
Daphne
Bholua
Tasmania
Lanceolata
34

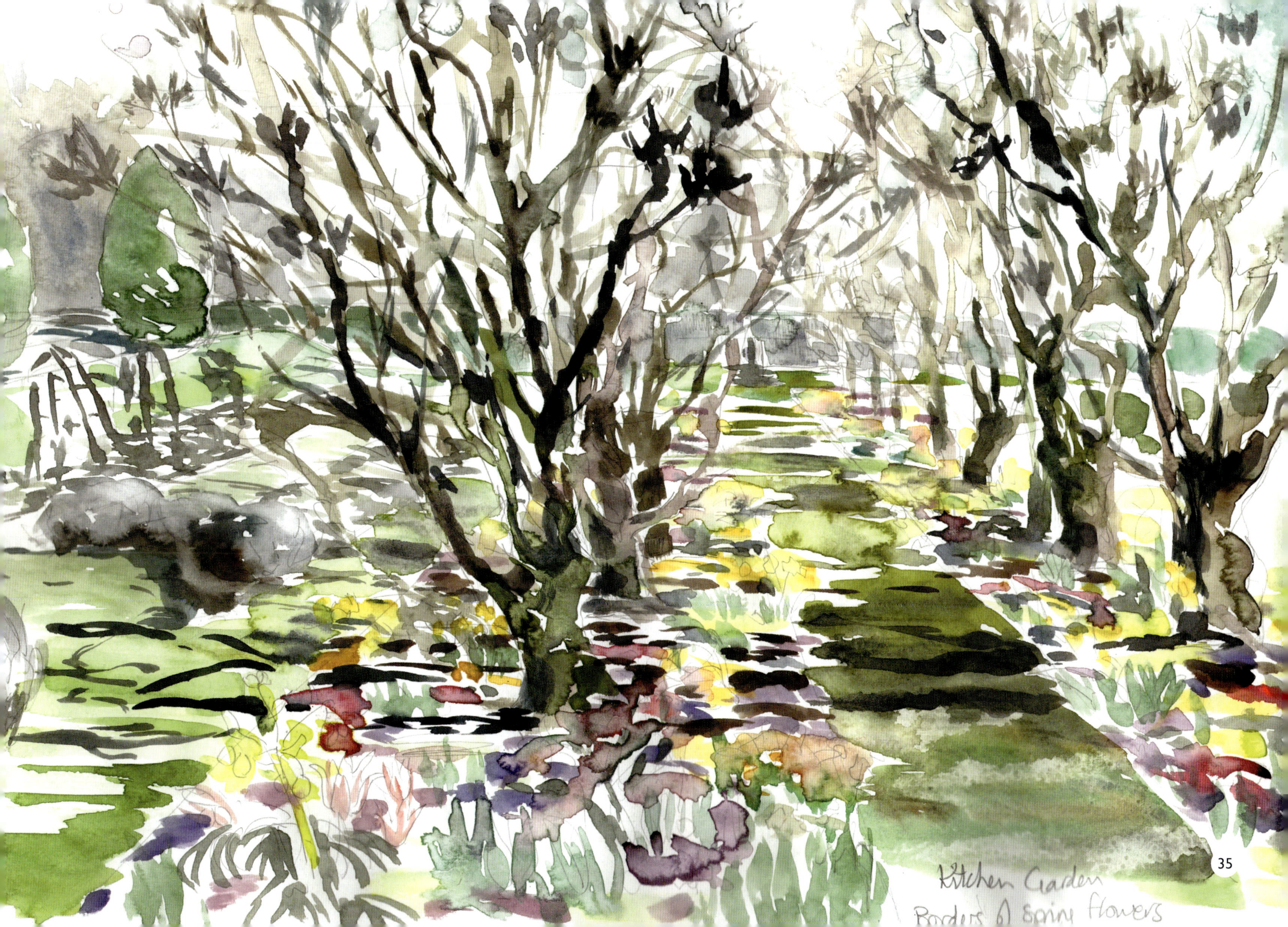

Kitchen Garden
Borders & Spring Flowers

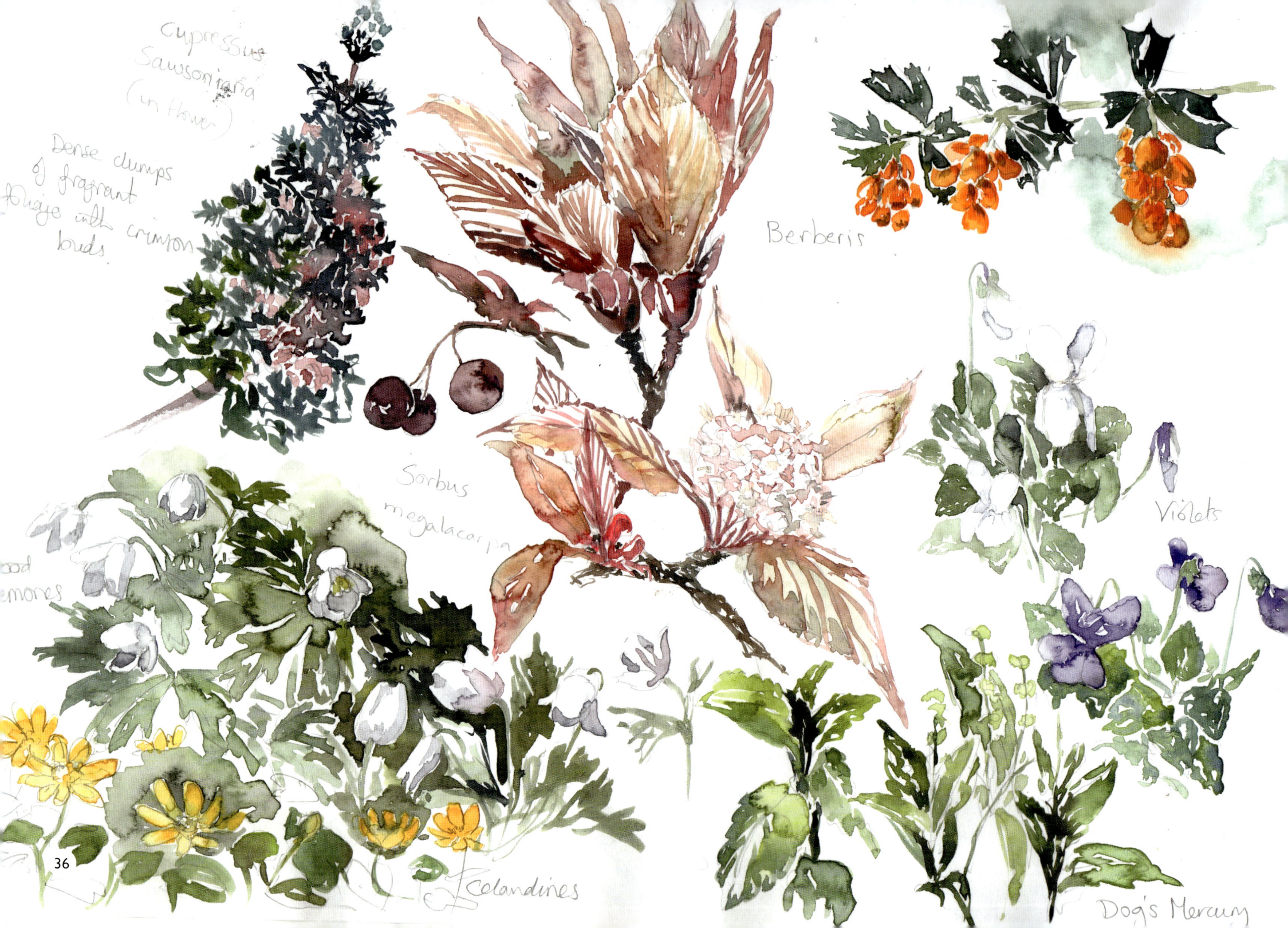

Cupressus
Sawsoniana
(in flower)

Dense clumps
of fragrant
foliage with crimson
buds.

Berberis

Sorbus
megalacarpa

Violets

wood
anemones

Celandines

Dog's Mercury

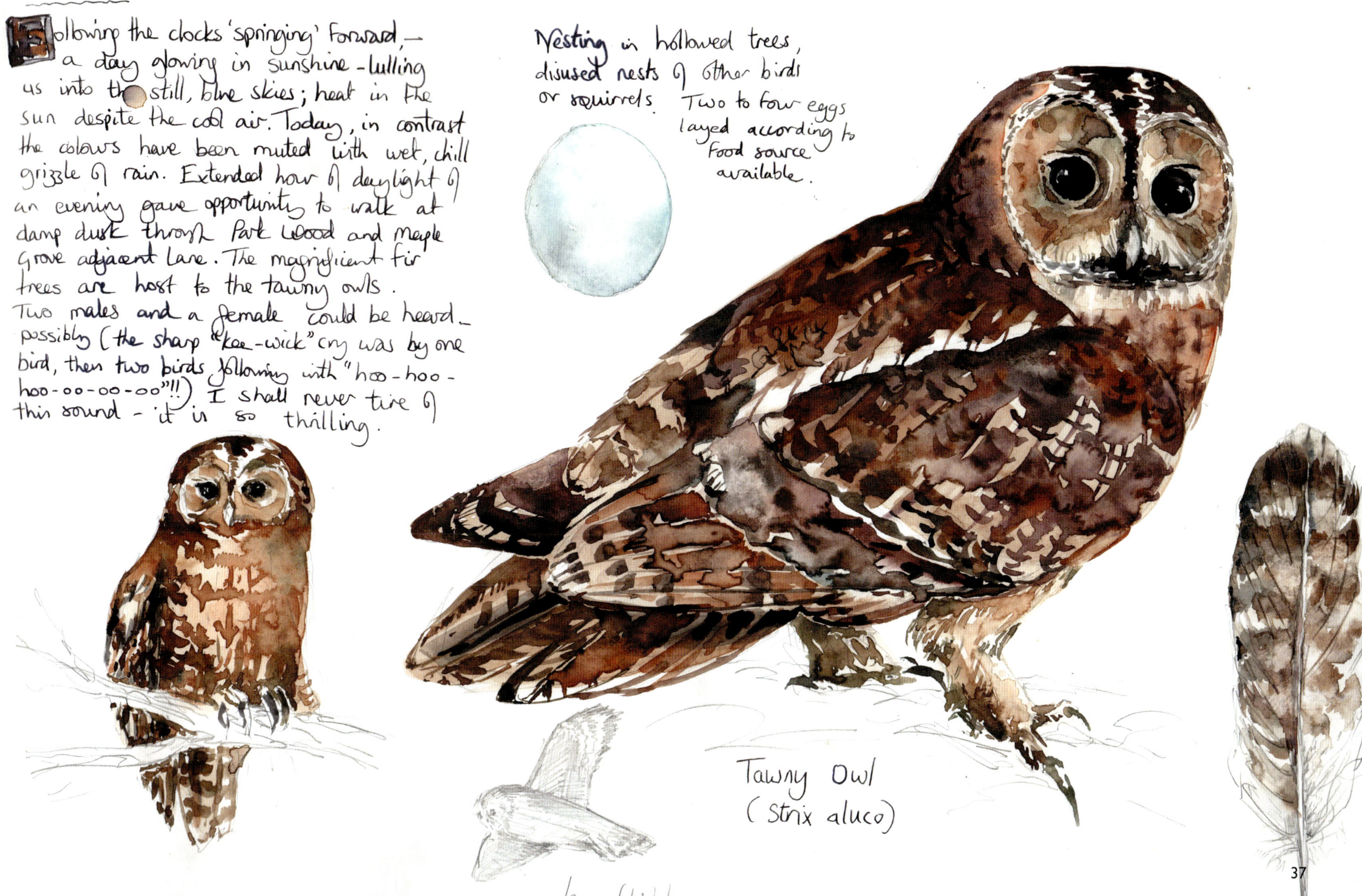

March 27th

Following the clocks 'springing' forward,— a day glowing in sunshine - lulling us into the still, blue skies; heat in the sun despite the cool air. Today, in contrast the colours have been muted with wet, chill grizzle of rain. Extended hour of daylight of an evening gave opportunity to walk at damp dusk through Park wood and Maple Grove adjacent Lane. The magnificent fir trees are host to the tawny owls. Two males and a female could be heard— possibly (the sharp "kee-wick" cry was by one bird, then two birds following with "hoo-hoo-hoo-oo-oo-oo"!!) I shall never tire of this sound - it is so thrilling.

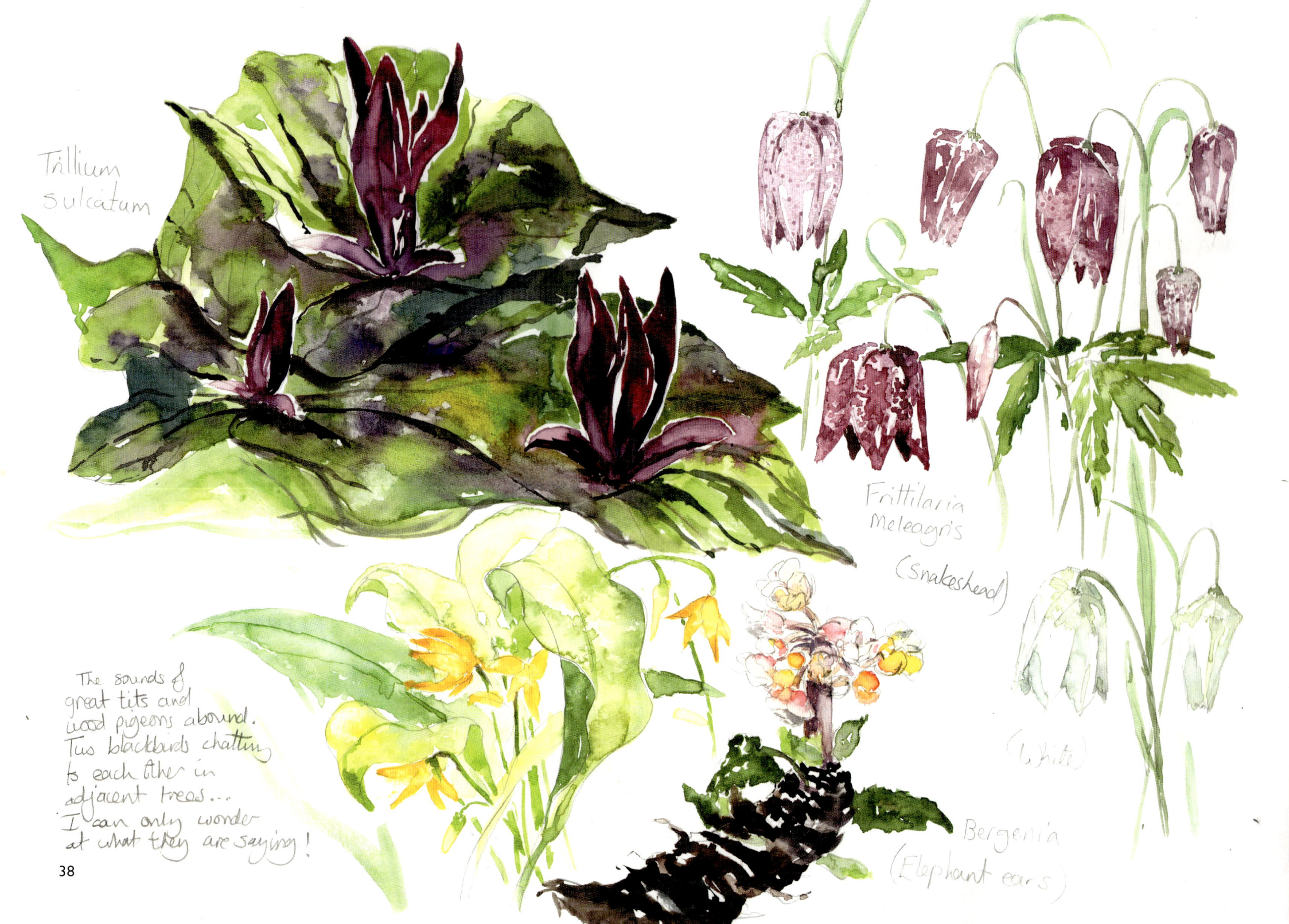

Trillium
sulcatum
Frittilaria
Meleagris
(Snakeshead)
(white)
Bergenia
(Elephant ears)
The sounds of
great tits and
wood pigeons abound.
Two blackbirds chatting
to each other in
adjacent trees...
I can only wonder
at what they are saying!
38

APRIL

Extracts from: The Tuft of Violets

'There was the healthy mass
Of dark delightful leaves, with their own breath
Of sylvan moss and grass; ....

From high above my head
The mated missel-thrush was singing proudly,
And through the dusky bed
The light-reflecting bee rejoicing loudly,
Kissing each modest face,
Sang to them well how beautiful they were,
Who in that slight embrace
Let fall upon the green a little tear.
                                        Ruth Pitter

'Oh, how this Spring of love resembleth
The uncertain glory of an April day!
Which now shows all the beauty of the sun
And by and bye a cloud takes all away."
                                        Two gent[of] Verona - Shakespeare

A song of Salutation
'Come forth ye blossoms!' - over hill and lea,
A breath of sweetness wantons with the sea;
And mid the smiles and tears of tender spring,
On dripping boughs I heard the throstle sing.
Ye cups and stars that strew the fair green field,
Ye wings of gold the prickly gorses yield;
Ye pensive bells to purple pageants born,
Ye milk-white may-buds of the mantling thorn;
Ye violet gems and eyes of sapphire blue,
Wan, flushing wind-flowers and shy elfin crew
Of every crannied wall - come forth! and fling
Your vernal showers around me while I sing.
                                        Edith Holden

April has arrived to a blaze of brilliant sunshine. Fresh, clear blue skies that is so dazzling against the wetness of land, making the spring flowers of yellows, blues and pinks emphatic in their presen With stillness as a backdrop it alerts the ears to every minuscule sound - the wood pigeons in yonder trees mellow in their call; chattering jolly blackbirds; striking, punctuated great tits; an underlyin drone note of bumble bees - I can even hear the saturated earth seeping away beneath the warmth of the sun. Not to be complacent, the nights' clear skies have brought forth the hardest of frosts!

39

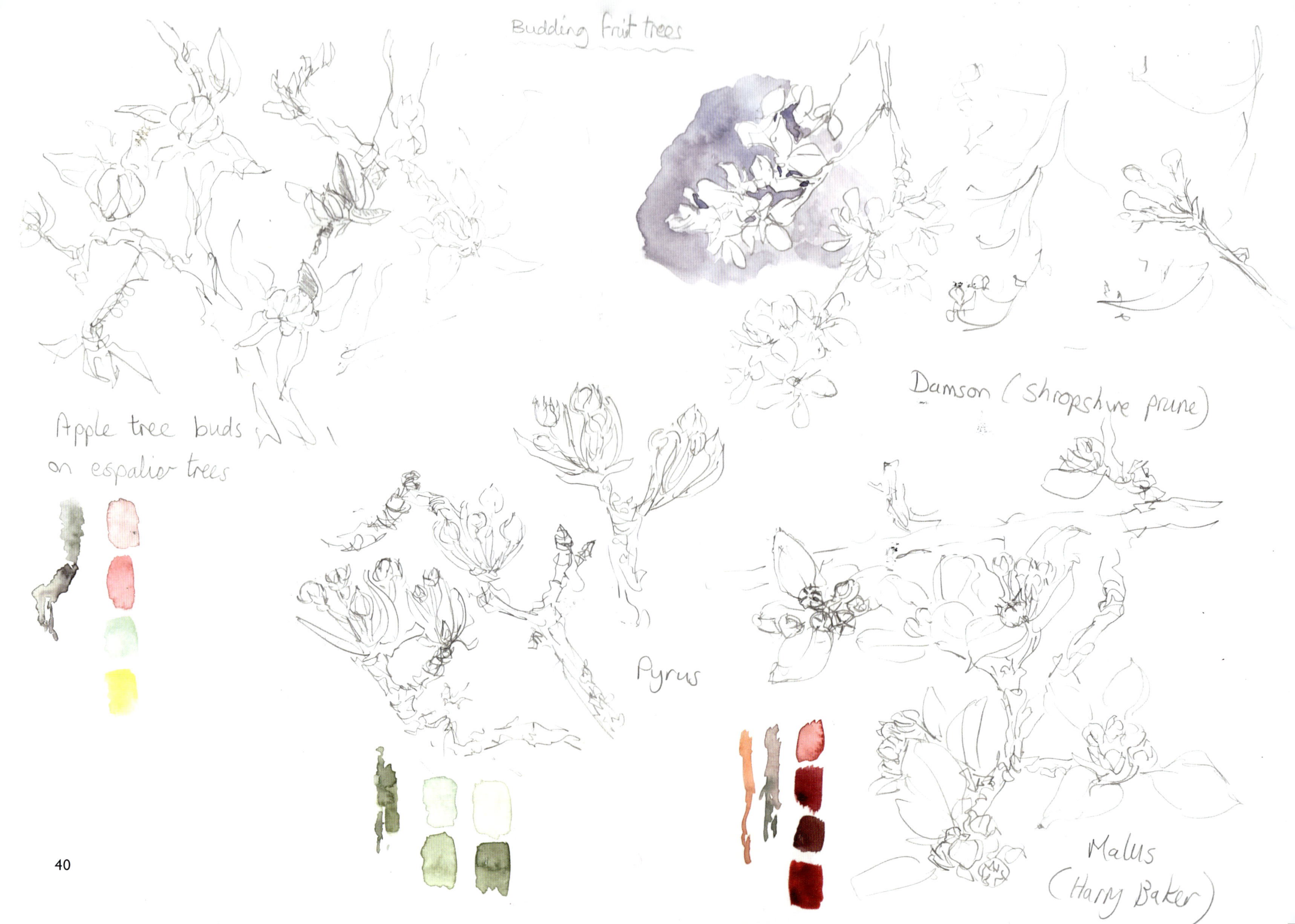

Budding fruit trees
Damson (Shropshire prune)
Apple tree buds
on espalier trees
Pyrus
Malus
(Harry Baker)
40

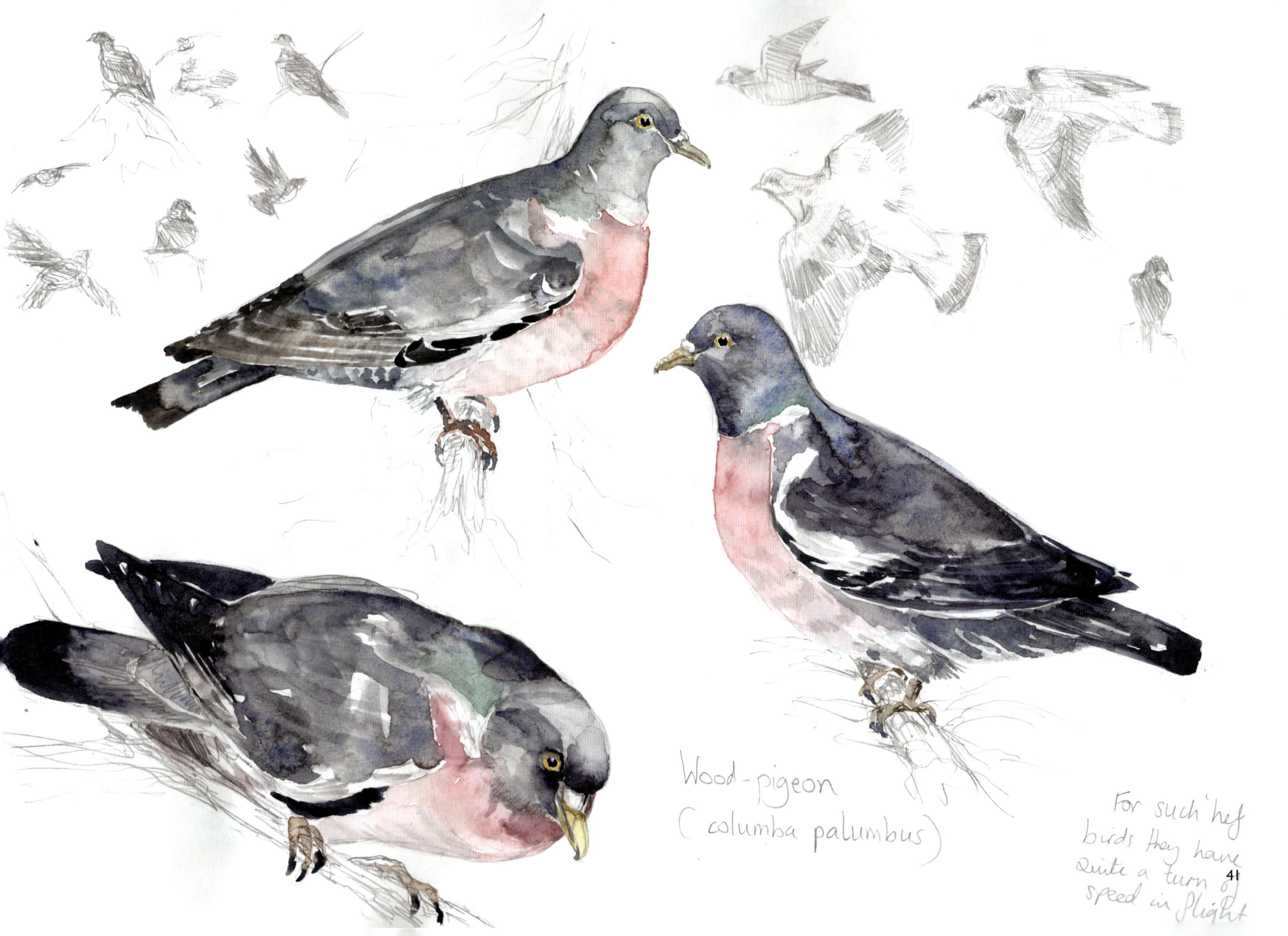

Wood-pigeon
(columba palumbus)
For such hef
birds they have
quite a turn of
speed in flight
41

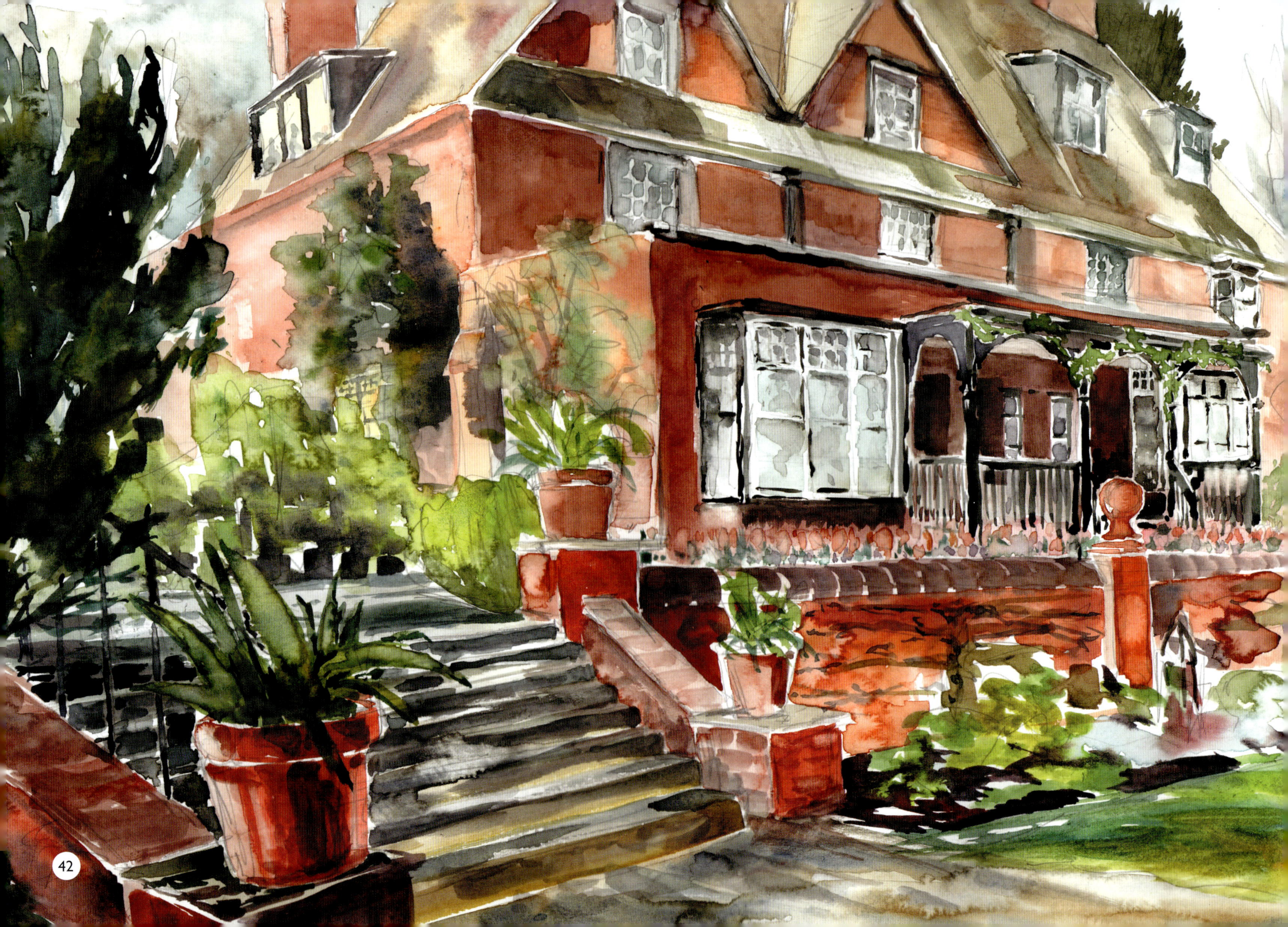

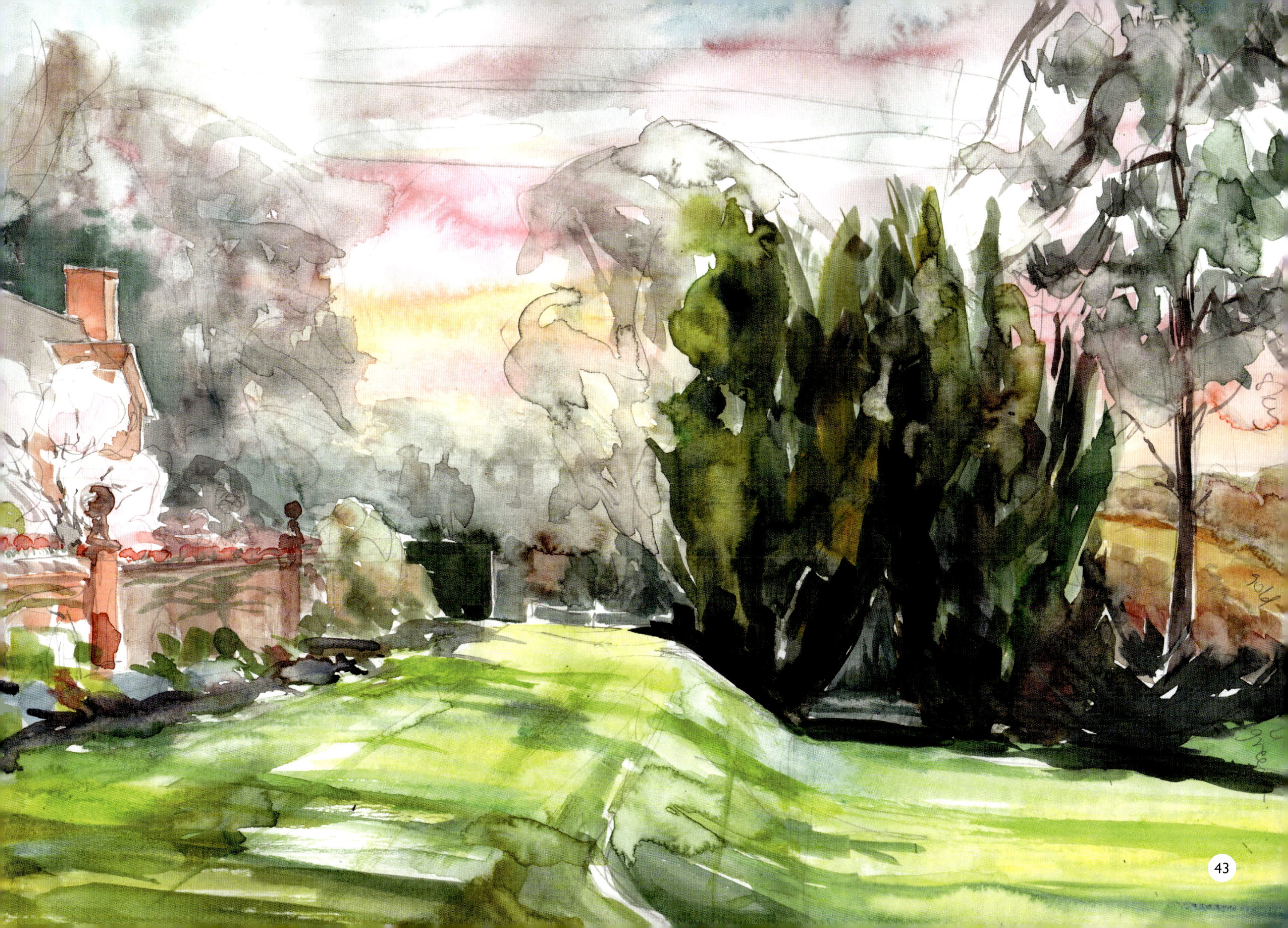

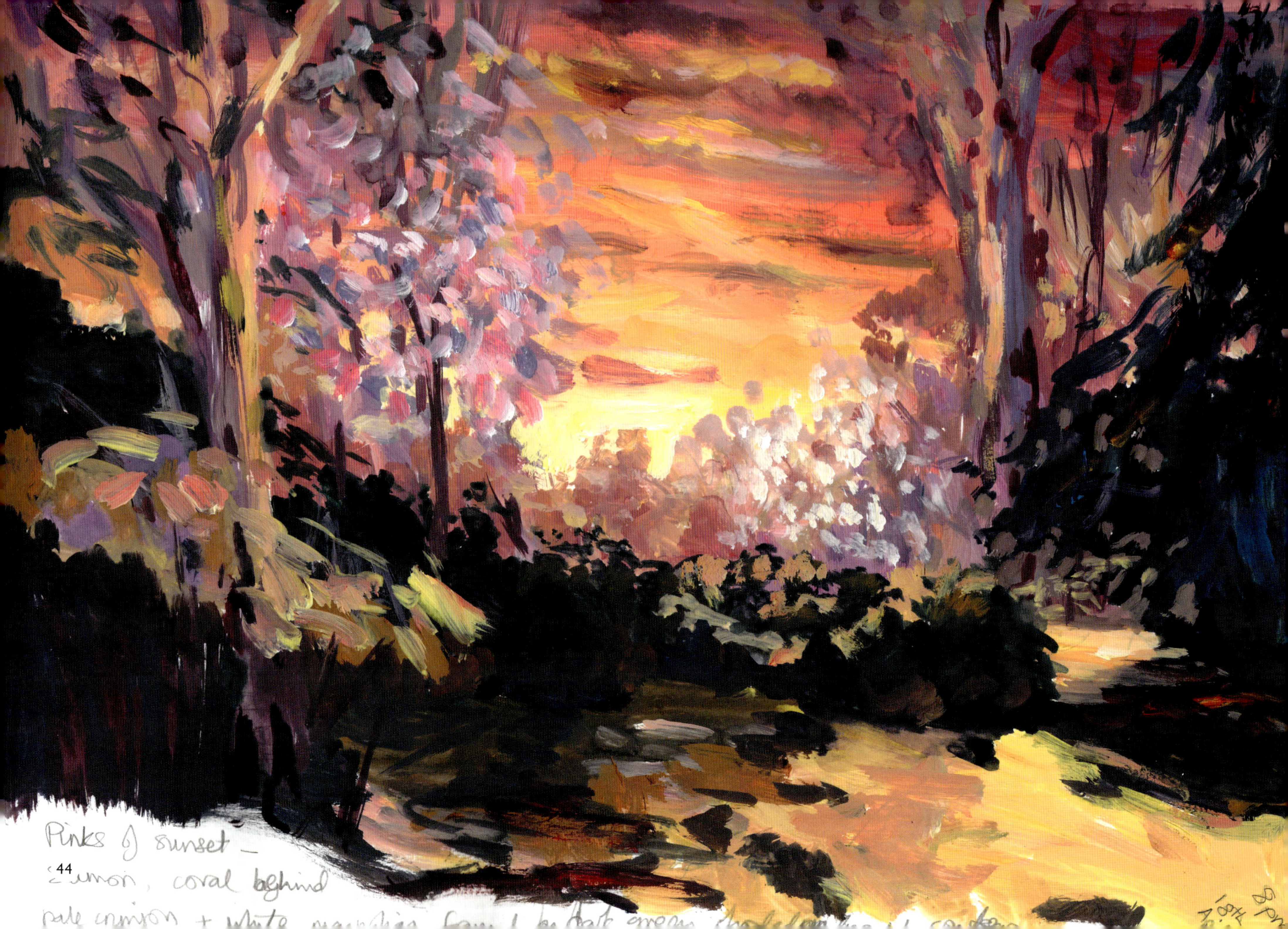

Pinks of sunset -
lemon, coral behind
pale crimson + white
44
7.48 pm

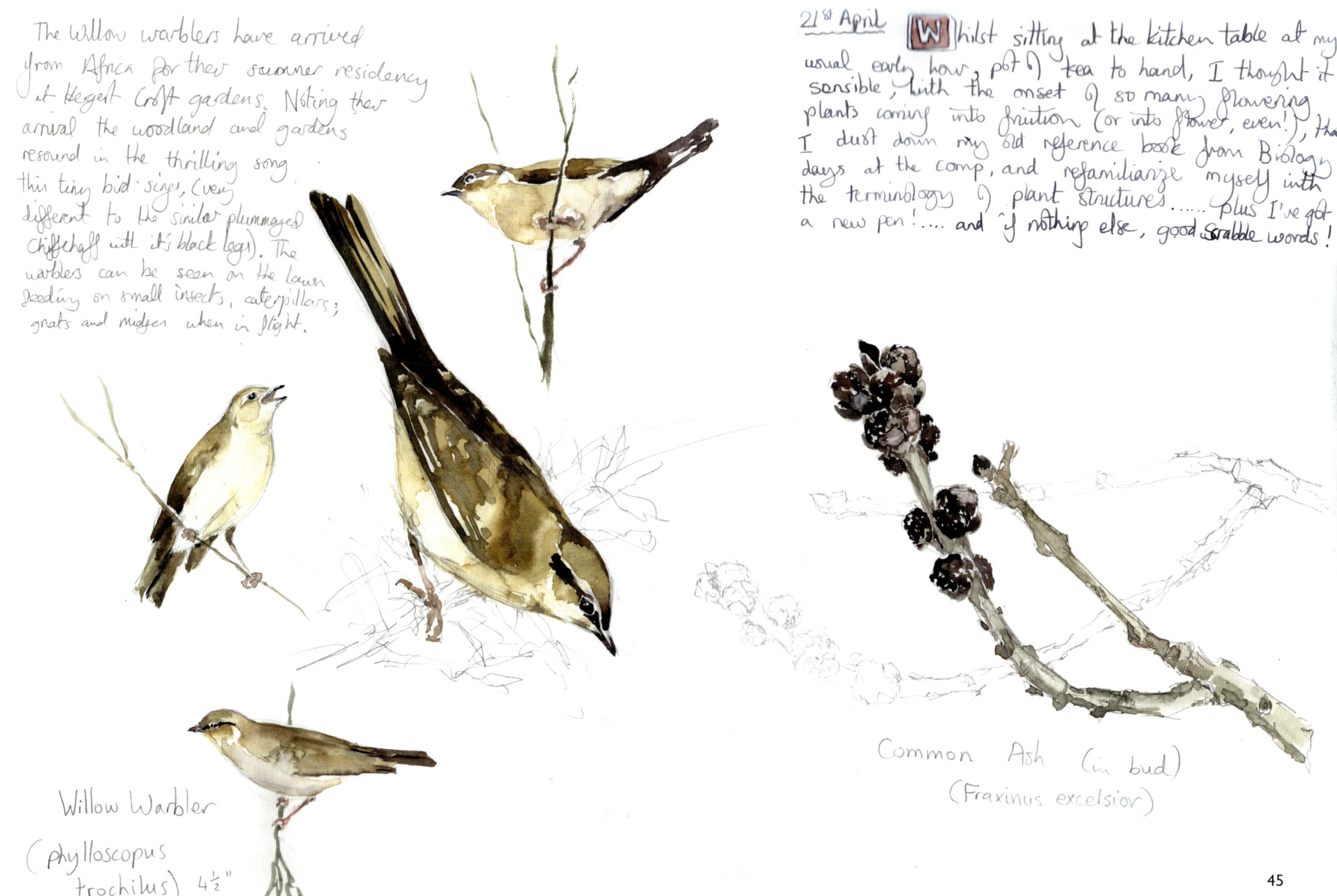

The willow warblers have arrived from Africa for their summer residency at Hergest Croft gardens. Noting their arrival the woodland and gardens resound in the thrilling song this tiny bird sings, (very different to the similar plummaged Chiffchaff with it's black legs). The warblers can be seen on the lawn feeding on small insects, caterpillars; gnats and midges when in flight.

21st April [W]hilst sitting at the kitchen table at my usual early hour, pot of tea to hand, I thought it sensible, with the onset of so many flowering plants coming into fruition (or into flower, even!), that I dust down my old reference book from Biology days at the comp, and refamiliarize myself with the terminology of plant structures...... plus I've got a new pen!.... and if nothing else, good scrabble words!

Willow Warbler

(Phylloscopus trochilus) 4½"

Common Ash (in bud)

(Fraxinus excelsior)

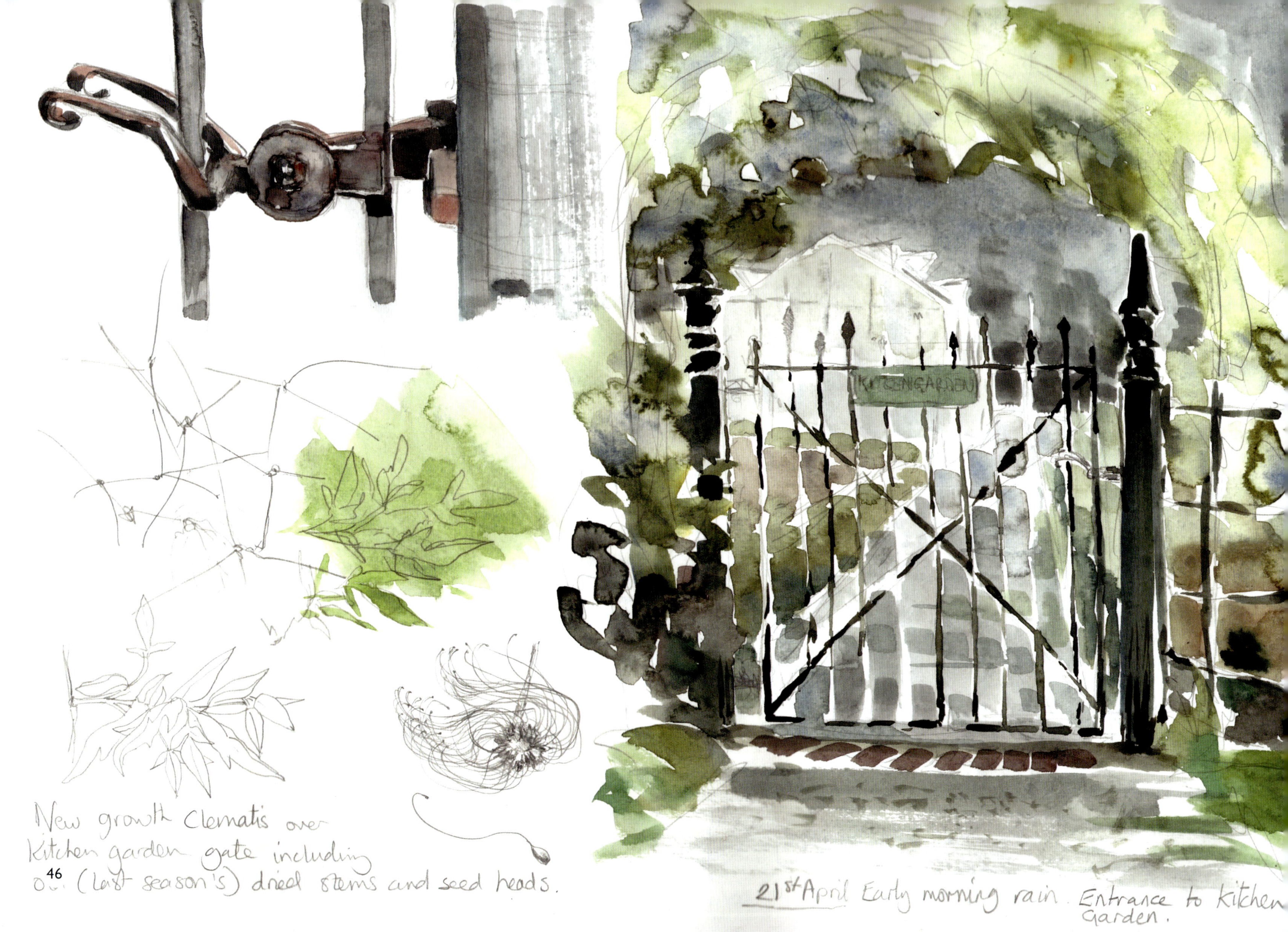
New growth clematis over
kitchen garden gate including
our (last season's) dried stems and seed heads.
46
21st April Early morning rain. Entrance to kitchen
Garden.

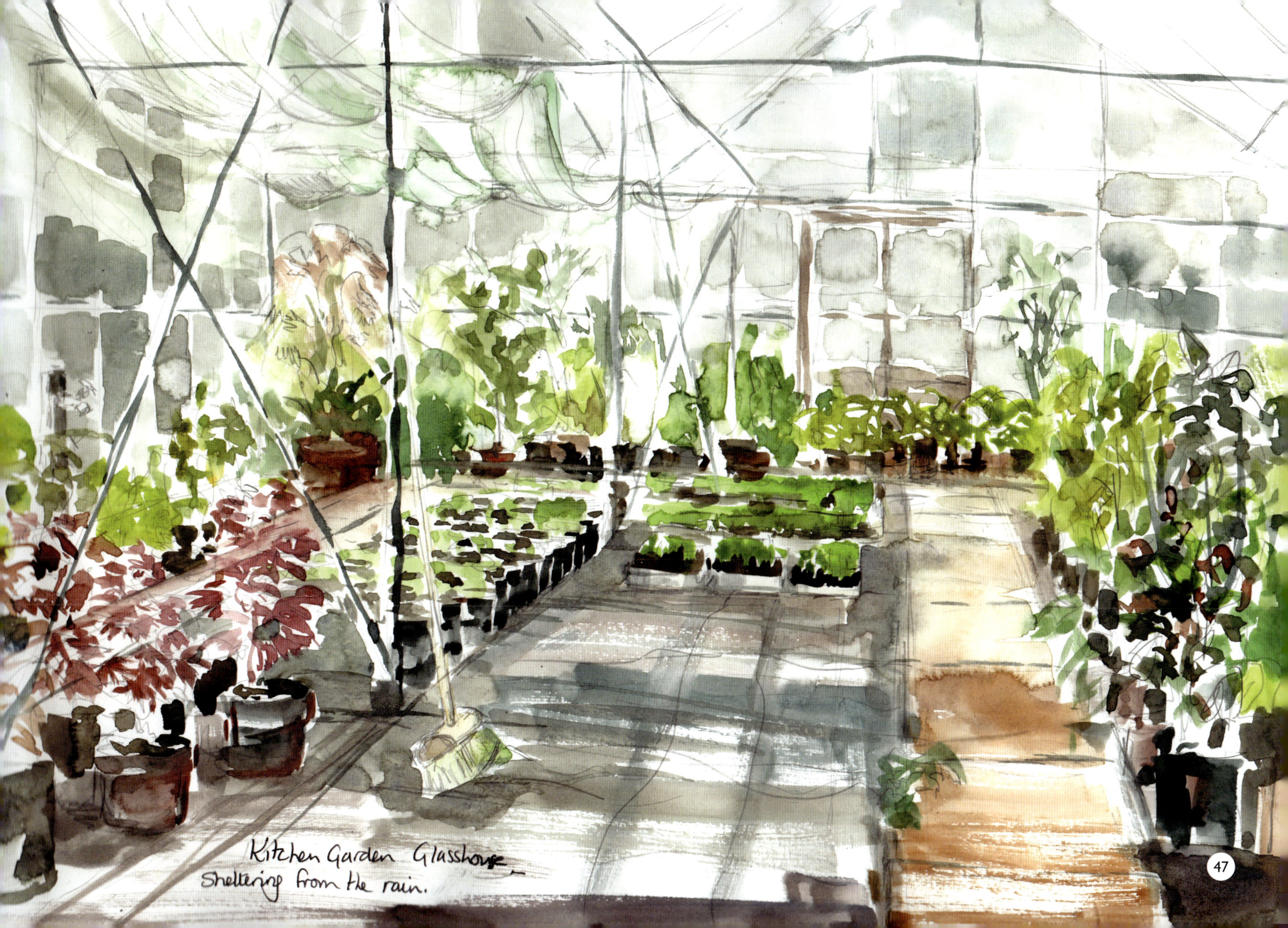
Kitchen Garden Glasshouse
sheltering from the rain.

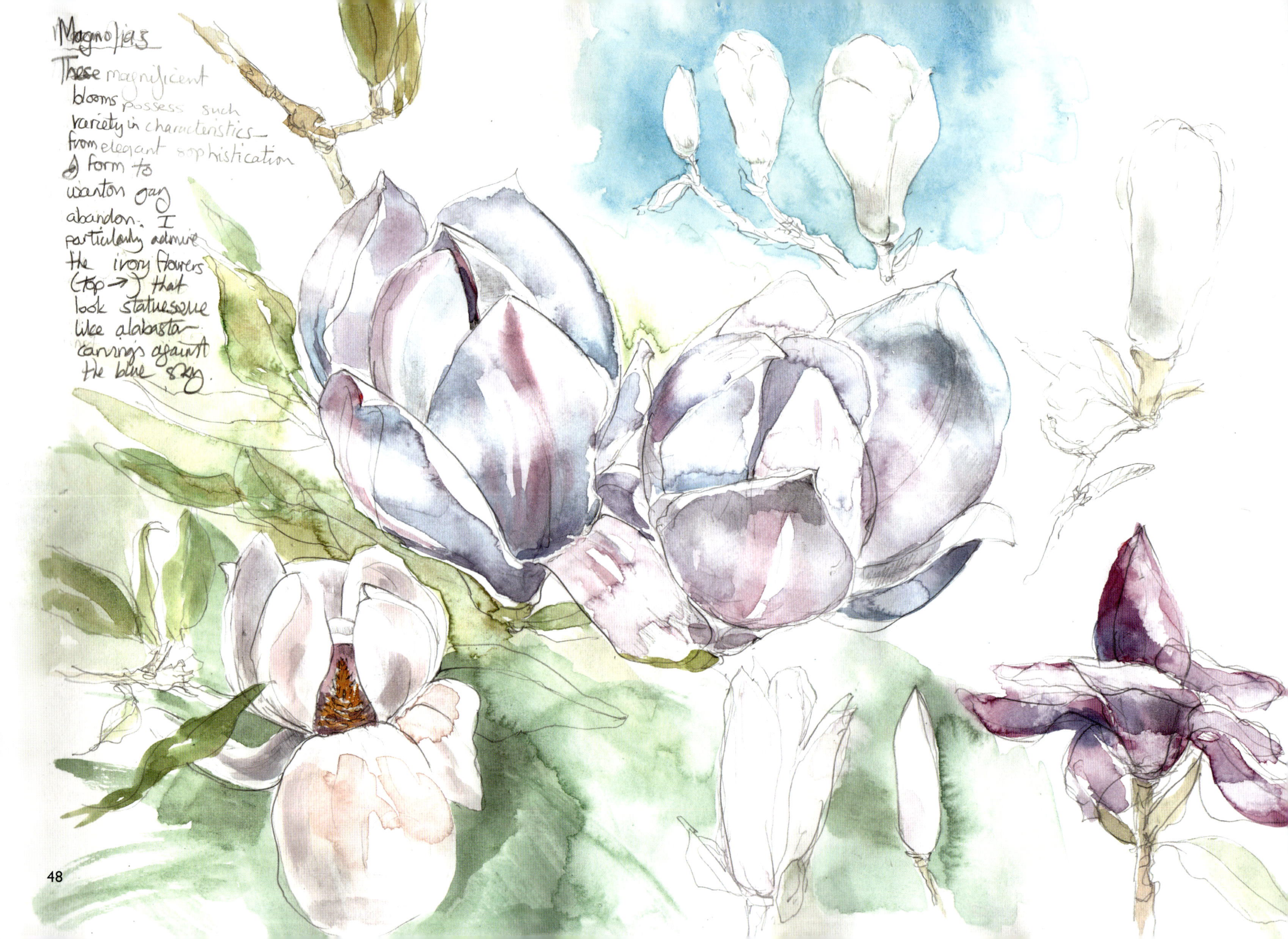

Magnolias
These magnificent blooms possess such variety in characteristics — from elegant sophistication of form to wanton gay abandon. I particularly admire the ivory flowers (top →) that look statuesque like alabaster carvings against the blue sky.

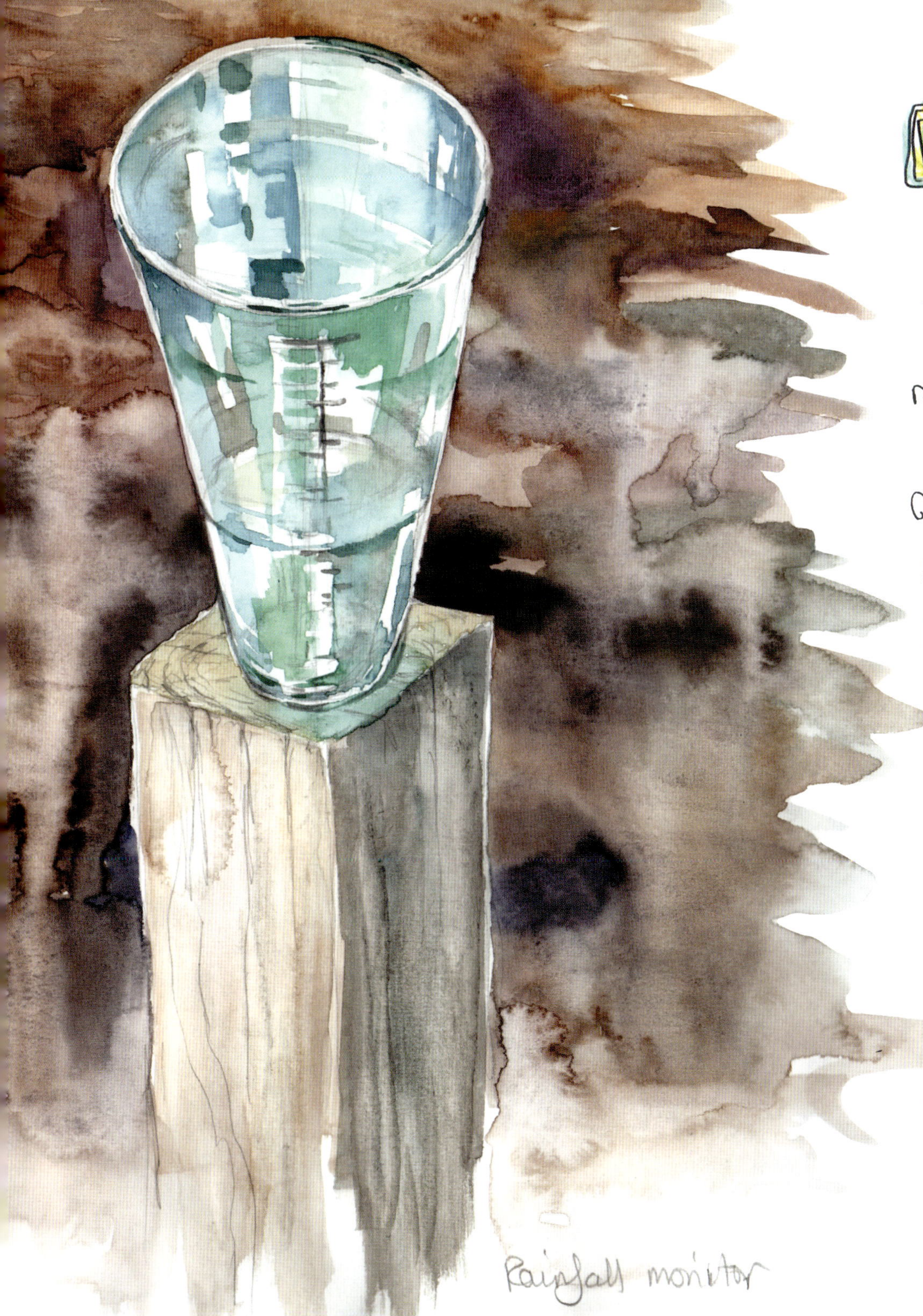

With the forthcoming Plant Fair this Spring Bank Holiday weekend, the gardeners, staff in the estate office, and the tearooms, are busy in preparations. There has been much activity weeding the beds and borders despite the considerable amount of rainfall April has received.

The gardens are looking spectacular. Cool palette of acid greens / blue greens / dark viridian greens, underlay additions of whites, pinks & crimson-red hue that have taken centre stage over the early spring yellows and blues.

The transformation has been rapid, yet seemless.

Every footstep one makes there is something new and exciting to observe — a small ground-cover plant; minuscule flowers hidden beneath leaves; fleshy foliage bursting forth; tree barks; buds of every kind and every colour sprouting from twiggy shrubs and trees, many in bloom before leaf; the canopies above; bird activity .... all is shifting!

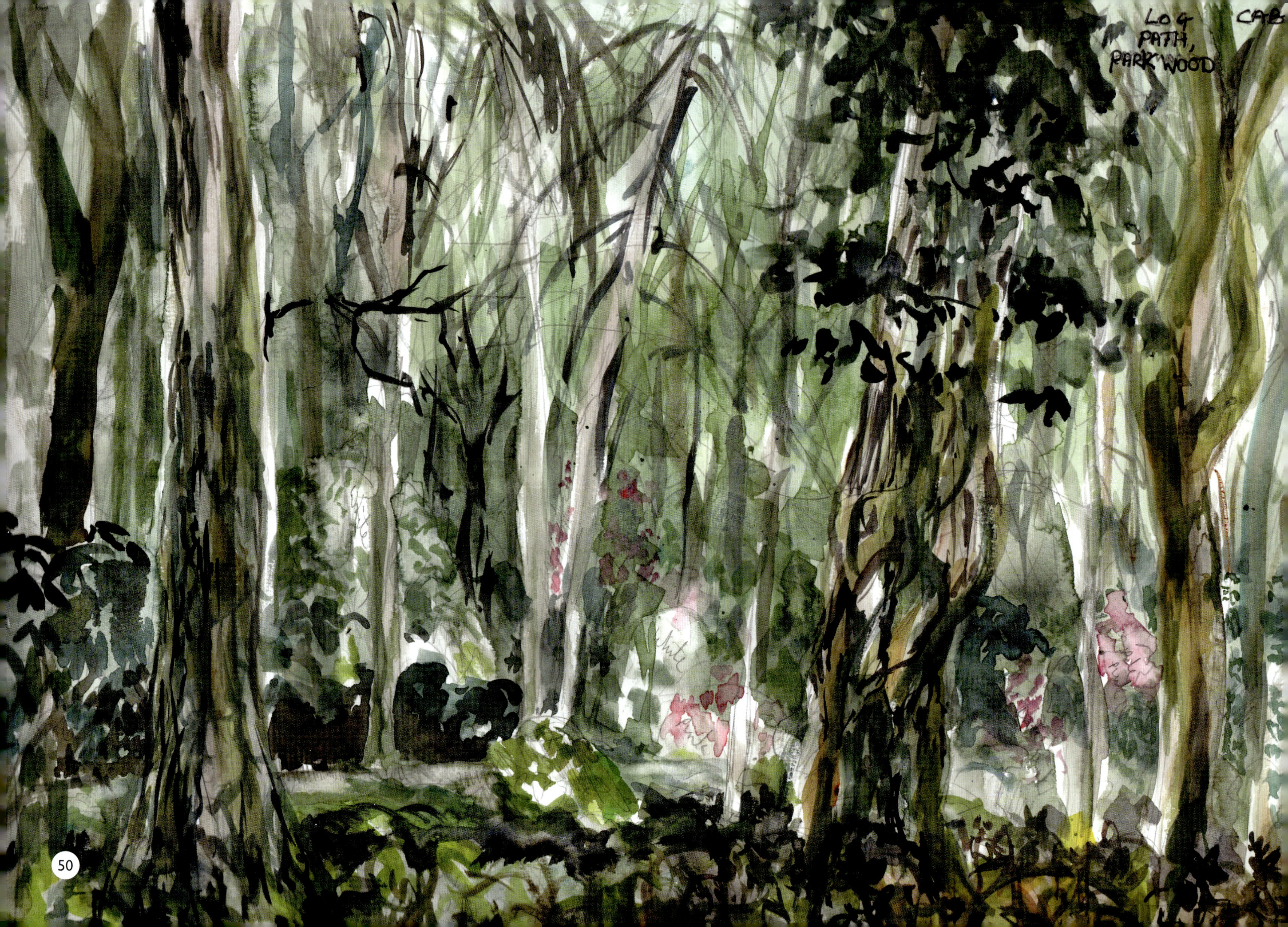

LOG PATH, PARK WOOD
CAB

MAY

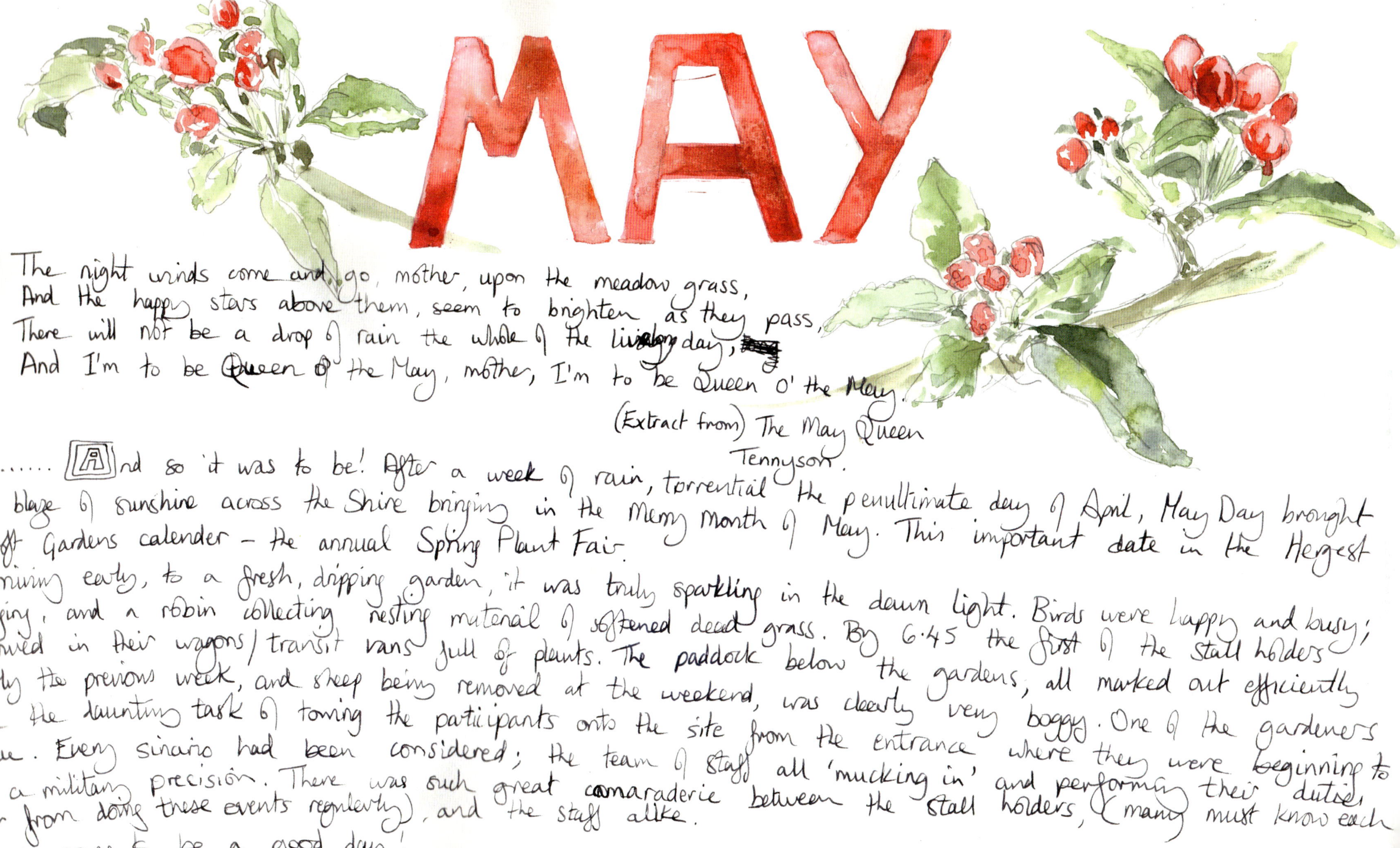

The night winds come and go, mother, upon the meadow grass,
And the happy stars above them, seem to brighten as they pass,
There will not be a drop of rain the whole of the livelong day,
And I'm to be Queen o' the May, mother, I'm to be Queen o' the May.

(Extract from) The May Queen
Tennyson.

...... And so it was to be! After a week of rain, torrential the penultimate day of April, May Day brought a blaze of sunshine across the Shire bringing in the Merry Month of May. This important date in the Hergest Gardens calender – the annual Spring Plant Fair. Arriving early, to a fresh, dripping garden, it was truly sparkling in the dawn light. Birds were happy and busy; singing, and a robin collecting nesting material of softened dead grass. By 6.45 the first of the stall holders arrived in their wagons / transit vans full of plants. The paddock below the gardens, all marked out efficiently early the previous week, and sheep being removed at the weekend, was clearly very boggy. One of the gardeners had the daunting task of towing the participants onto the site from the entrance where they were beginning to queue. Every sinario had been considered; the team of staff all 'mucking in' and performing their duties a military precision. There was such great camaraderie between the stall holders, (many must know each other from doing these events regularly), and the staff alike.
It was going to be a good day!

'Who doffs his coat on a winter's day,
will gladly put it on in May'.

'Change not a clout
till May be out!'

'Be it weal or be it woe, beans blow 'fore
May doth go.'

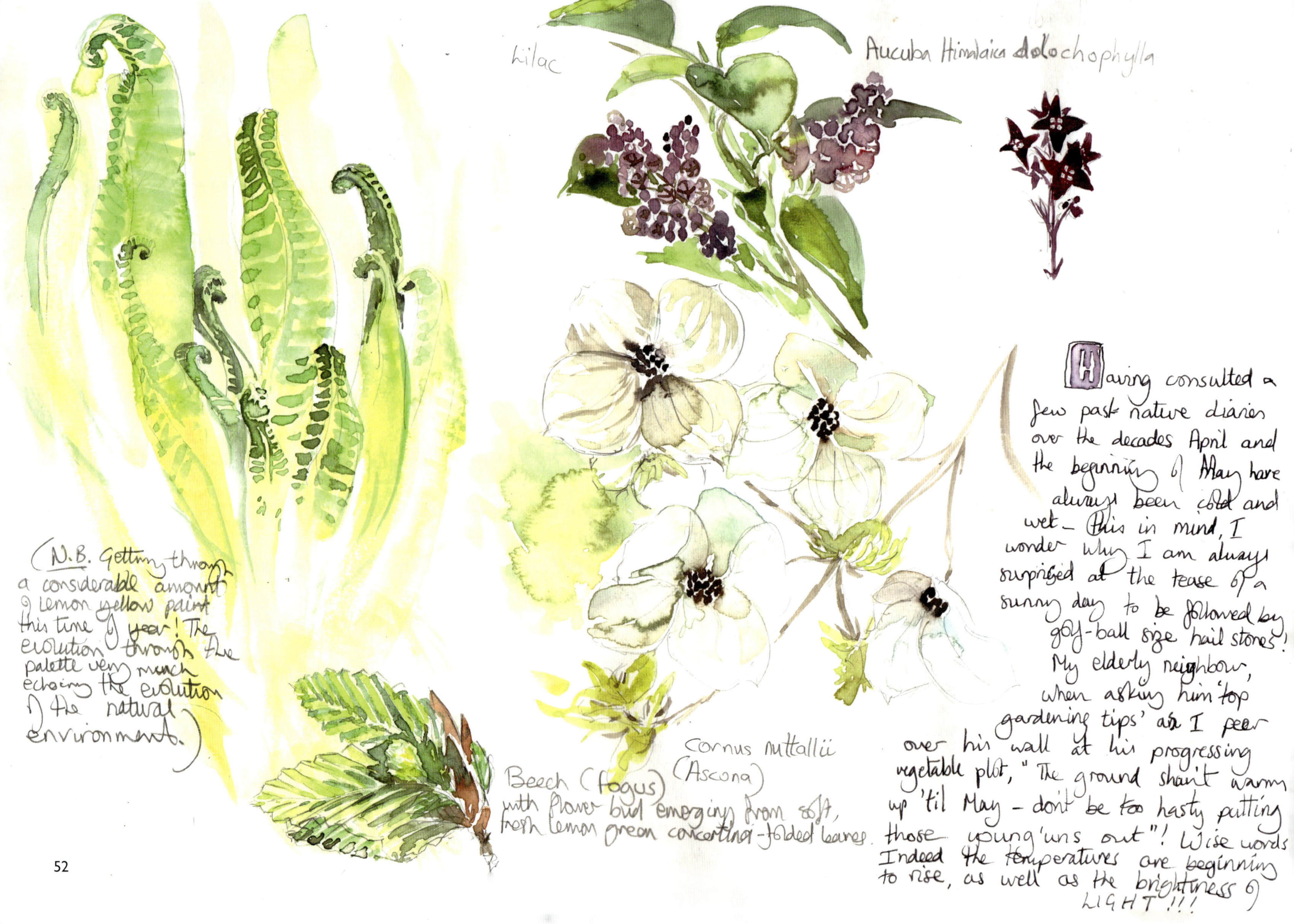

Lilac
Aucuba Himalaica dolochophylla
(N.B. Getting through a considerable amount of lemon yellow paint this time of year! The evolution through the palette very much echoing the evolution of the natural environment.)
Cornus nuttallii (Ascona)
Beech (fagus) with flower bud emerging from soft, fresh lemon green concertina-folded leaves.
Having consulted a few past nature diaries over the decades April and the beginning of May have always been cold and wet — this in mind, I wonder why I am always surprised at the tease of a sunny day to be followed by golf-ball size hail stones! My elderly neighbour, when asking him 'top gardening tips' as I peer over his wall at his progressing vegetable plot, "The ground shan't warm up 'til May — don't be too hasty putting those young 'uns out"! Wise words indeed the temperatures are beginning to rise, as well as the brightness of LIGHT !!!

52

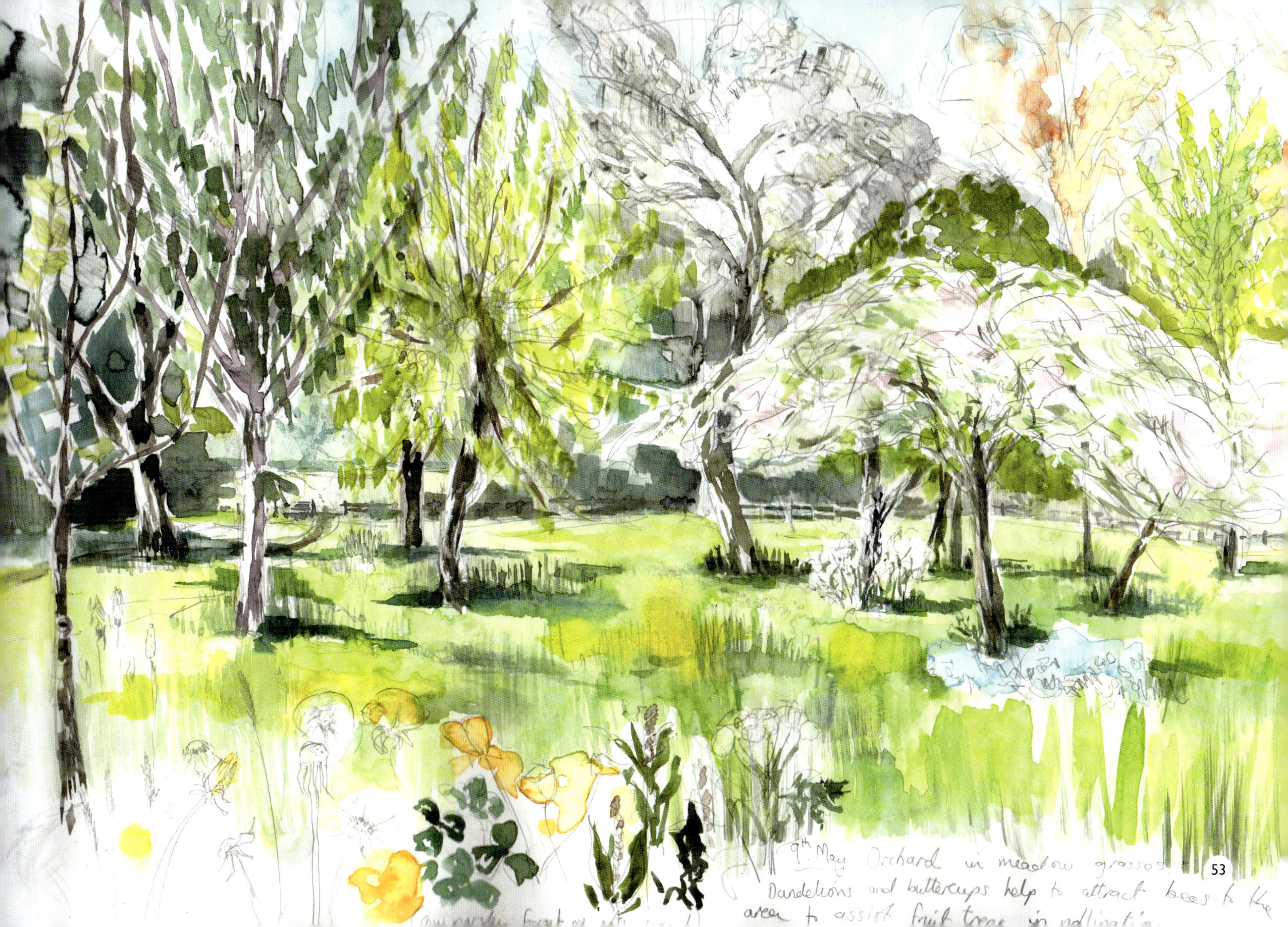

9th May Orchard in meadow grasses.
Dandelions and buttercups help to attract bees to the
area to assist fruit trees in pollination.

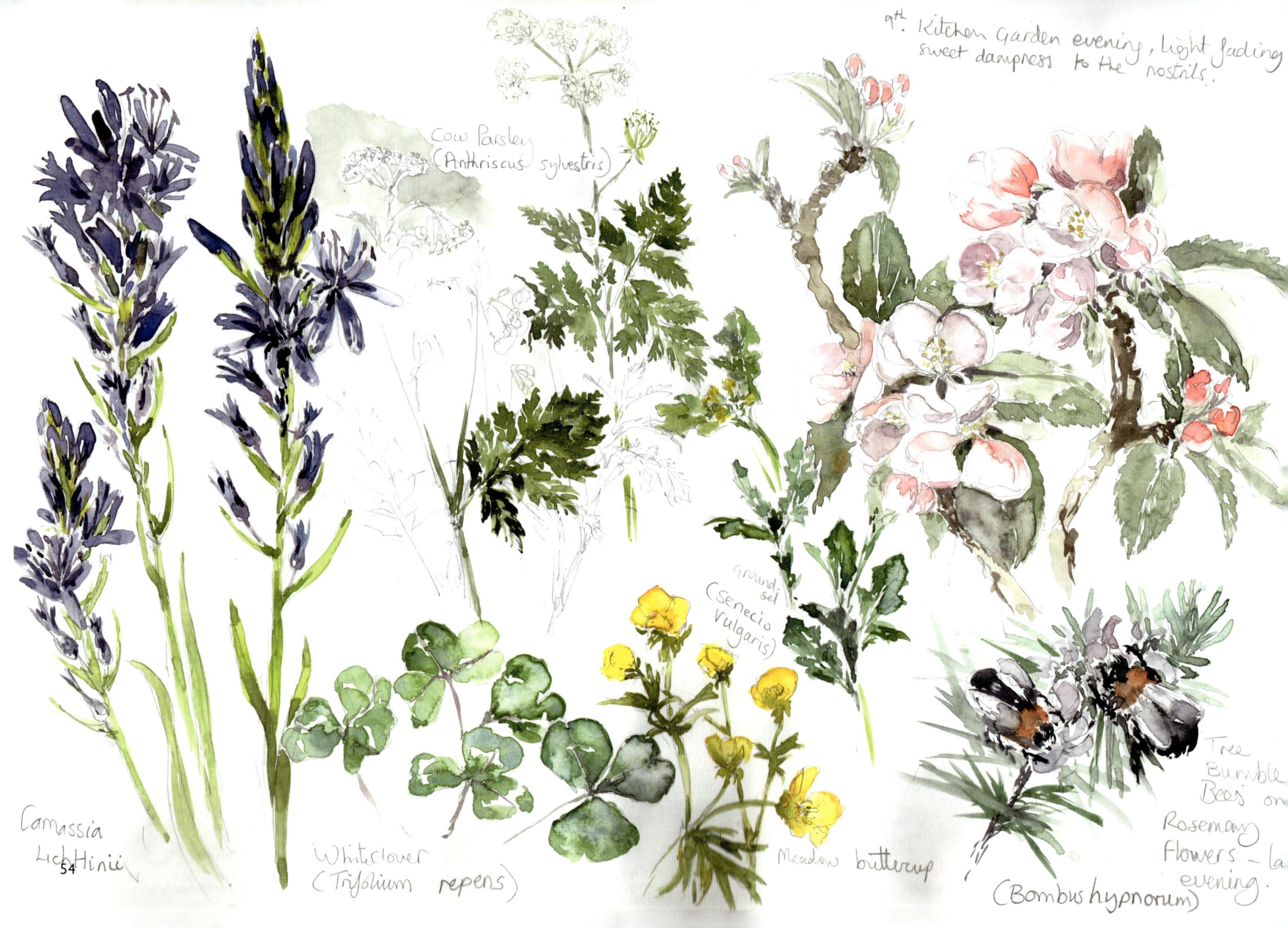

9th. Kitchen Garden evening, light fading
sweet dampness to the nostrils.
Cow Parsley
(Anthriscus sylvestris)
Ground sel
(Senecio vulgaris)
Camassia
Lichtlinii
54
Whiteclover
(Trifolium repens)
Meadow buttercup
Tree Bumble Bees on Rosemary Flowers - late evening.
(Bombus hypnorum)

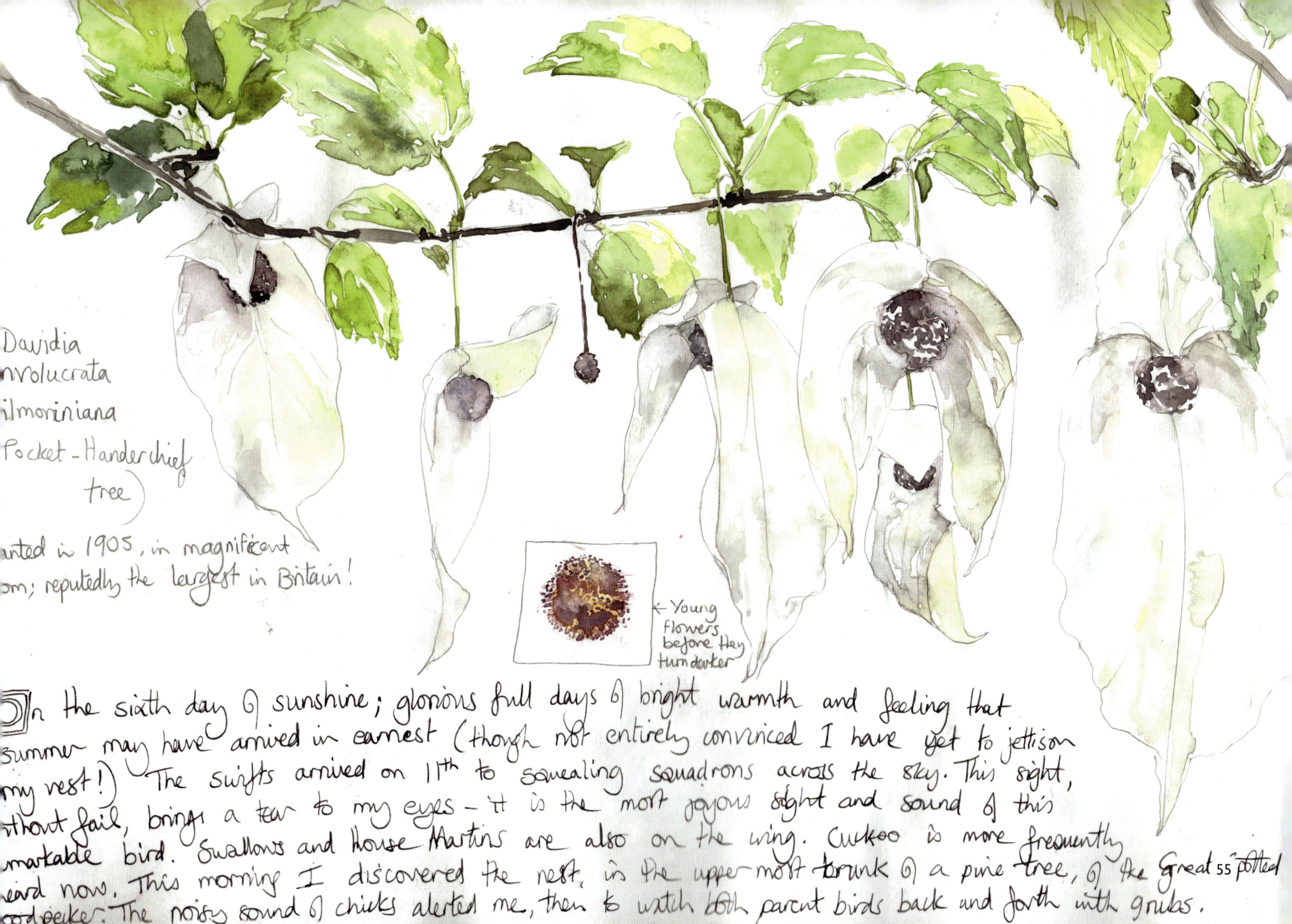

Davidia
involucrata
vilmoriniana
(Pocket-Handkerchief
tree)

anted in 1905, in magnificent
om; reputedly the largest in Britain!

← Young
flowers
before they
turn darker

On the sixth day of sunshine; glorious full days of bright warmth and feeling that
summer may have arrived in earnest (though not entirely convinced I have yet to jettison
my vest!) The swifts arrived on 11th to squealing squadrons across the sky. This sight,
without fail, brings a tear to my eyes - it is the most joyous sight and sound of this
remarkable bird. Swallows and House Martins are also on the wing. Cuckoo is more frequently
heard now. This morning I discovered the nest, in the upper-most trunk of a pine tree, of the Great Spotted
Woodpecker. The noisy sound of chicks alerted me, then to watch both parent birds back and forth with grubs.

55

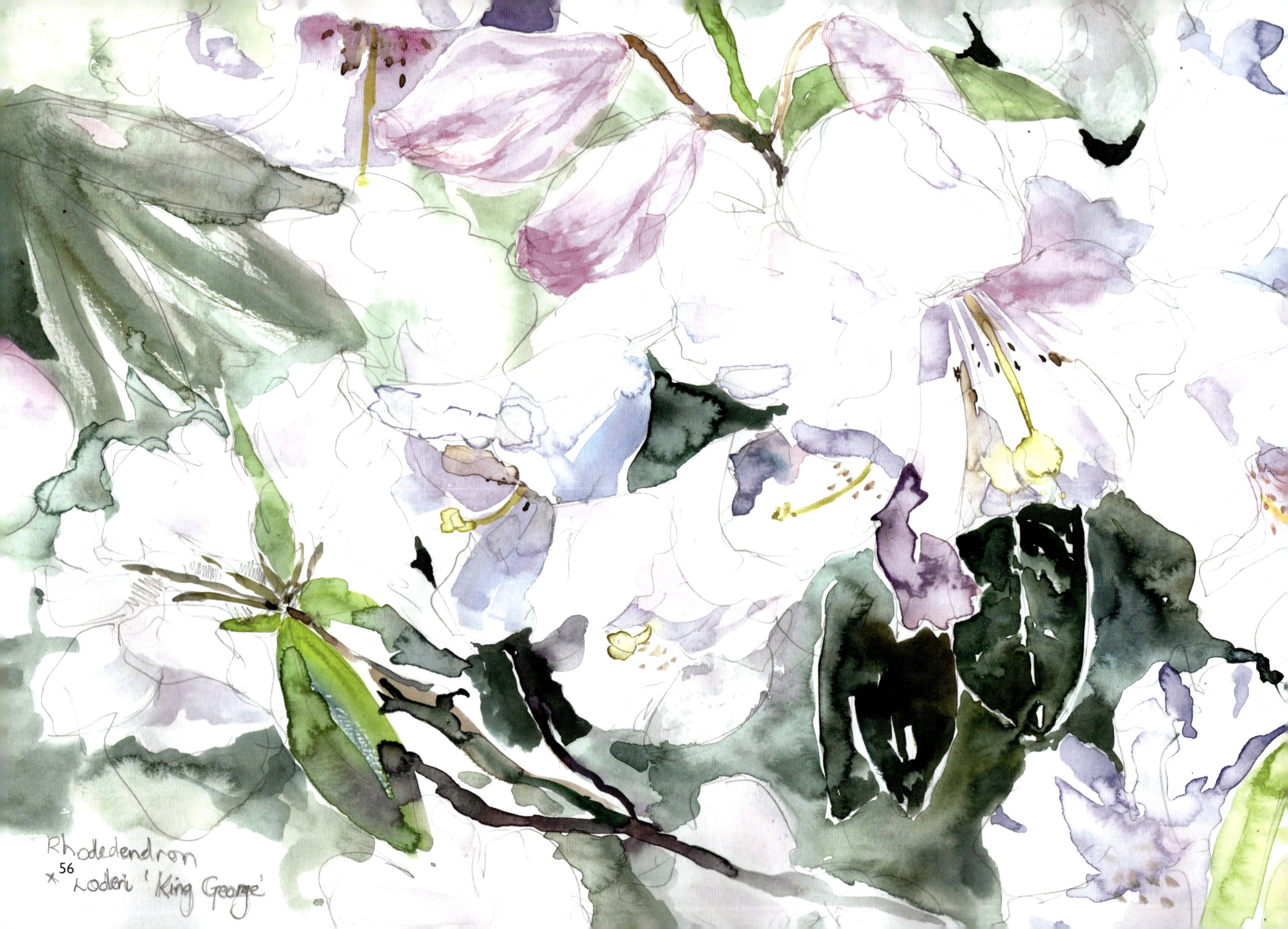
Rhododendron
x Loderi 'King George'
56

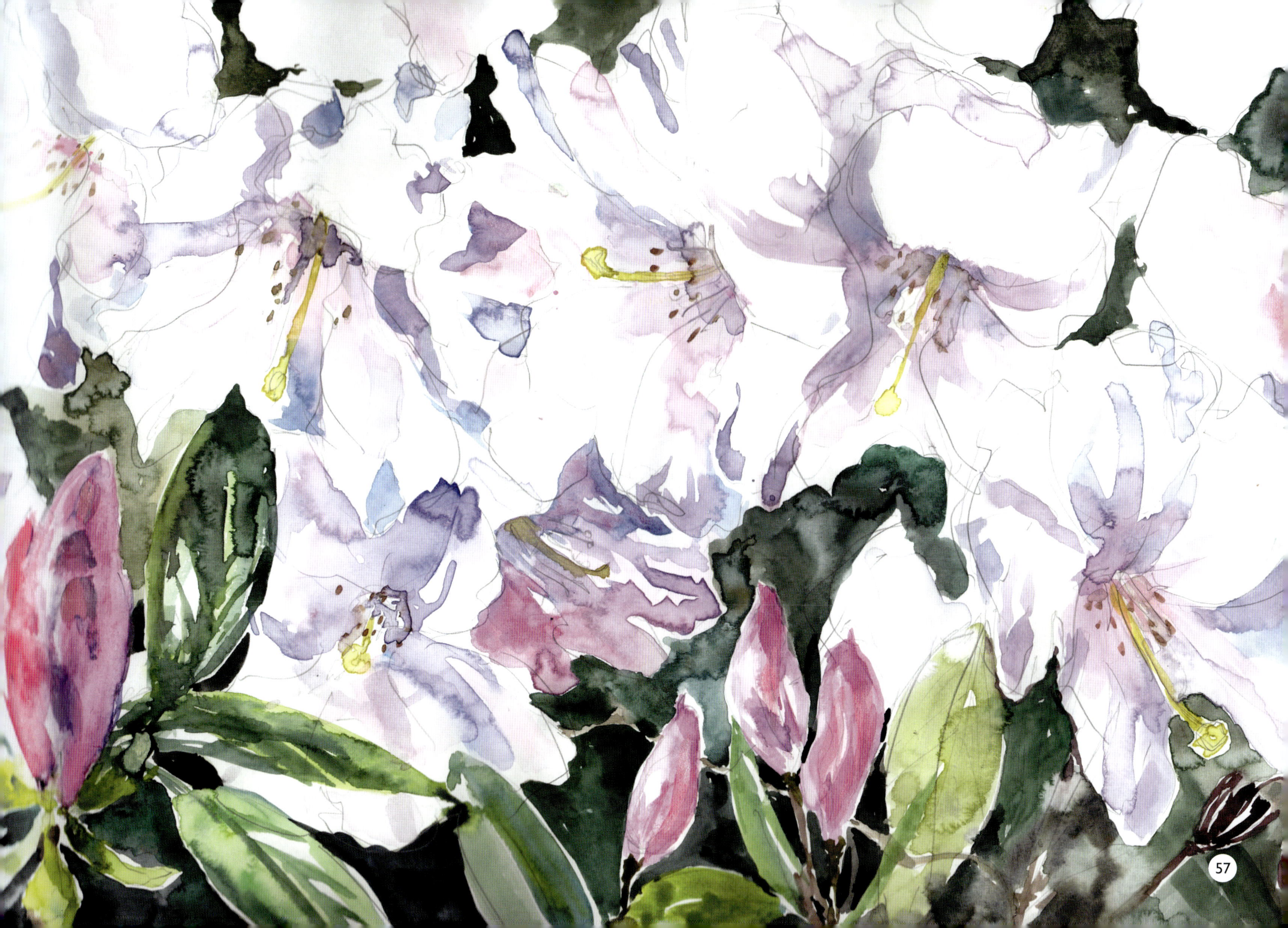

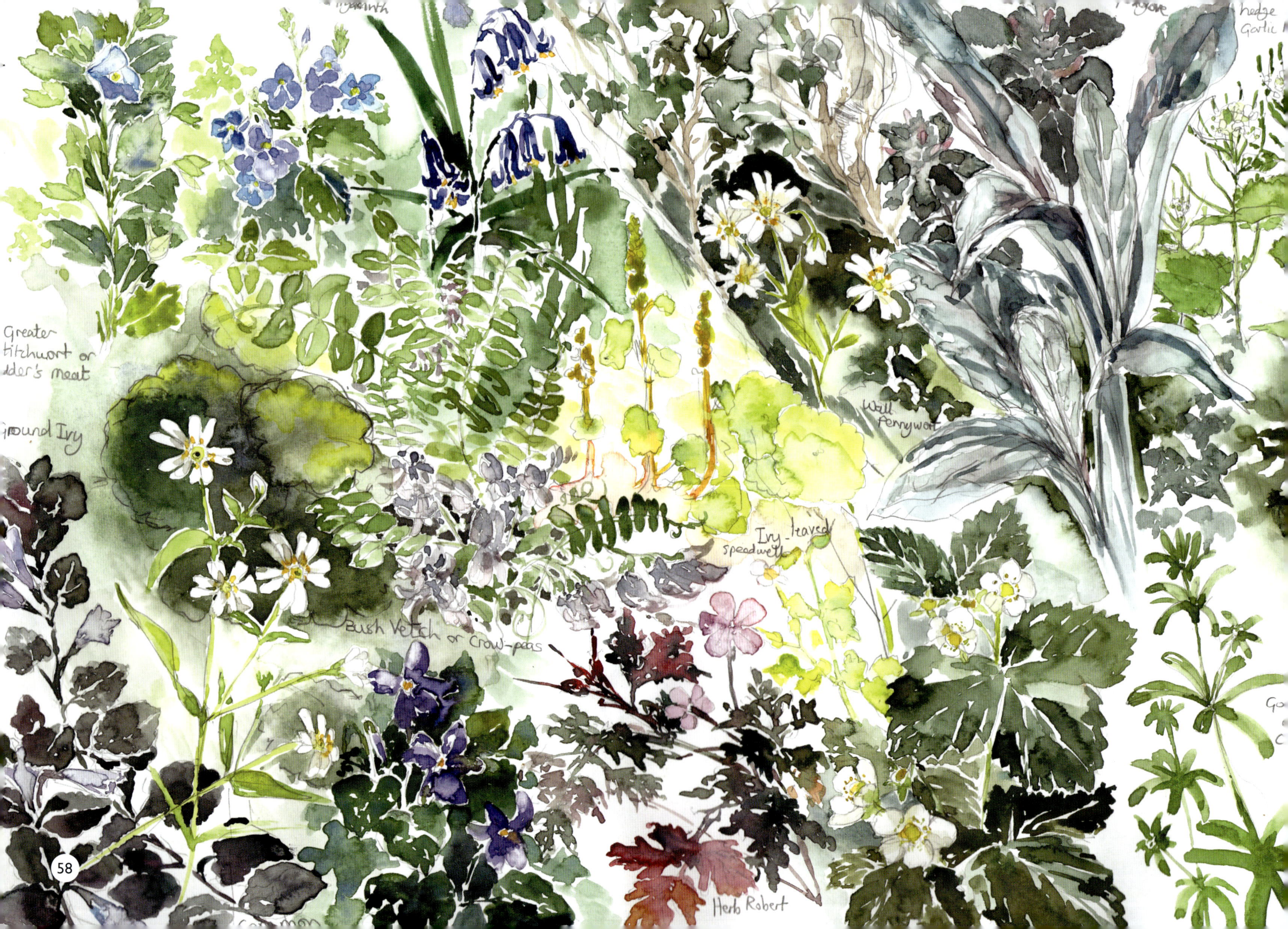
hedge
Garlic
Greater
stitchwort or
adder's meat
ground Ivy
Wall
Pennywort
Ivy-leaved
speedwell
Bush Vetch or Crow-peas
Herb Robert

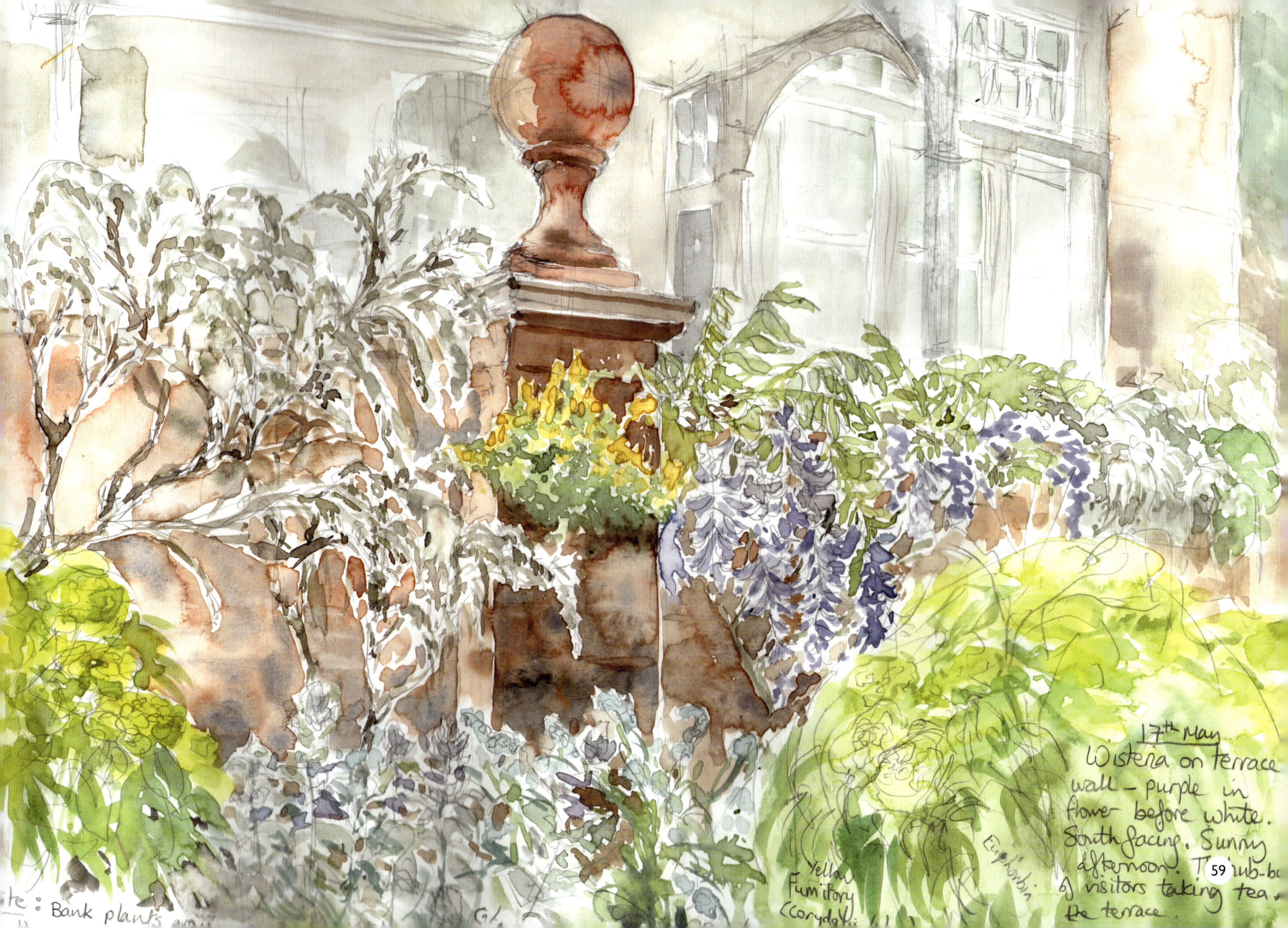
17th May
Wisteria on terrace
wall — purple in
flower before white.
South facing. Sunny
afternoon. The shrub-b..
b) visitors taking tea
the terrace.
Yellow
Fumitory
(Corydalis
Euphorbia
te: Bank plants
59

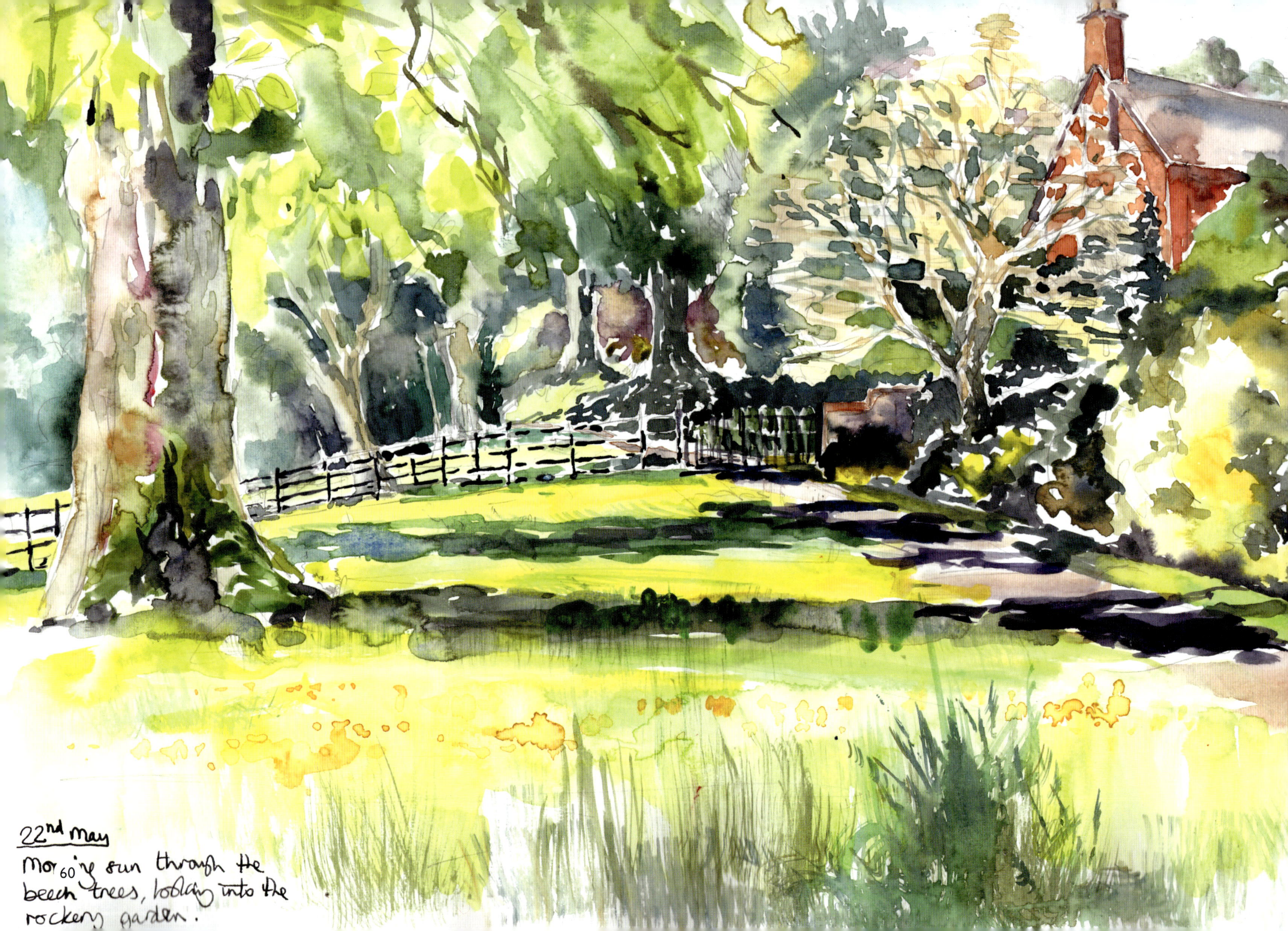

22nd May
Morning sun through the beech trees, looking into the rockery garden.

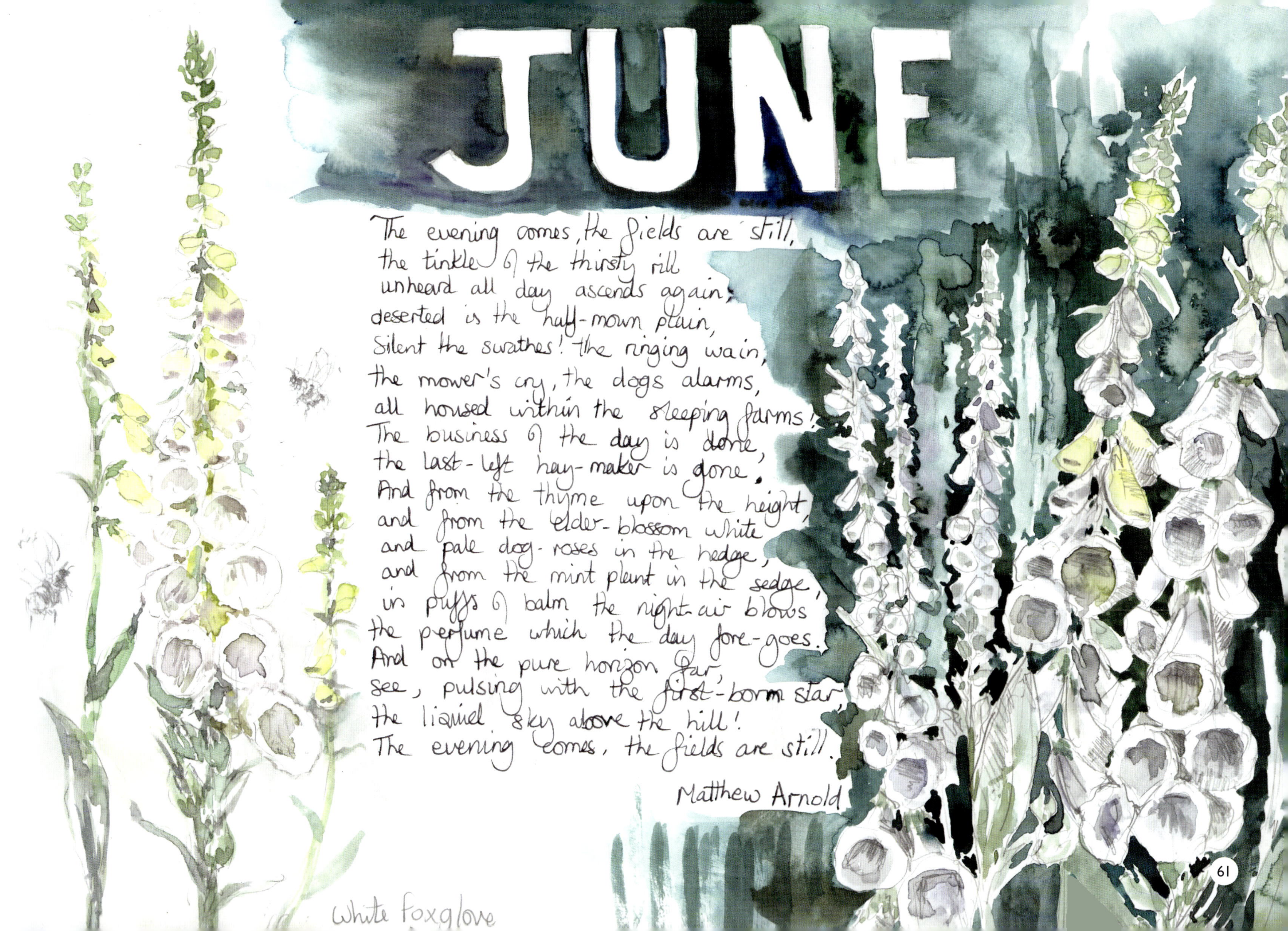

JUNE

The evening comes, the fields are still,
the tinkle of the thirsty rill
unheard all day ascends again;
deserted is the half-mown plain,
Silent the swathes! the ringing wain,
the mower's cry, the dogs alarms,
all housed within the sleeping farms!
The business of the day is done,
the last-left hay-maker is gone.
And from the thyme upon the height,
and from the elder-blossom white
and pale dog-roses in the hedge,
and from the mint-plant in the sedge,
in puffs of balm the night-air blows
the perfume which the day fore-goes.
And on the pure horizon far,
see, pulsing with the first-born star,
the liquid sky above the hill!
The evening comes, the fields are still.

Matthew Arnold

White Foxglove

Irises — Kitchen Garden   4th June - very hot afternoon

tall
gold/purple

short
pale lavender

tall darker
yellow

62

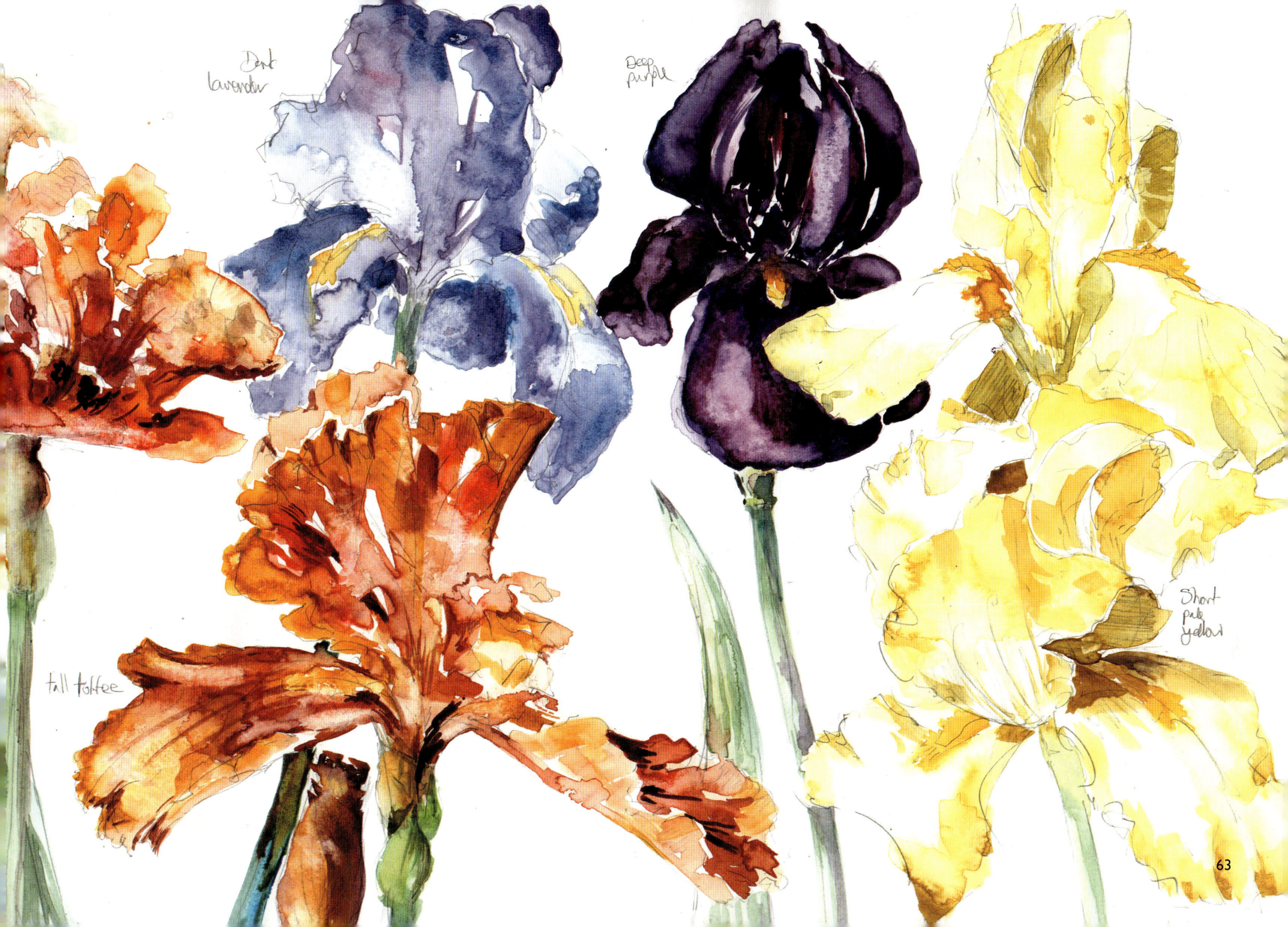

Dark
lavender
Deep
purple
tall toffee
Short
pale
yellow
63

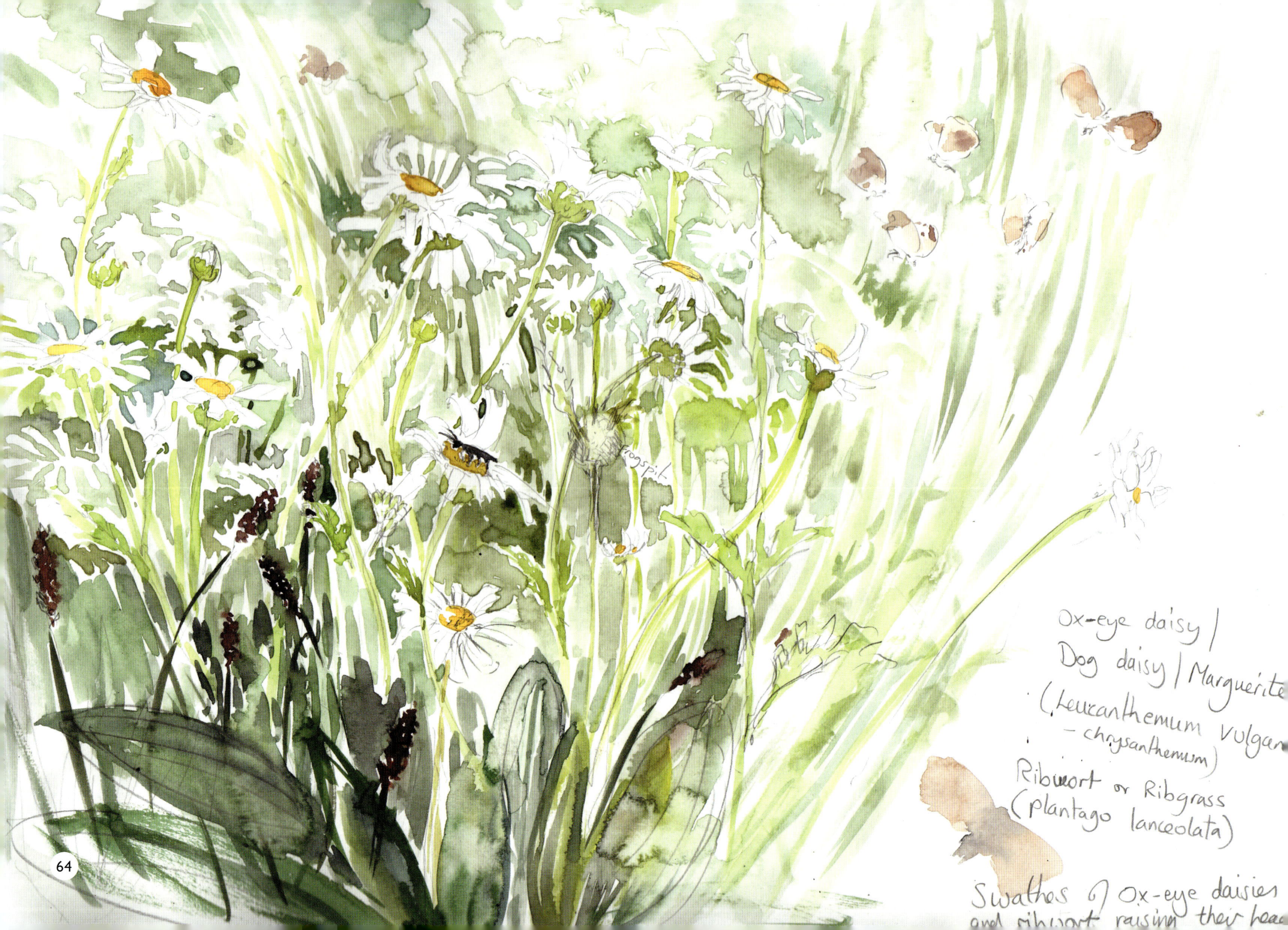

Frogspit
Ox-eye daisy /
Dog daisy / Marguerite
(Leucanthemum vulgan
— chrysanthemum)
Ribwort or Ribgrass
(plantago lanceolata)
Swathes of Ox-eye daisies
and ribwort raising their hea

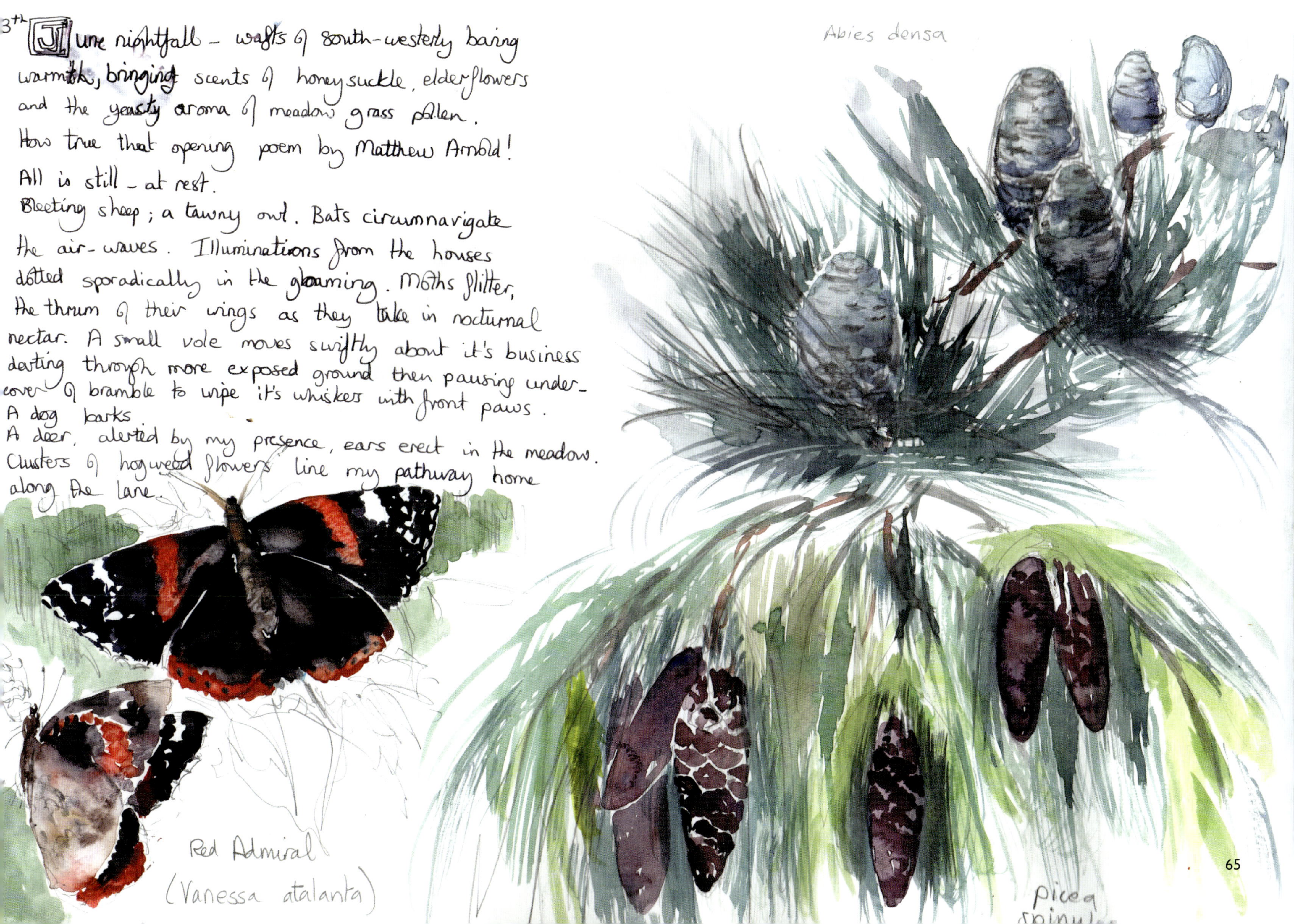

3rd June nightfall – wafts of south-westerly bearing warmth, bringing scents of honeysuckle, elderflowers and the yeasty aroma of meadow grass pollen.
How true that opening poem by Matthew Arnold!
All is still – at rest.
Bleeting sheep; a tawny owl. Bats circumnavigate the air-waves. Illuminations from the houses dotted sporadically in the gloaming. Moths flitter, the thrum of their wings as they take in nocturnal nectar. A small vole moves swiftly about it's business darting through more exposed ground then pausing under-cover of bramble to wipe it's whiskers with front paws.
A dog barks.
A deer, alerted by my presence, ears erect in the meadow. Clusters of hogweed flowers line my pathway home along the lane.

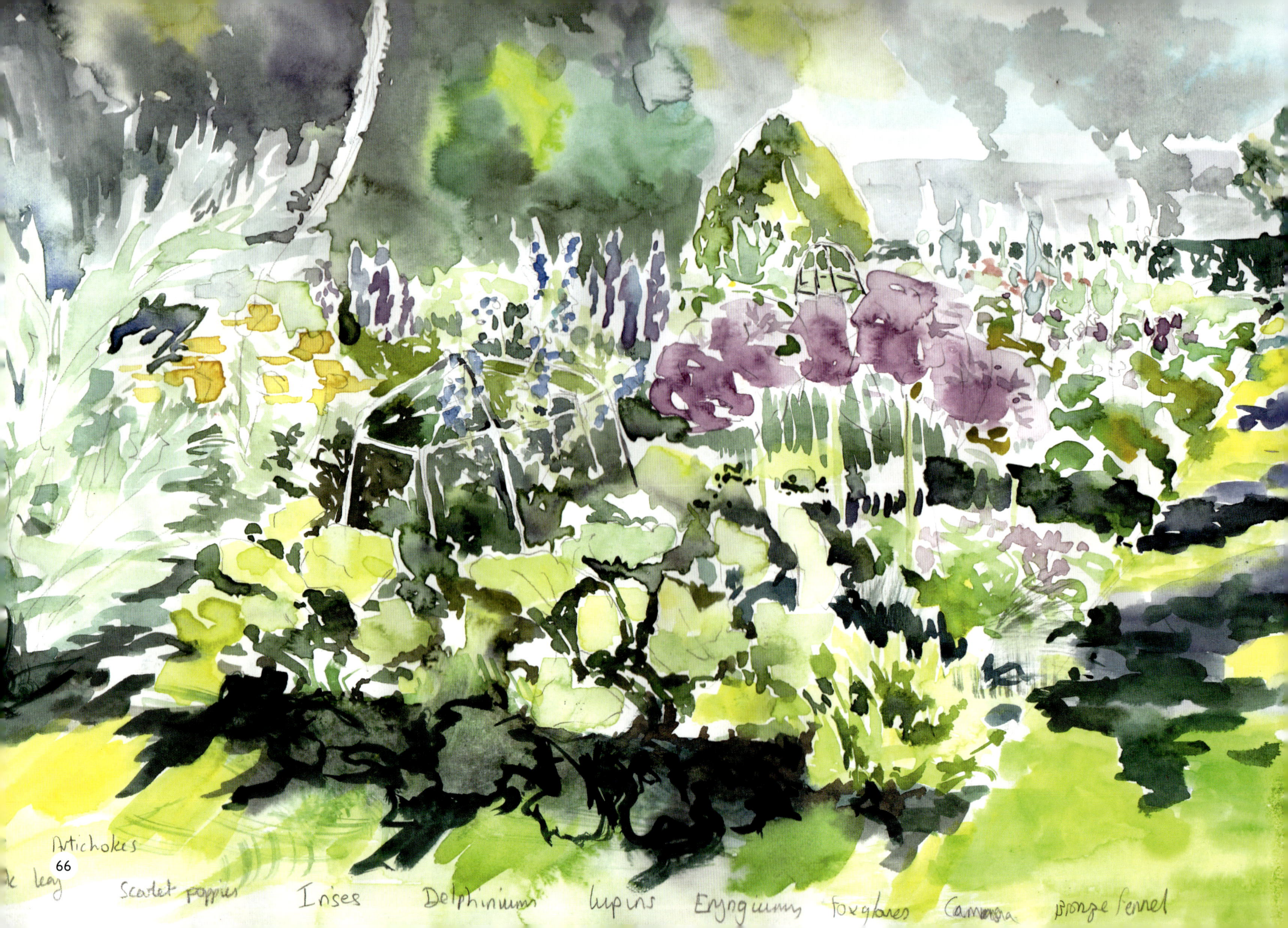

Artichokes
66
k leaf   Scarlet poppies   Irises   Delphiniums   lupins   Eryngiums   foxgloves   Camassia   bronze fennel

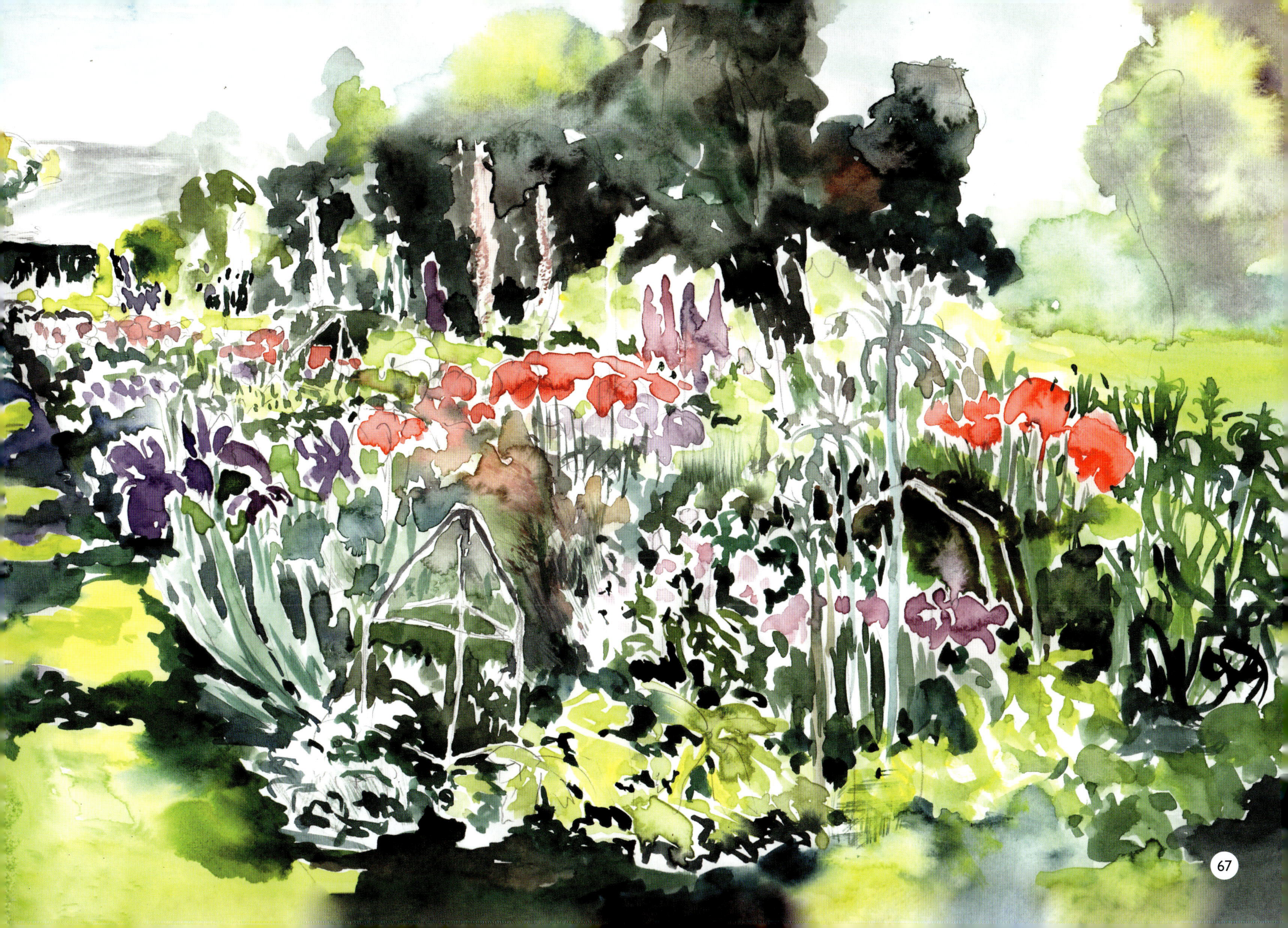

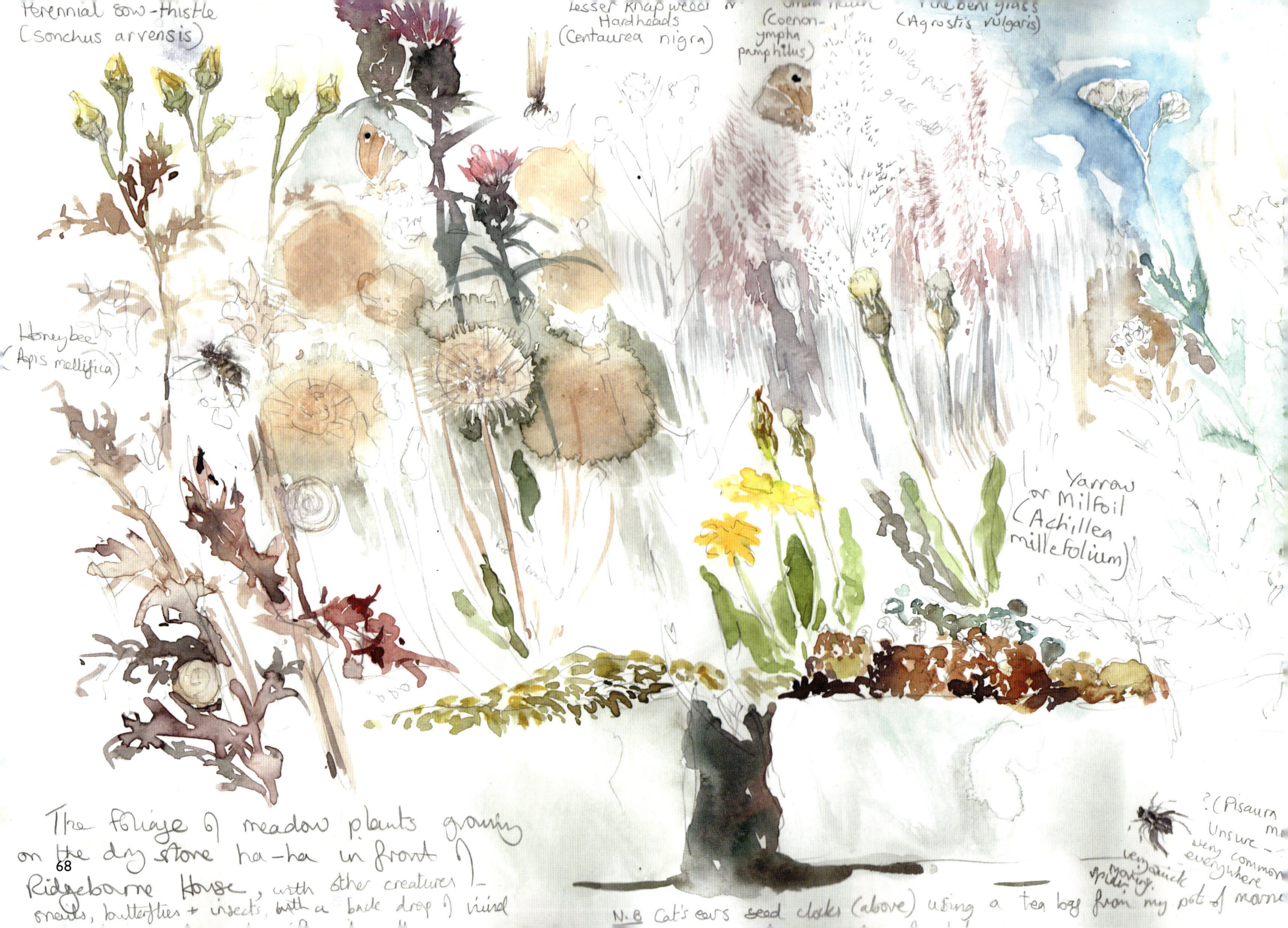

Perennial sow-thistle
(Sonchus arvensis)
Lesser Knapweed /
Hardheads
(Centaurea nigra)
Small Heath
(Coenon-
ympha
pamphilus)
Fine bent grass
(Agrostis vulgaris)
Honeybee
(Apis mellifica)
Dulcy pink grass seed
Yarrow
or Milfoil
(Achillea
millefolium)
?(Pisaura m...
Unsure -
very common
everywhere
very quick
moving
spider.
The foliage of meadow plants growing
on the dry stone ha-ha in front of
Ridgeborne House, with other creatures -
snails, butterflies + insects, with a back drop of vivid
N.B Cat's ears seed clocks (above) using a tea bag from my pot of morn...

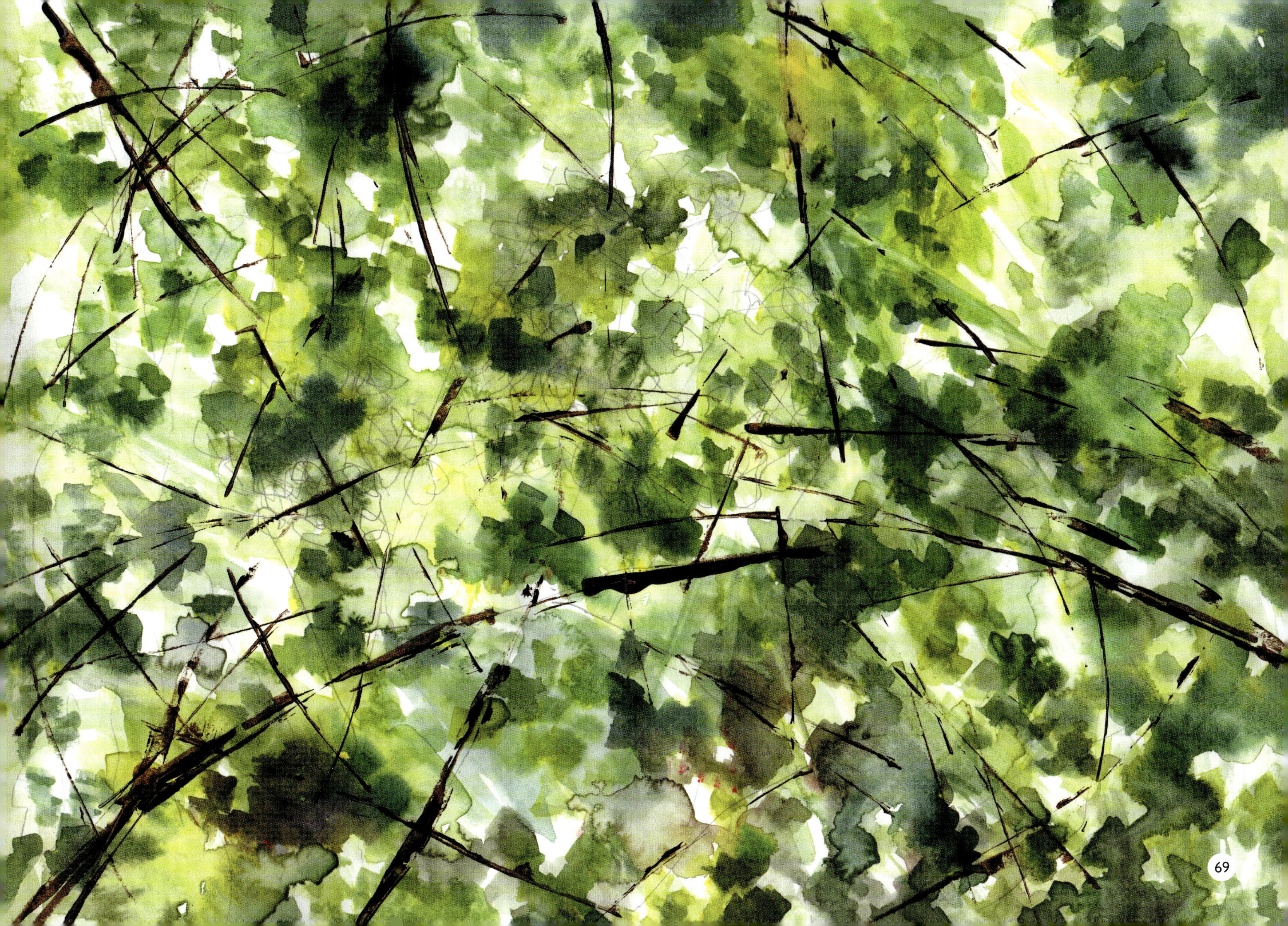

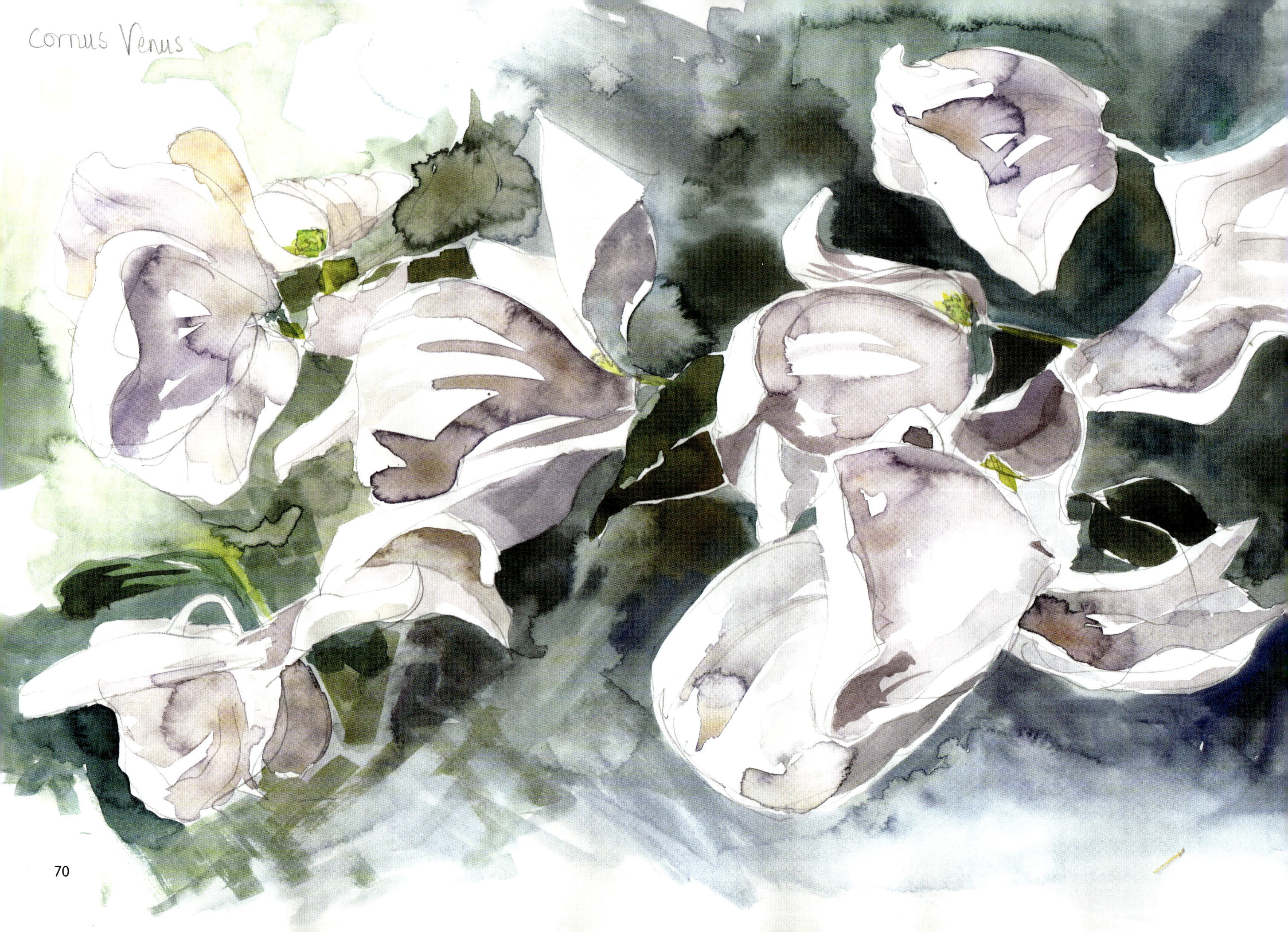

Cornus Venus

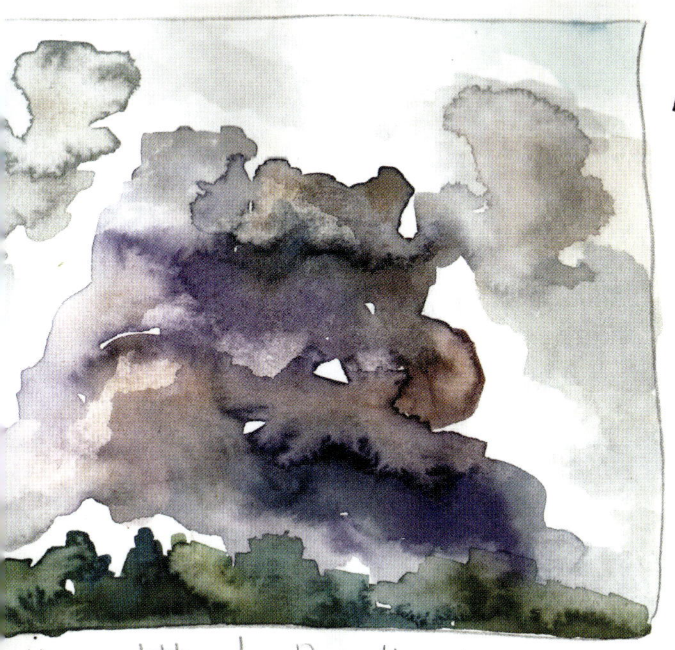

...milar palette to the thunderous sky
...s day.

.B
Thoughts on collage material —
layering colours between drying —
base colour let dry, re-paint
fluid watery mark-making.
practise depths of pigment —
effects for clouds/leaves/
areas of multi layered effects.

Artist's sentiments to which I concur:

'In the 'Trattato della pittura' he stresses the importance of the painter getting out in the country, experiencing it at first hand (by no means a universal practise amongst Renaissance artists.) It is presented like a pilgrimage: you must 'quit your home in town, and leave your family and friends, and go over the mountains and valleys into the country'. You must 'expose yourself to the fierce heat of the sun'. It would be easier, he says, to get everything second-hand, from other artists' paintings or from some poetic description in a book — 'wouldn't that be more convenient, and less tiring, since you can stay in a cold place without moving about and exposing yourself to 'illness?' But, if you did only that, your soul could not experience, through the 'window' of the eye, the inspiring beauties of the countryside: 'it could not recieve the reflections of bright places; it could not see the shady valleys'. The proper way to experience nature, he insists, is alone. 'While you are alone you are entirely your own'. The painter should 'withdraw apart, the better to study the forms of natural objects'. He should 'remain solitary, especially when he is intent on studying and considering those things which continually appear before his eyes, and which furnish material to be carefully stored up in the memory'. This desire for solitude, Leonardo warns, will not be understood by others! 'I tell you, you will be thought crazy'.

Leonardo da Vinci (1490)
extract from The flights of the mind
Charles Nicholl

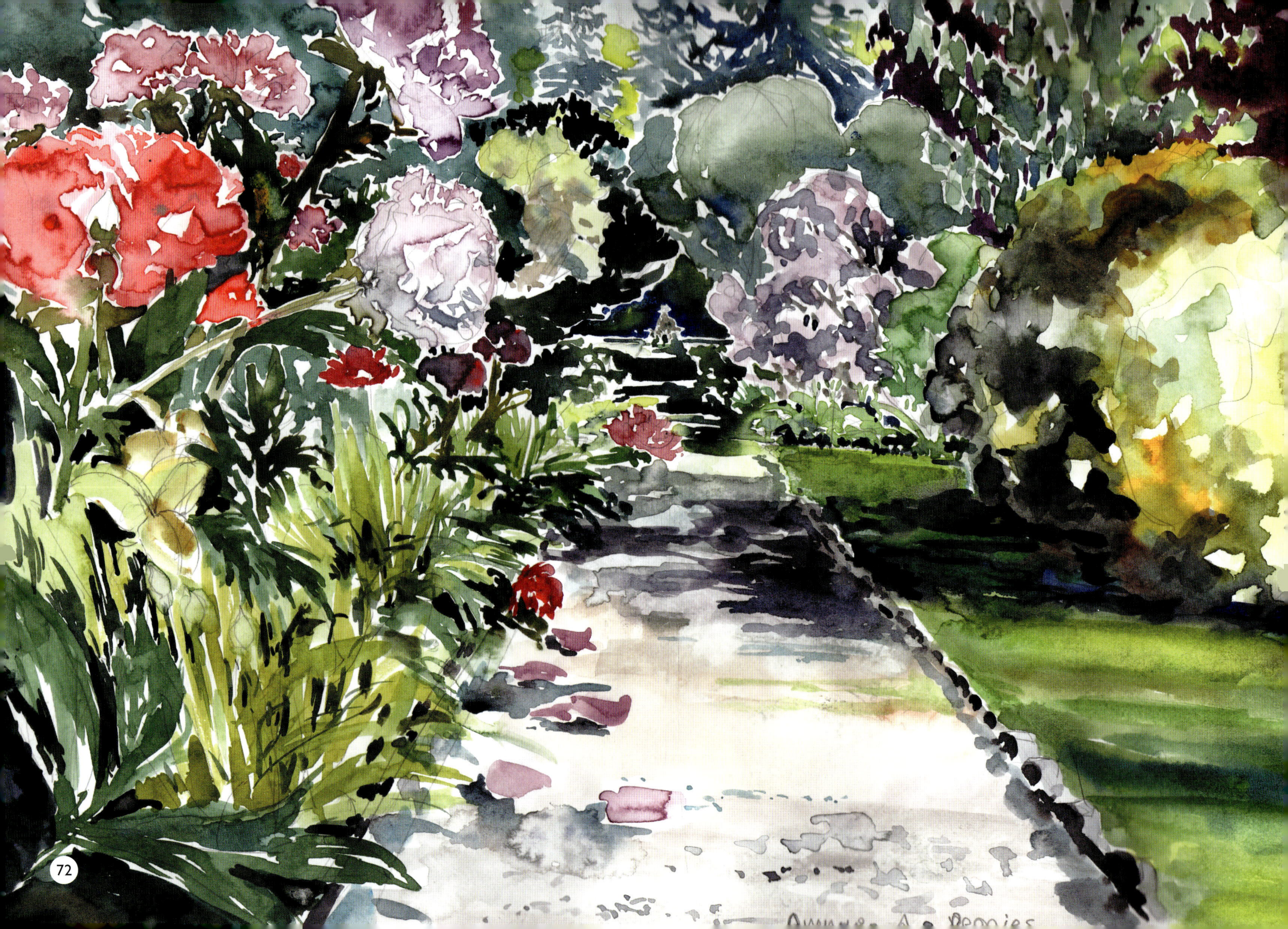
Poppies

JULY

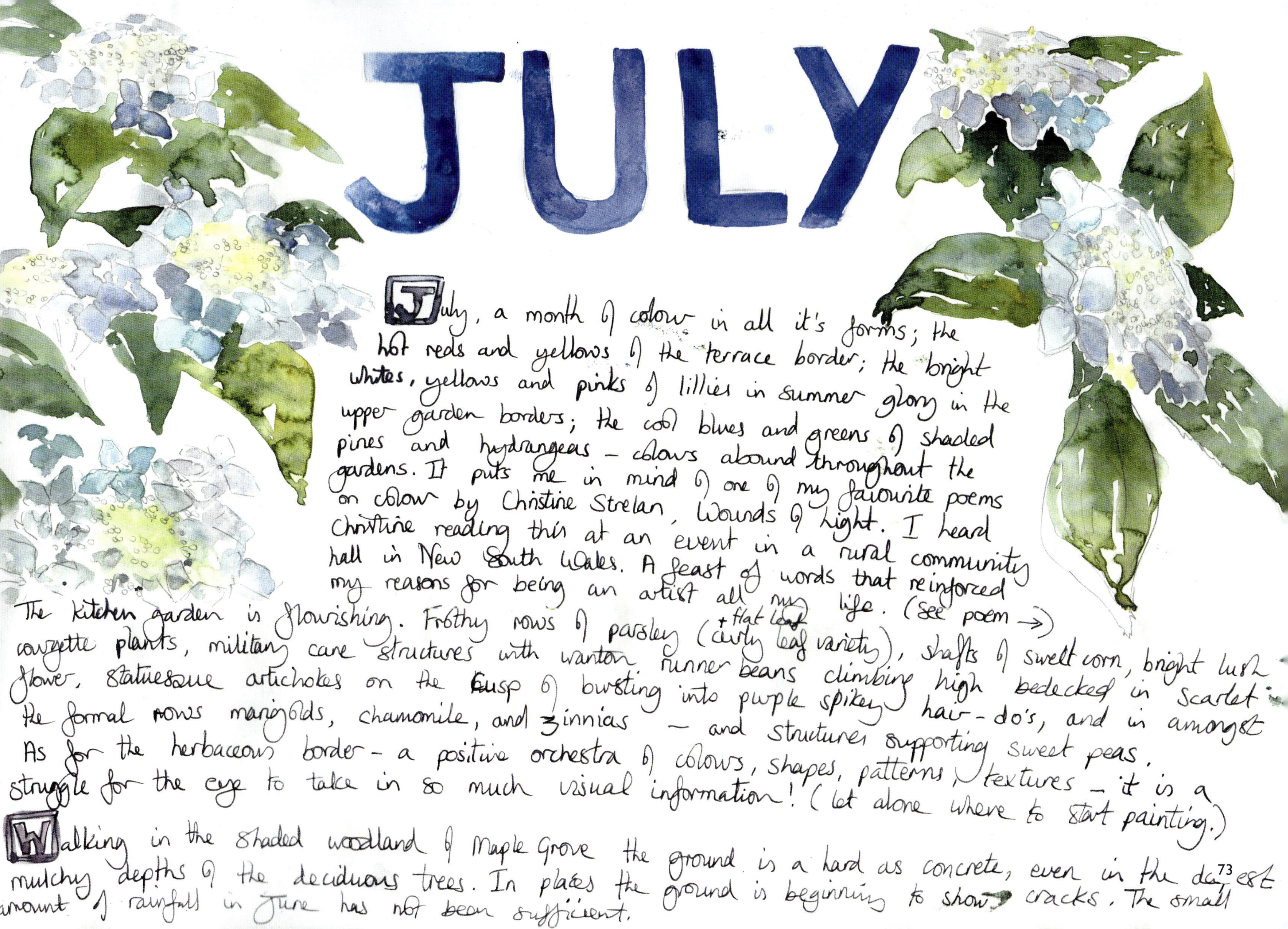

July, a month of colour in all it's forms; the hot reds and yellows of the terrace border; the bright whites, yellows and pinks of lillies in summer glory in the upper garden borders; the cool blues and greens of shaded pines and hydrangeas — colours abound throughout the gardens. It puts me in mind of one of my favourite poems on colour by Christine Strelan, Wounds of Light. I heard Christine reading this at an event in a rural community hall in New South Wales. A feast of words that reinforced my reasons for being an artist all my life. (see poem →)

The kitchen garden is flourishing. Frothy rows of parsley (curly leaf variety + flat leaf), shafts of sweet corn, bright lush courgette plants, military cane structures with wanton runner beans climbing high bedecked in scarlet flower, statuesque artichokes on the cusp of bursting into purple spikey hair-do's, and in amongst the formal rows marigolds, chamomile, and zinnias — and structures supporting sweet peas. As for the herbaceous border — a positive orchestra of colours, shapes, patterns, textures — it is a struggle for the eye to take in so much visual information! (let alone where to start painting.)

Walking in the shaded woodland of Maple Grove the ground is a hard as concrete, even in the dampest mulchy depths of the deciduous trees. In places the ground is beginning to show cracks. The small amount of rainfall in June has not been sufficient.

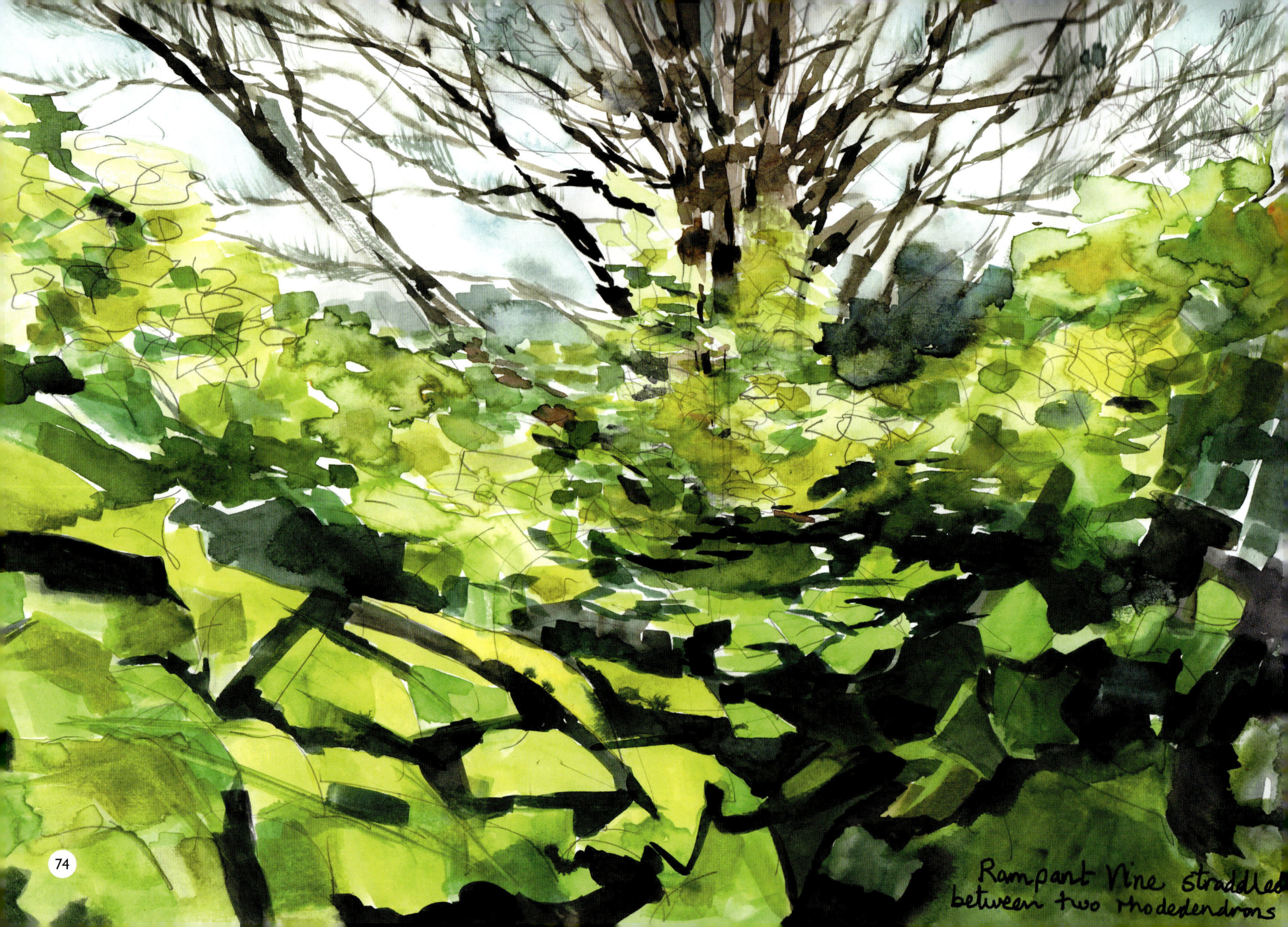

74
Rampant Vine straddled
between two rhododendrons

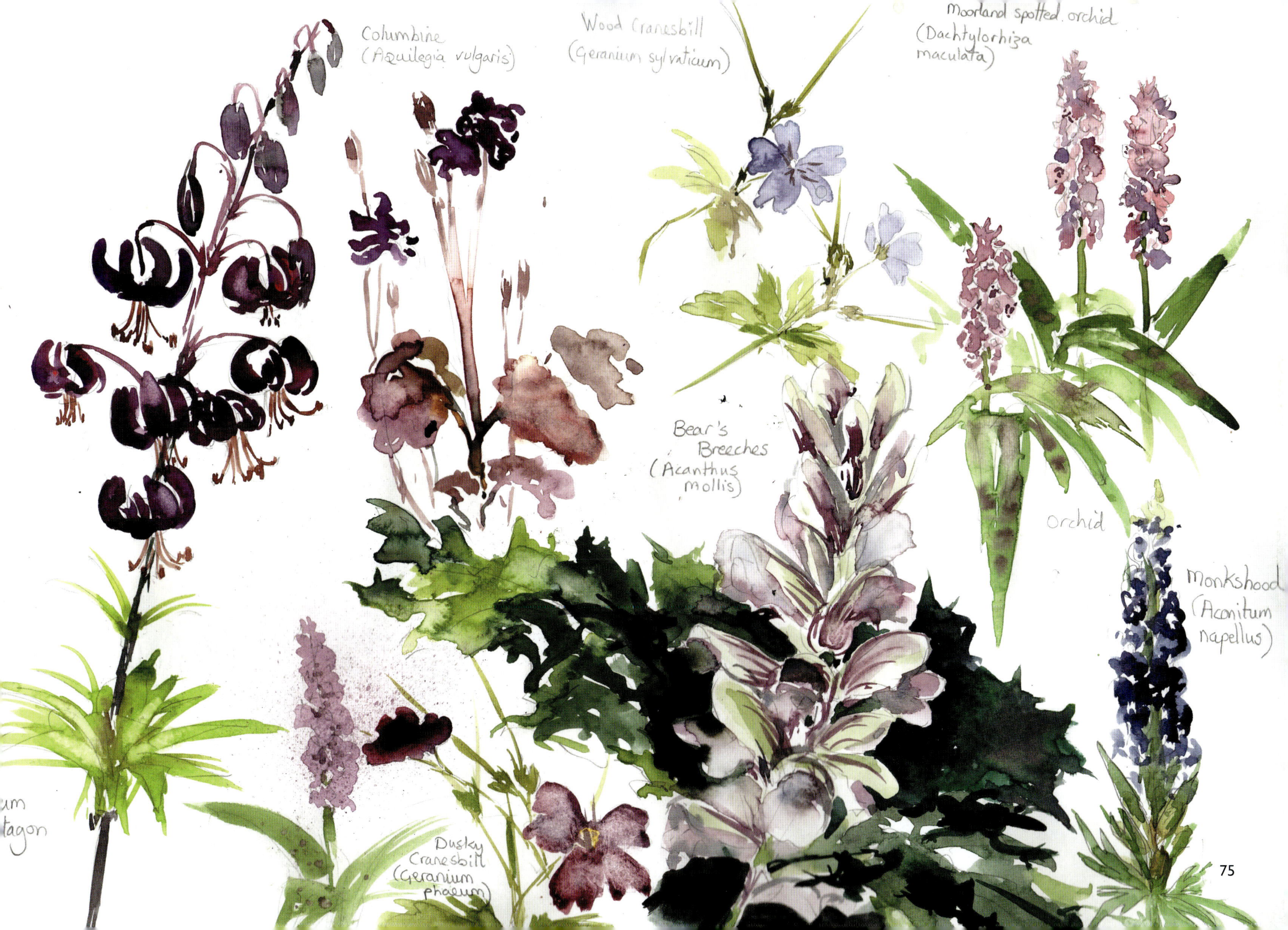

Columbine
(Aquilegia vulgaris)
Wood Cranesbill
(Geranium sylvaticum)
Moorland spotted. orchid
(Dachtylorhiza
maculata)
Bear's
Breeches
(Acanthus
mollis)
orchid
Monkshood
(Aconitum
napellus)
Dusky
Cranesbill
(Geranium
phaeum)
um
tagon

In nature nothing stands still. Each day new buds will open, other flower heads will droop, seeds will be scattered, leaves will droop where other flowers will rise. As too with the evolving gardening calendar. The extensive swathes of grasses and undergrowth, seemingly 'wild' in appearance, are managed; knowing when to leave fallow and when to cut back is an art in itself.

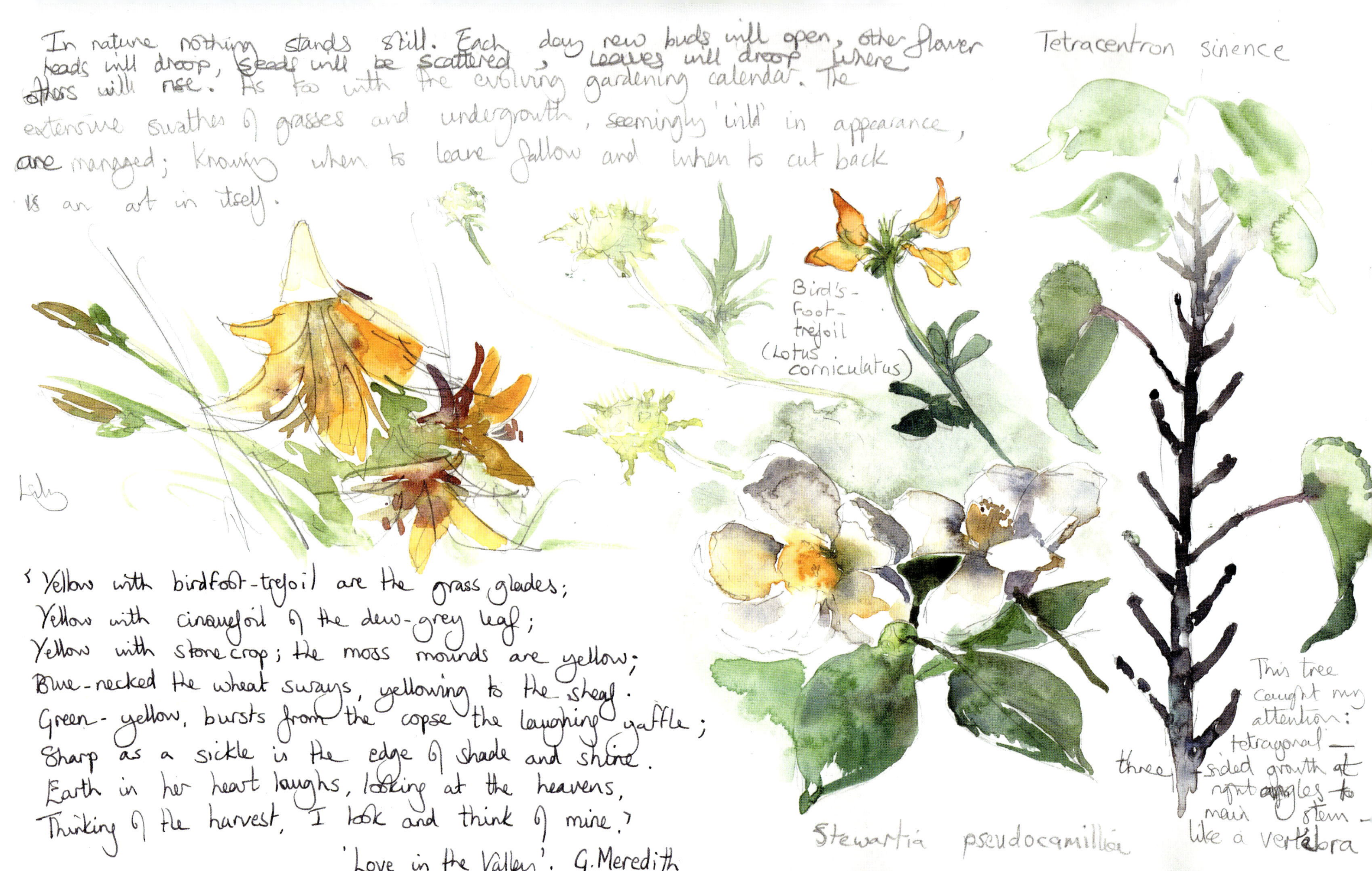

' Yellow with birdfoot-trefoil are the grass glades;
Yellow with cinquefoil of the dew-grey leaf;
Yellow with stonecrop; the moss mounds are yellow;
Blue-necked the wheat sways, yellowing to the sheaf:
Green-yellow, bursts from the copse the laughing yaffle;
Sharp as a sickle is the edge of shade and shine.
Earth in her heart laughs, looking at the heavens,
Thinking of the harvest, I look and think of mine.'
            'Love in the Valley'. G. Meredith

N.B. Bird's-foot-trefoil — country\folk names:— 'Lady's-shoes-and-stockings', 'crow-toes', 'God-Almighty's-thumb-and-finger', 'bacon-and-eggs'.

N.B. 'yaffle', (line 5) is the old country name for green woodpecker.
* I particularly enjoy line 6 — it describes strong summer light so succinctly.

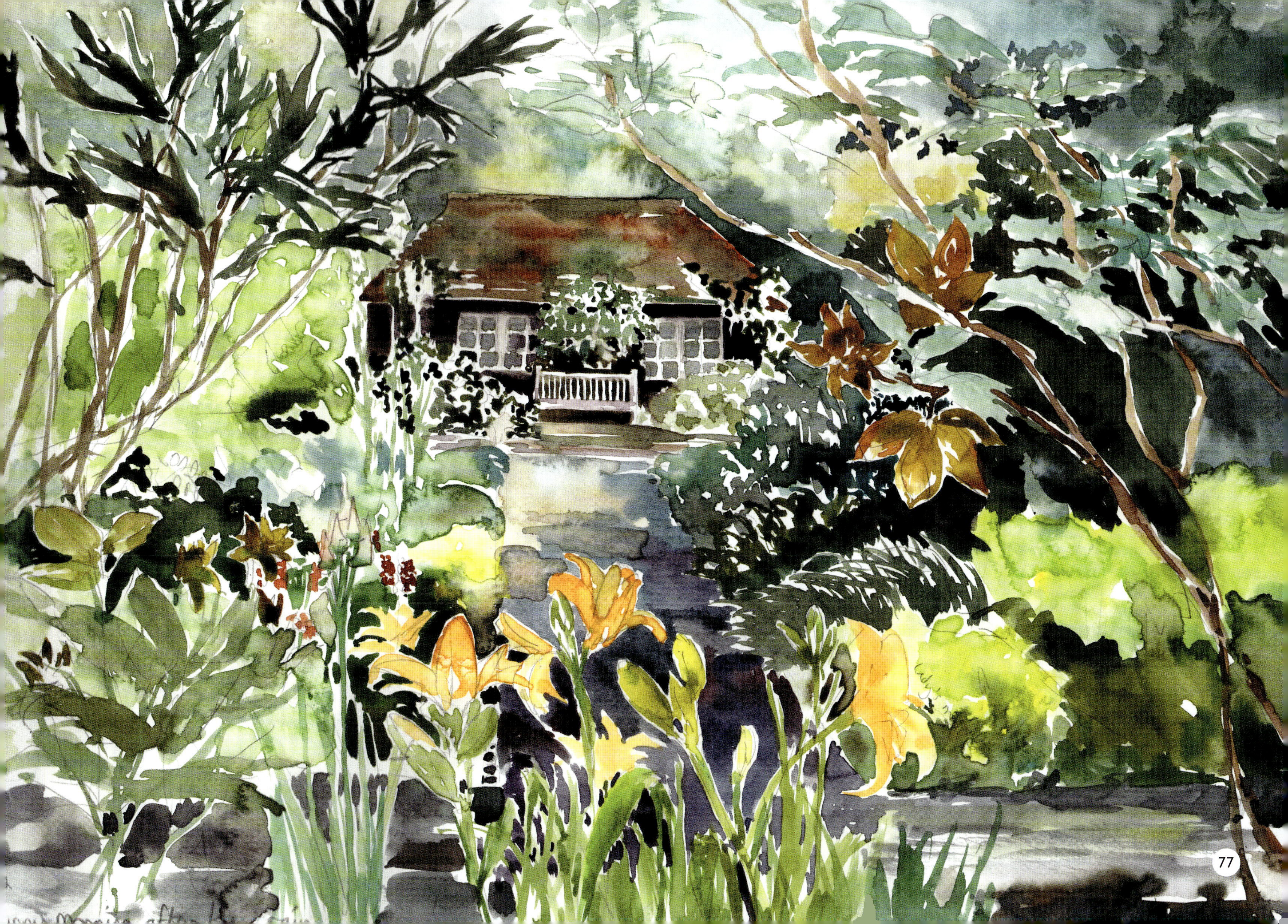

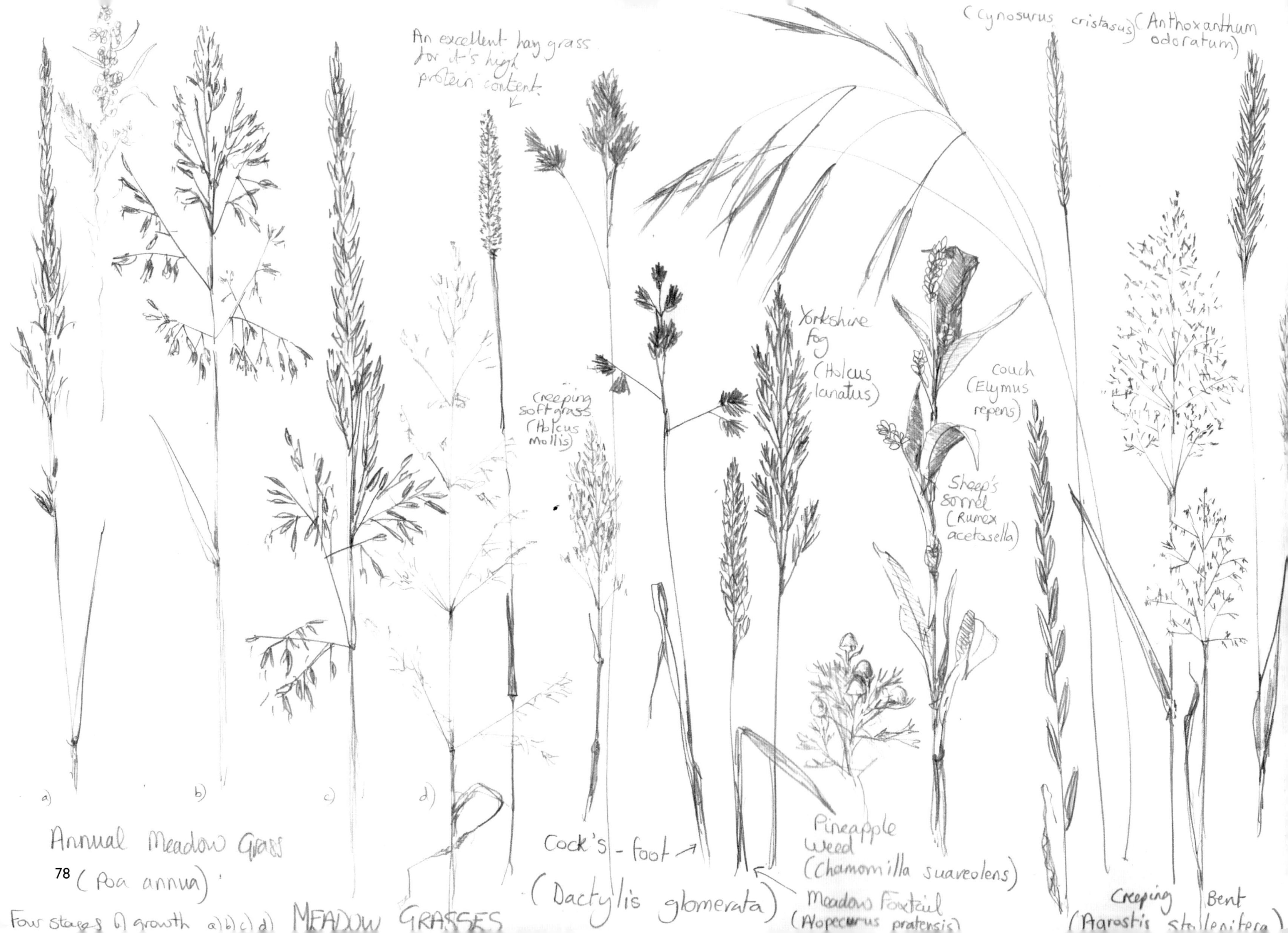
An excellent hay grass for it's high protein content.
(Cynosurus cristasus)
(Anthoxanthum odoratum)
creeping soft grass (Holcus mollis)
Yorkshire fog (Holcus lanatus)
Couch (Elymus repens)
Sheep's sorrel (Rumex acetosella)
Annual Meadow Grass
78
(Poa annua).
Four stages of growth a) b) c) d)
MEADOW GRASSES
Cock's - foot →
(Dactylis glomerata)
Pineapple Weed (Chamomilla suaveolens)
Meadow Foxtail (Alopecurus pratensis)
Creeping Bent (Agrostis stolonifera)
a)
b)
c)
d)

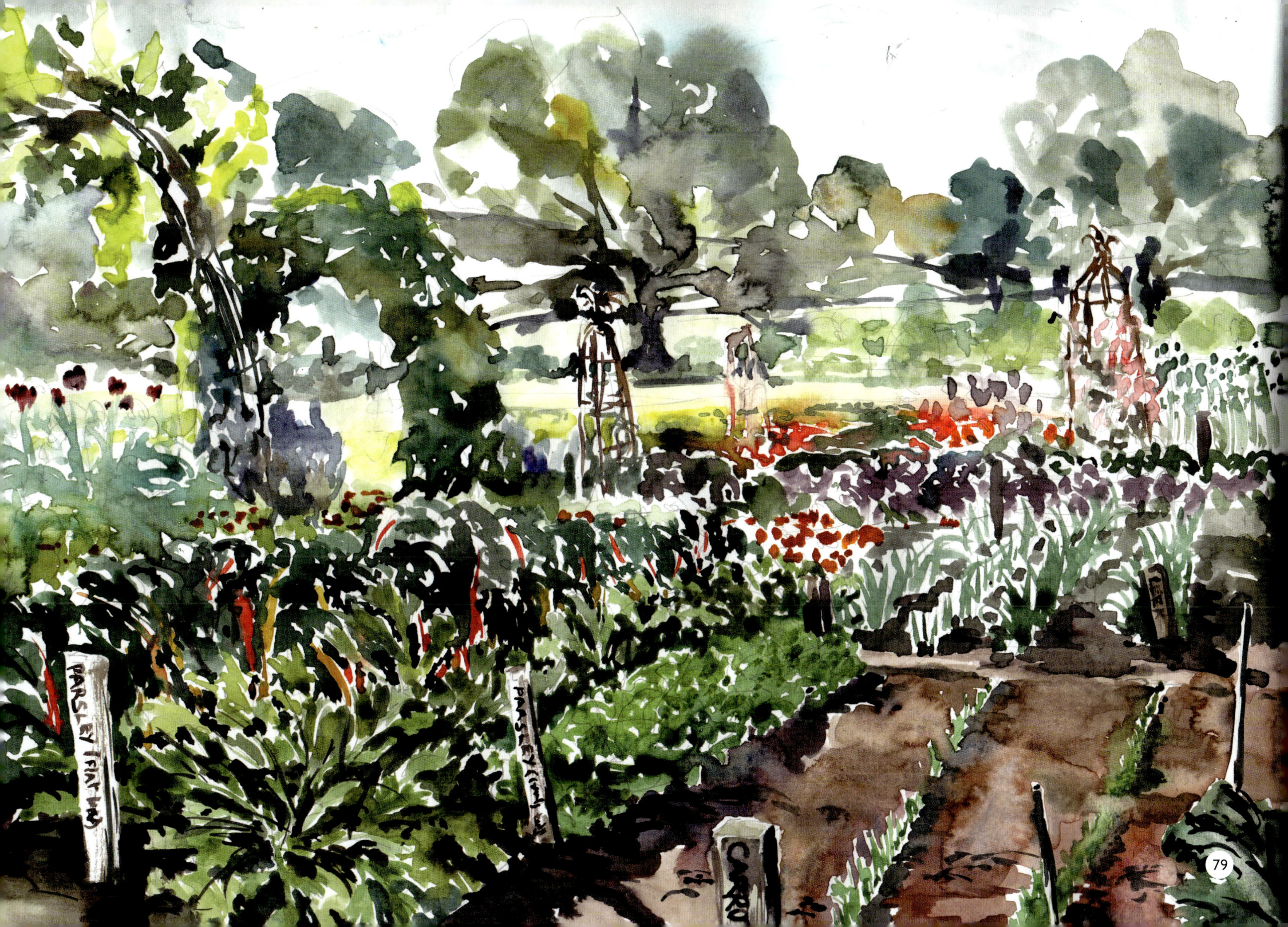

PARSLEY (FLAT LEAF)
PARSLEY (CURLED)
CARROT
LEEK

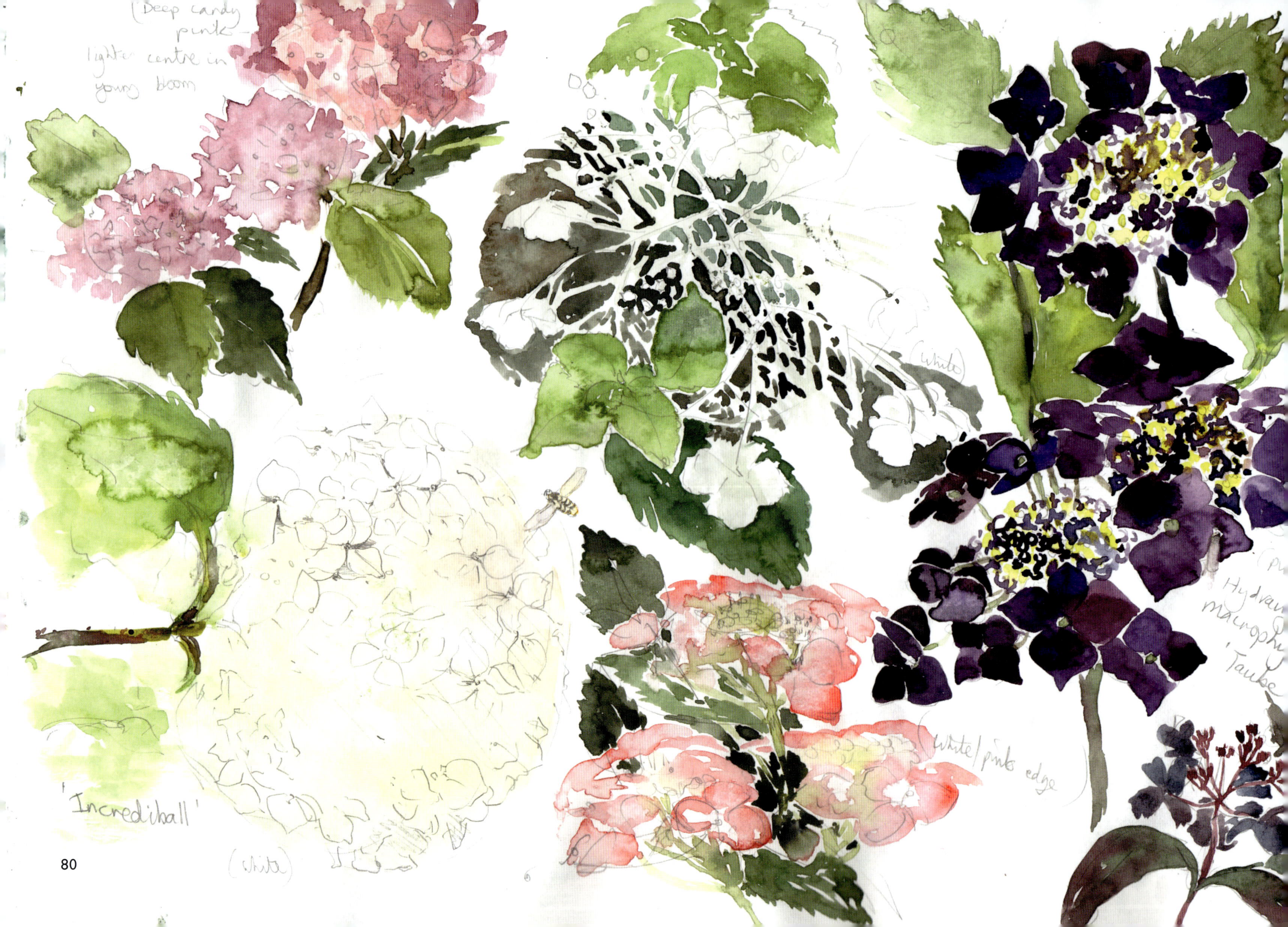
(Deep candy
pink —
lighter centre in
young bloom

'Incrediball'

(White)

(White)

white/pink edge

Hydran
macrophy
'Taube'

80

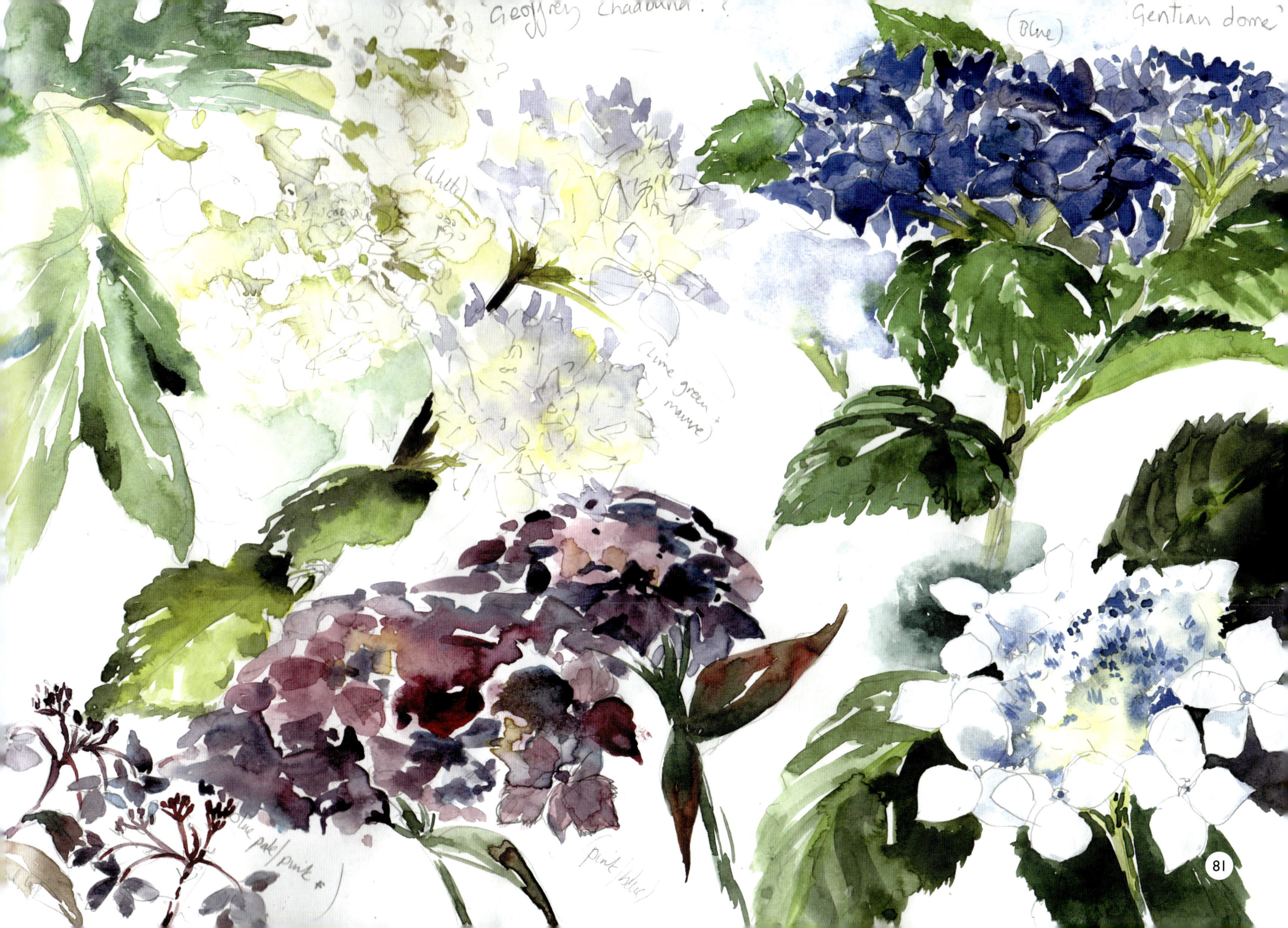

Geoffrey Chadbund :
(Blue)
'Gentian dome'
(white)
(Lime green + mauve)
blue pale/pink
pink/blue
81

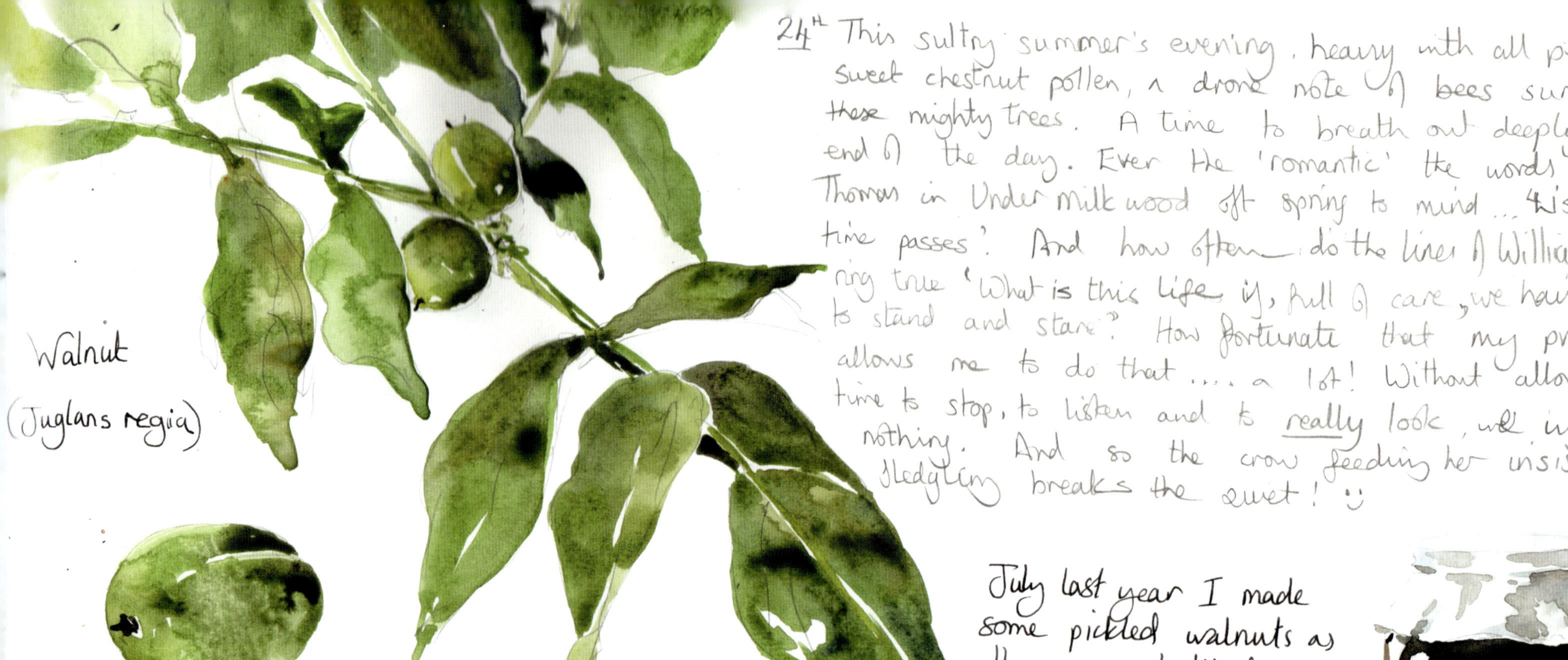

Walnut

(Juglans regia)

24th This sultry summer's evening, heavy with all pervasive sweet chestnut pollen, a drone note of bees surrounding these mighty trees. A time to breath out deeply at the end of the day. Ever the 'romantic' the words of Dylan Thomas in Under milk wood oft spring to mind ... "Listen ... time passes". And how often do the lines of William. H. Davies ring true 'What is this life if, full of care, we have no time to stand and stare'? How fortunate that my profession allows me to do that .... a lot! Without allowing ourselves time to stop, to listen and to really look, we will see nothing. And so the crow feeding her insistent fledgling breaks the quiet! :)

"A thing that I regret..... is that I have never in my life planted a walnut." (George Orwell 'A good word for the Vicar of Bray' 1946)

July last year I made some pickled walnuts as there was plentiful supply from a friend's garden! I suspect I was slightly late harvesting the green fruits as the kernels had started to form their surrounding hard shell. Consequently they are a tad crunchy, but no less lacking in flavour.

Such a versatile species. Interestingly growth beneath trees is often stunted or limited due to allelopathy. Walnut trees produce a range of chemicals in the leaves, fruits and roots, the most prevalent of these being juglone. When the leaves fall and decompose the chemicals enter the soil inhibiting other growth, reducing competition and giving the walnut an advantage in it's survival.

I have also made the richest of dark umber inks for drawing, from the blackened husks, as well as natural dyes for my spun wool. The dye possesses a natural mordant so no pre-mordanting is required to fix dye.

82

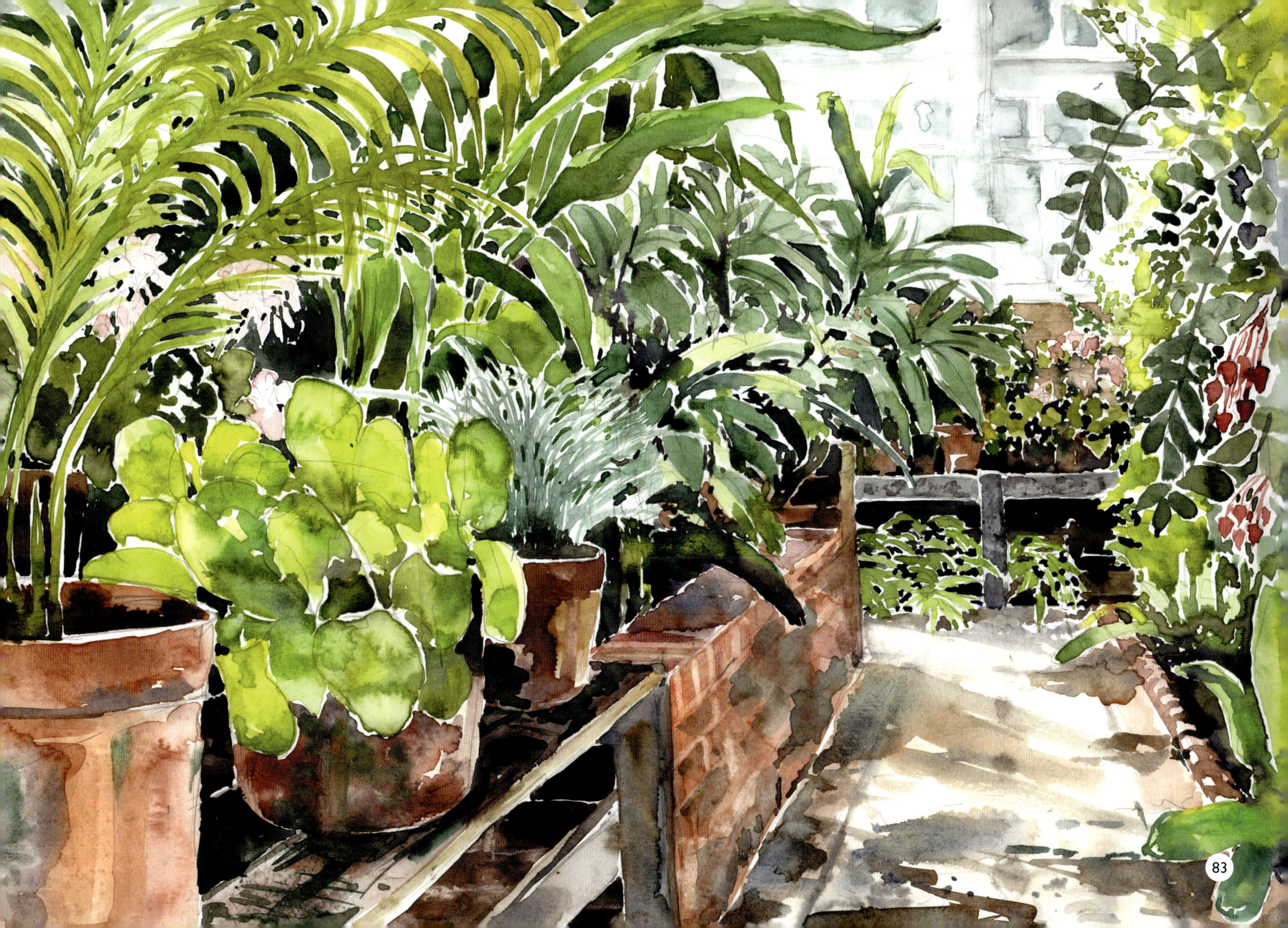

AUGUST

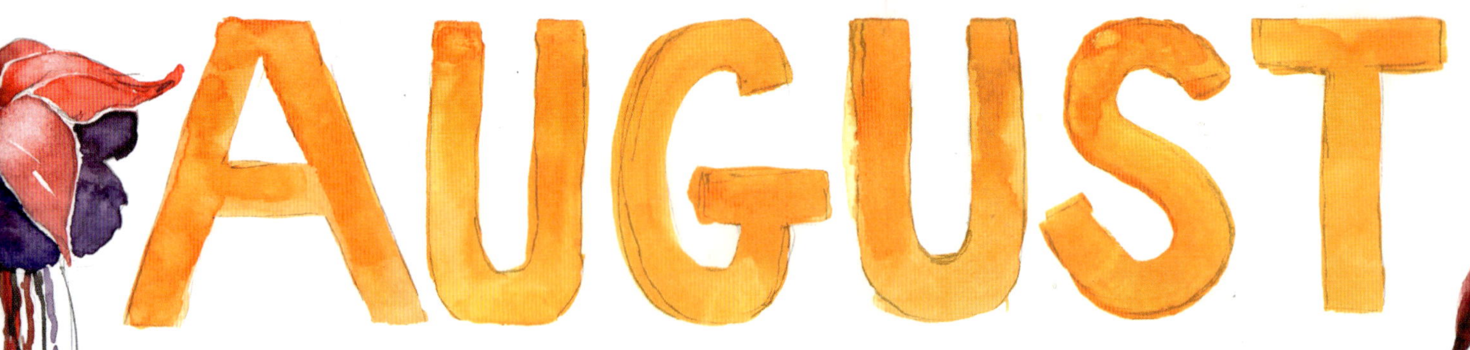

"There are painters who transform the sun into a yellow spot, but there are others who, thanks to their art and their intelligence, transform a yellow spot into the sun."

Pablo Picasso

<u>4th August</u> A still, sultry morning, a morning reluctant to commit to any particular weather. The dense cloud-covered sky, above and beyond, forms the perfect back cloth for the swirling dance of swallows and house martins. (My recent painting of Herbert Court witnessed the bountiful nests of house martins along the eaves - there were so many it looked like a swarm of bees around the house.) Quiet when the birds move to another piece of sky, but for the everpresent crows cawing from time to time, and a blackbird. A squirrel behind me alerting my presence as it clucks at me, gesticulating with it's tail. The nearby beech trees are shedding husks - falling through the branches it sounds like rain. And in yonder fields the drone of the hay making machinery.

84

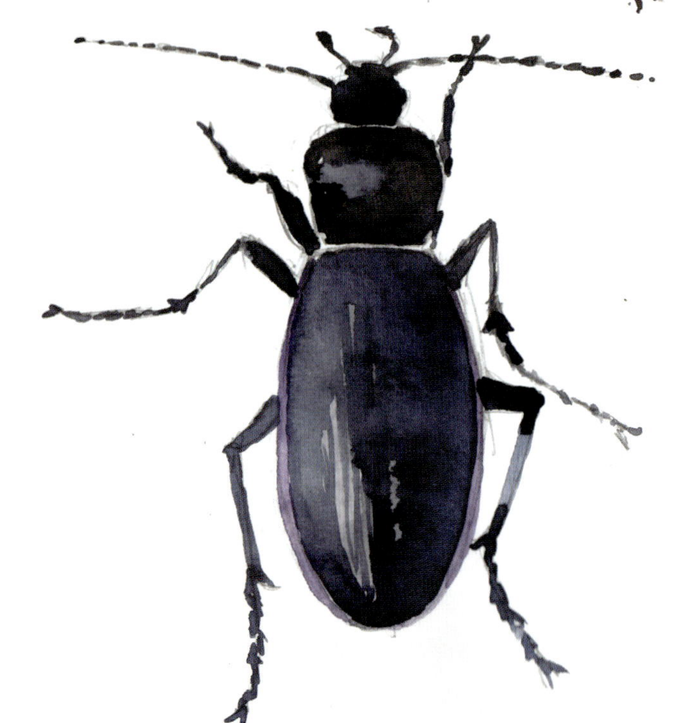

Ground beetle - Carabus problematicus

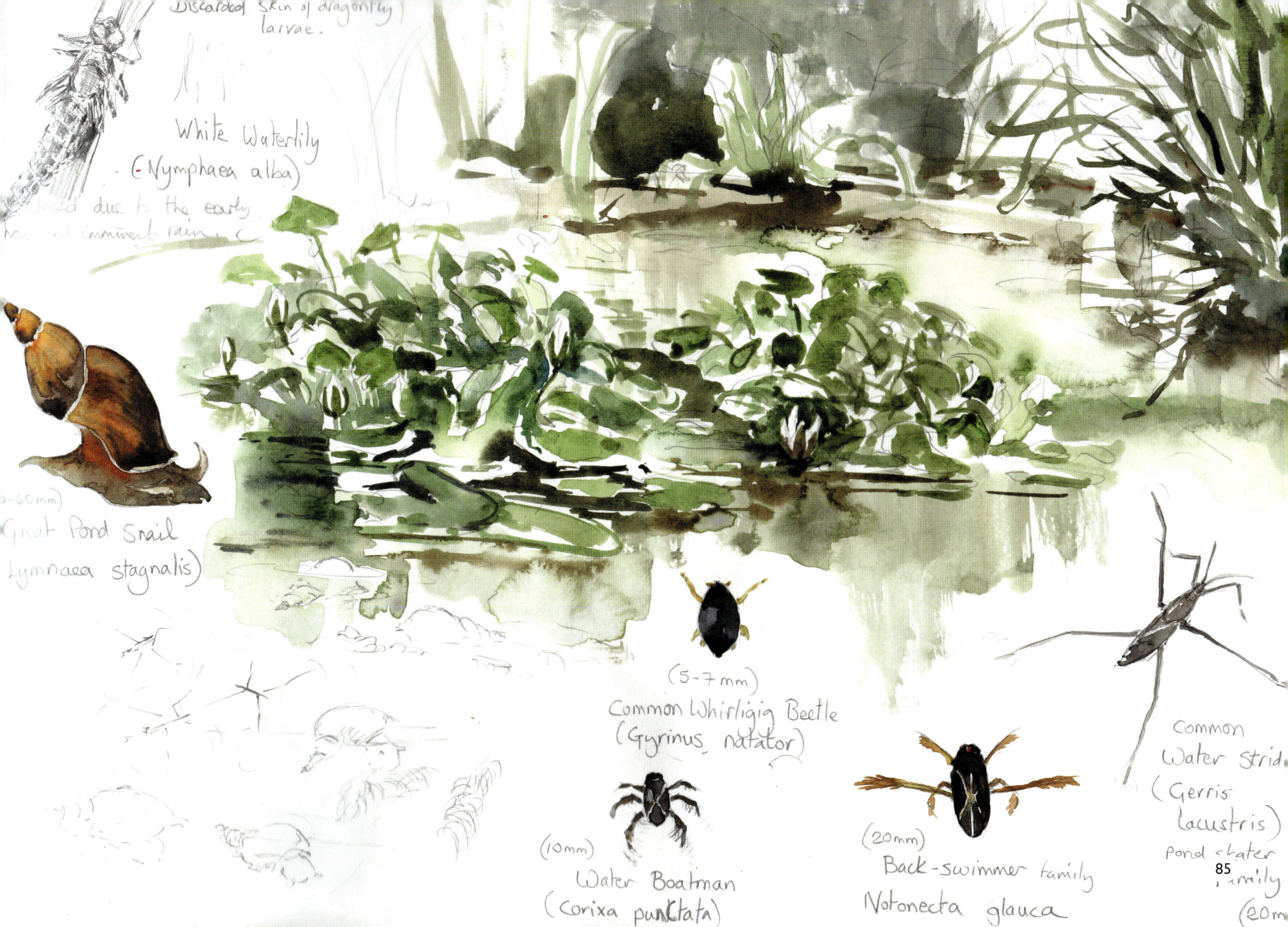

Discarded skin of dragonfly larvae.
White Waterlily
(Nymphaea alba)
Closed due to the early hour and imminent rain.
0-60mm)
(Great Pond Snail Lymnaea stagnalis)
(5-7mm)
Common Whirligig Beetle
(Gyrinus natator)
(10mm)
Water Boatman
(Corixa punctata)
(20mm)
Back-swimmer family
Notonecta glauca
Common Water strider
(Gerris lacustris)
Pond skater family
(20m
85

5th [T]orrential rain all day today.
Useful time spent reading up about pond life following yesterday's drawing. Collecting jam jars of pond life was my teenage pastime; cycling across the moors in Somerset, haversack rattling with jars, net across handlebars, and to get home proceeding to look at small pipette drops of stagnant water on a glass slide under the microscope. Only today, following nearly fifty years, have I realised that my knowledge of waterboatmen has been incorrect! They are in fact Back-Swimmers; swimming on their backs/upside down, unlike water boatmen that swim on their fronts. Both insects, indeed the order of 'Bugs' (Heteroptera) fly at night! I never knew that. The water-strider also ventures on to land, so isn't just a water dweller. The dragonfly larvae (giant dragonfly and Brown dragonfly) take one and two years to develop respectively. The female dragonfly lays eggs near the water against reeds and these develop into predacious larvae, even capturing small fish. When large enough they climb out of their subterranean depths of pond-matter to mutate from sinister larvae body into stunning, radiant dragonfly; (their large-eyed swivelling heads as adults do look like military jet pilots, I think.)

The electric blue of the Giant Dragonfly has the very same radiance as a kingfisher I inadvertently disturbed on the River Arrow near Hergest Court last week. It was perched on a boulder waiting for a passing morsel, patiently. What a spectacle!

Whilst on the subject of mis-informed naming, many associate the 'Bulrush' as the dark solid seed case on a stem = [drawing]. This in, in fact also known as Reed Mace (Great) or Cat's tail.

86 Bulrush (Lesser) / lesser Reedmace — longer, more wispy.

Reed Mace, not in the gardens at the Croft, does however grow around the Pond of Legend at Hergest Court, along with tall tales!

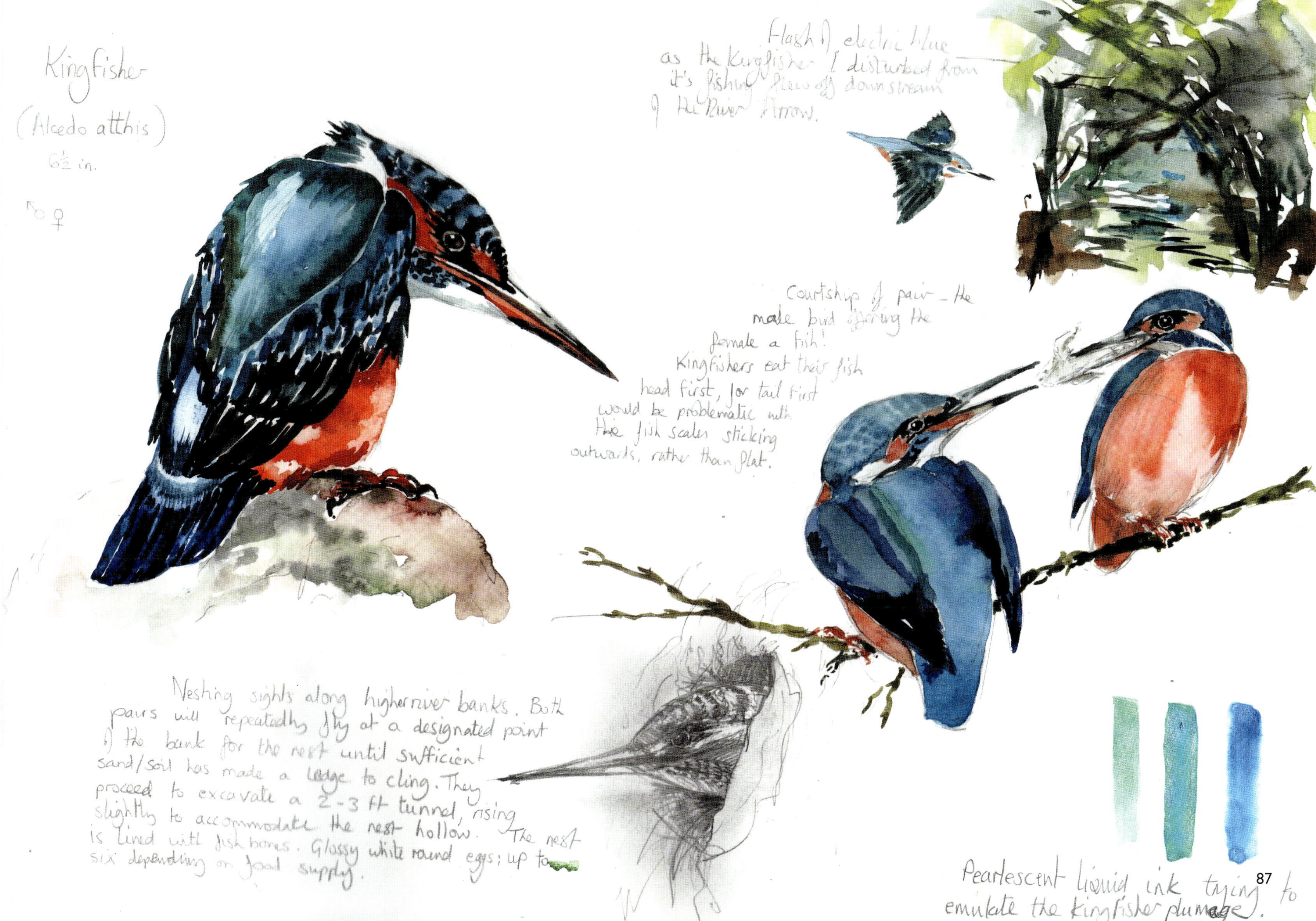

Kingfisher
(Alcedo atthis)
6½ in.
♂ ♀

Flash of electric blue
as the Kingfisher I disturbed from
it's fishing perch off downstream
of the River Arrow.

Courtship of pair – the
male bird offering the
female a fish!
Kingfishers eat their fish
head first, for tail first
would be problematic with
their fish scales sticking
outwards, rather than flat.

Nesting sights along higher river banks. Both
pairs will repeatedly fly at a designated point
of the bank for the nest until sufficient
sand/soil has made a ledge to cling. They
proceed to excavate a 2-3 ft tunnel, rising
slightly to accommodate the nest hollow. The nest
is lined with fish bones. Glossy white round eggs; up to
six depending on food supply.

Pearlescent liquid ink trying to
emulate the kingfisher plumage.

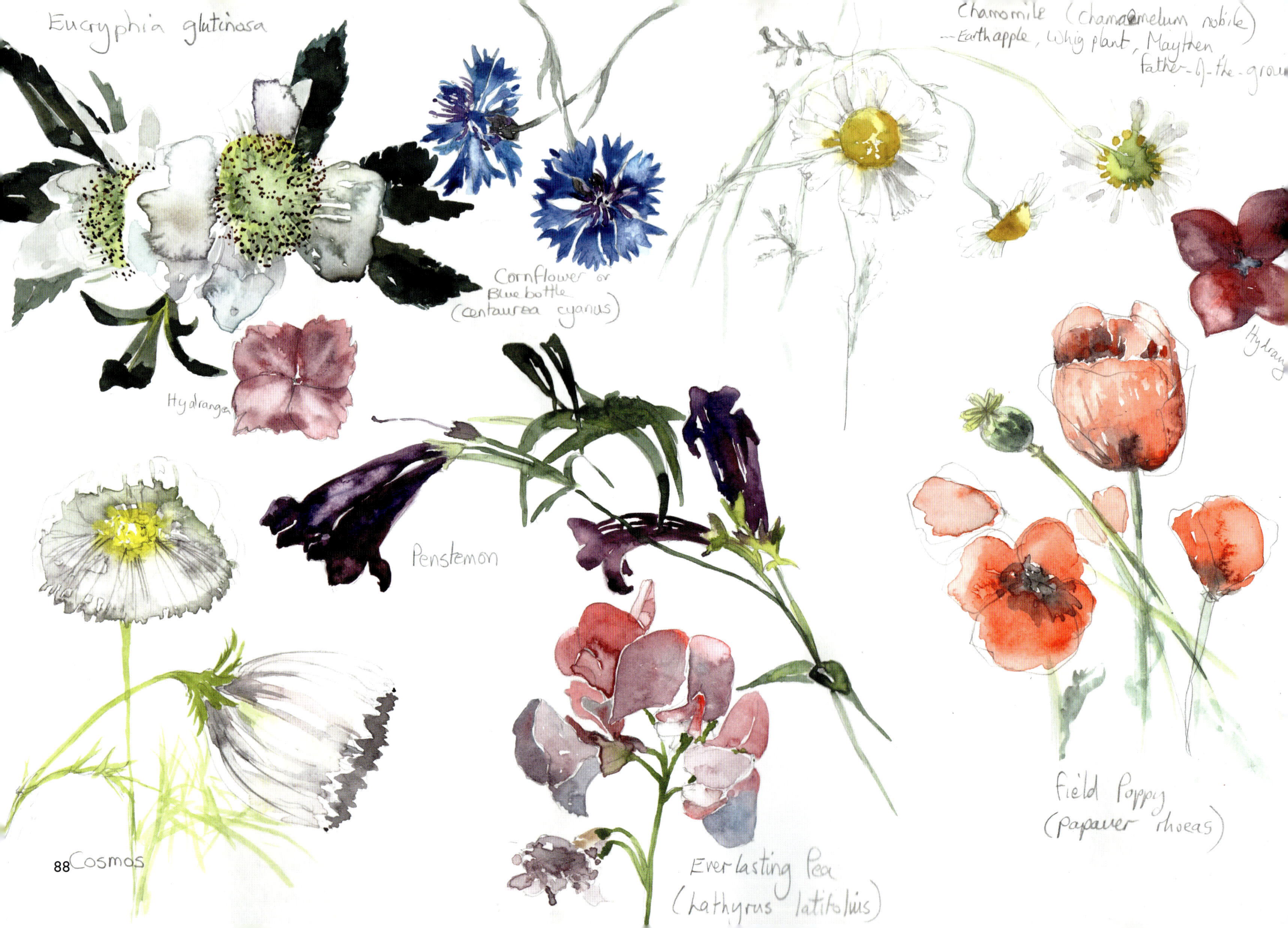

Eucryphia glutinosa
Chamomile (Chamaemelum nobile)
—Earthapple, Whig plant, Maythen
Father-of-the-ground
Cornflower or
Blue bottle
(Centaurea cyanus)
Hydrangea
Hydrangea
Penstemon
Field Poppy
(Papaver rhoeas)
88 Cosmos
Everlasting Pea
(Lathyrus latifoluis)

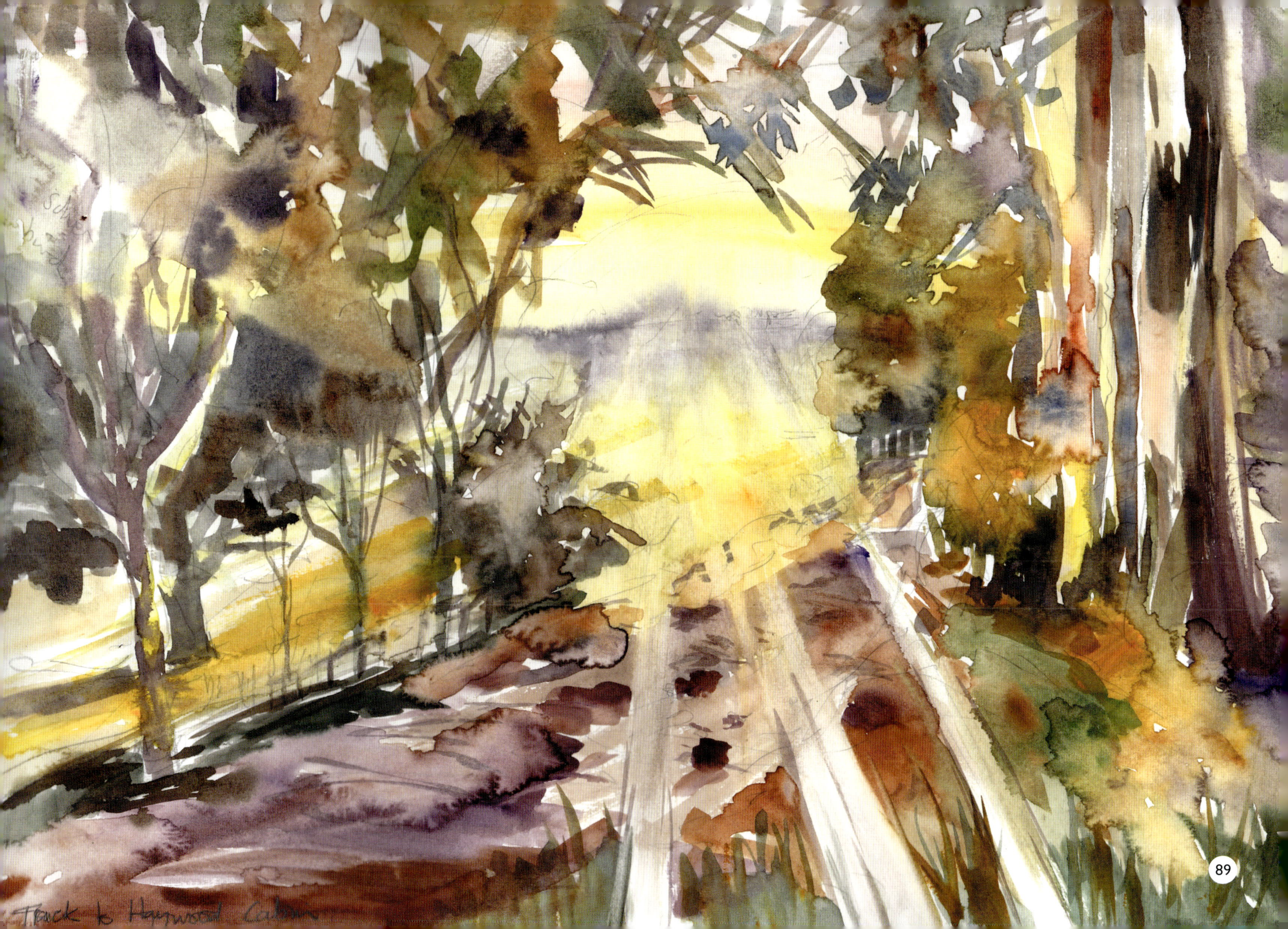
Track to Haywood Column

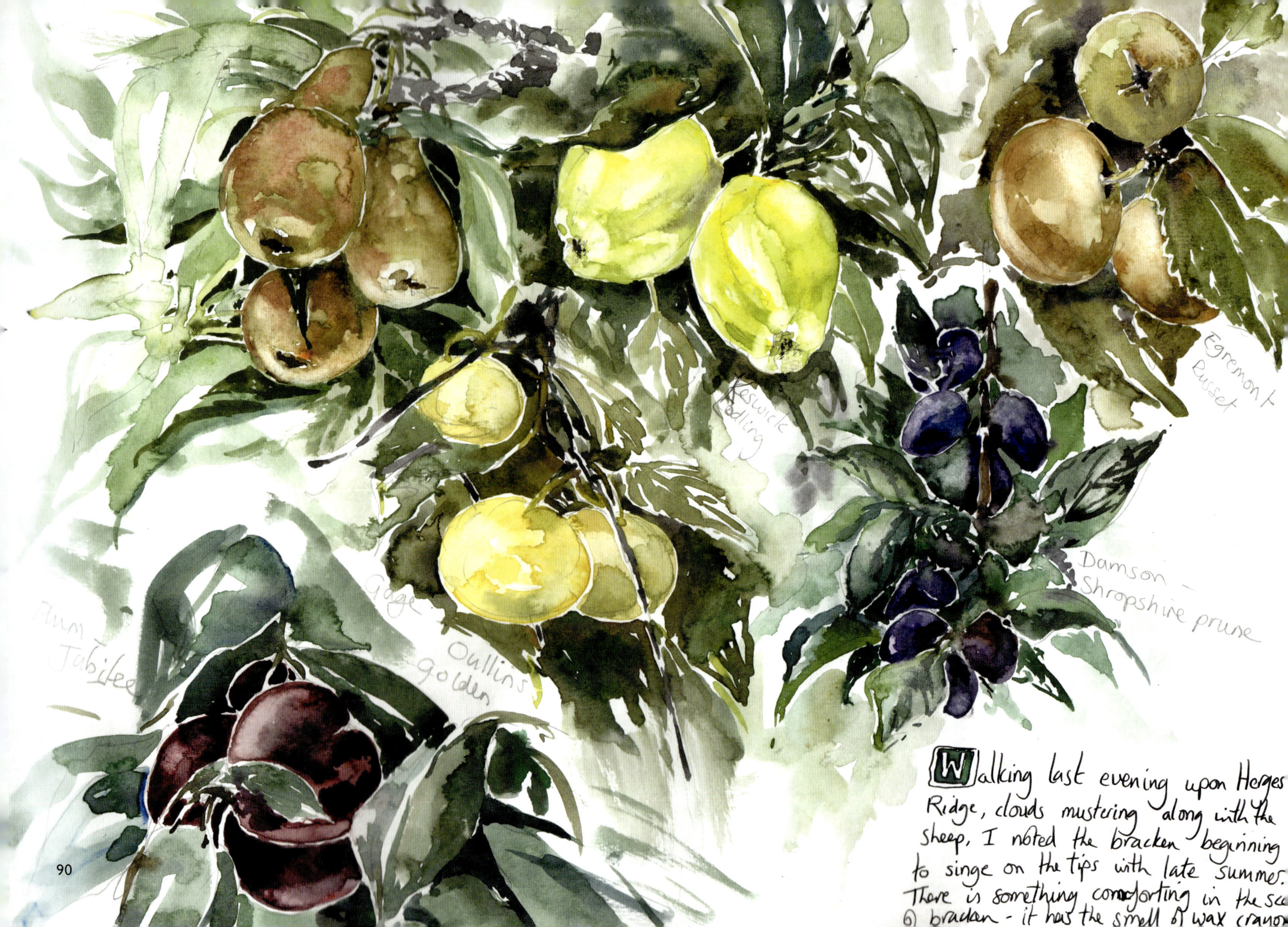
Egremont
Russet
Keswick
Codling
Damson –
Shropshire prune
Plum
Jubilee
Gage
Oullins
Golden
90
Walking last evening upon Herges
Ridge, clouds mustering along with the
sheep, I noted the bracken beginning
to singe on the tips with late summer.
There is something comforting in the sce
of bracken – it has the smell of wax crayon

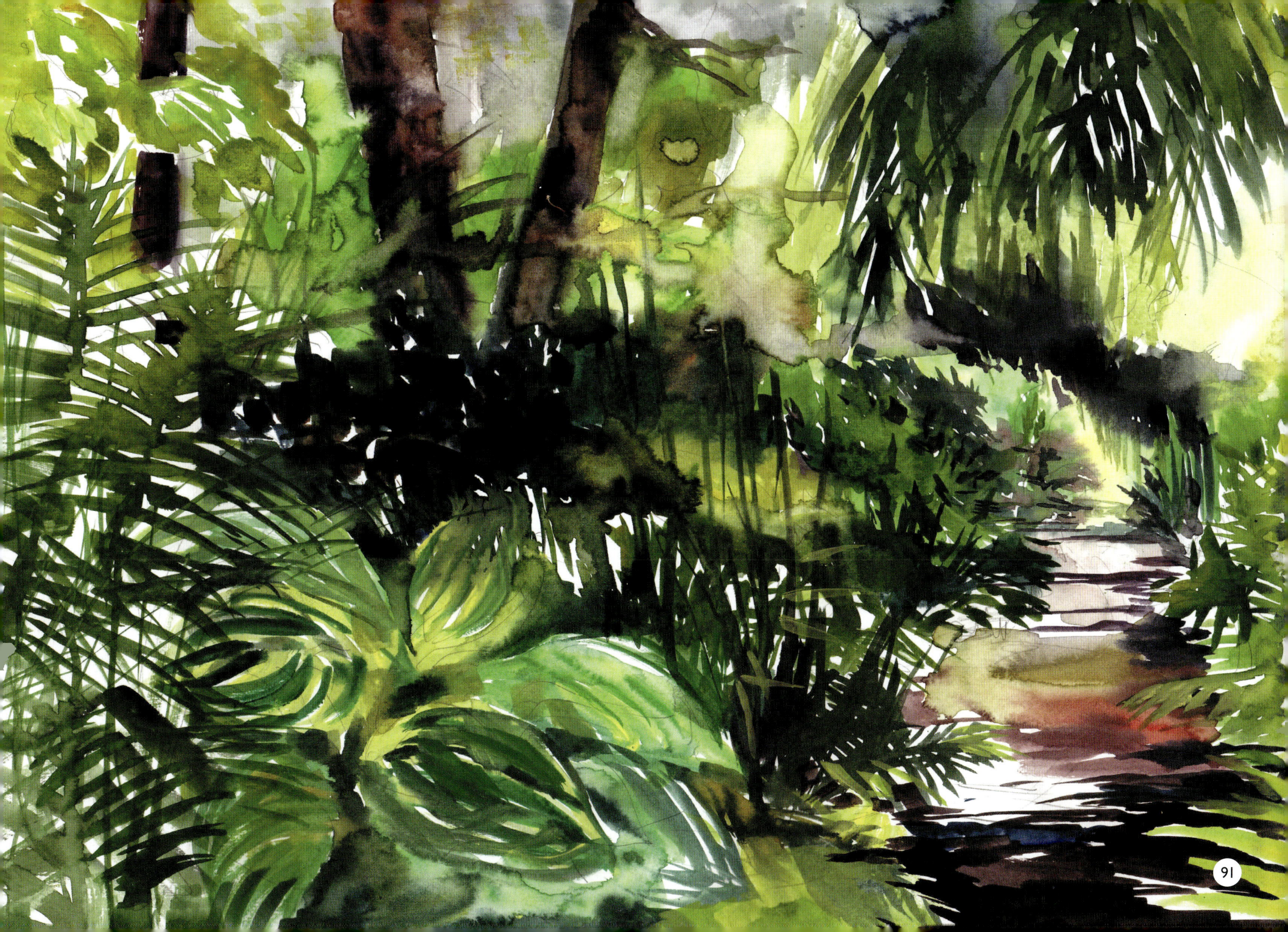

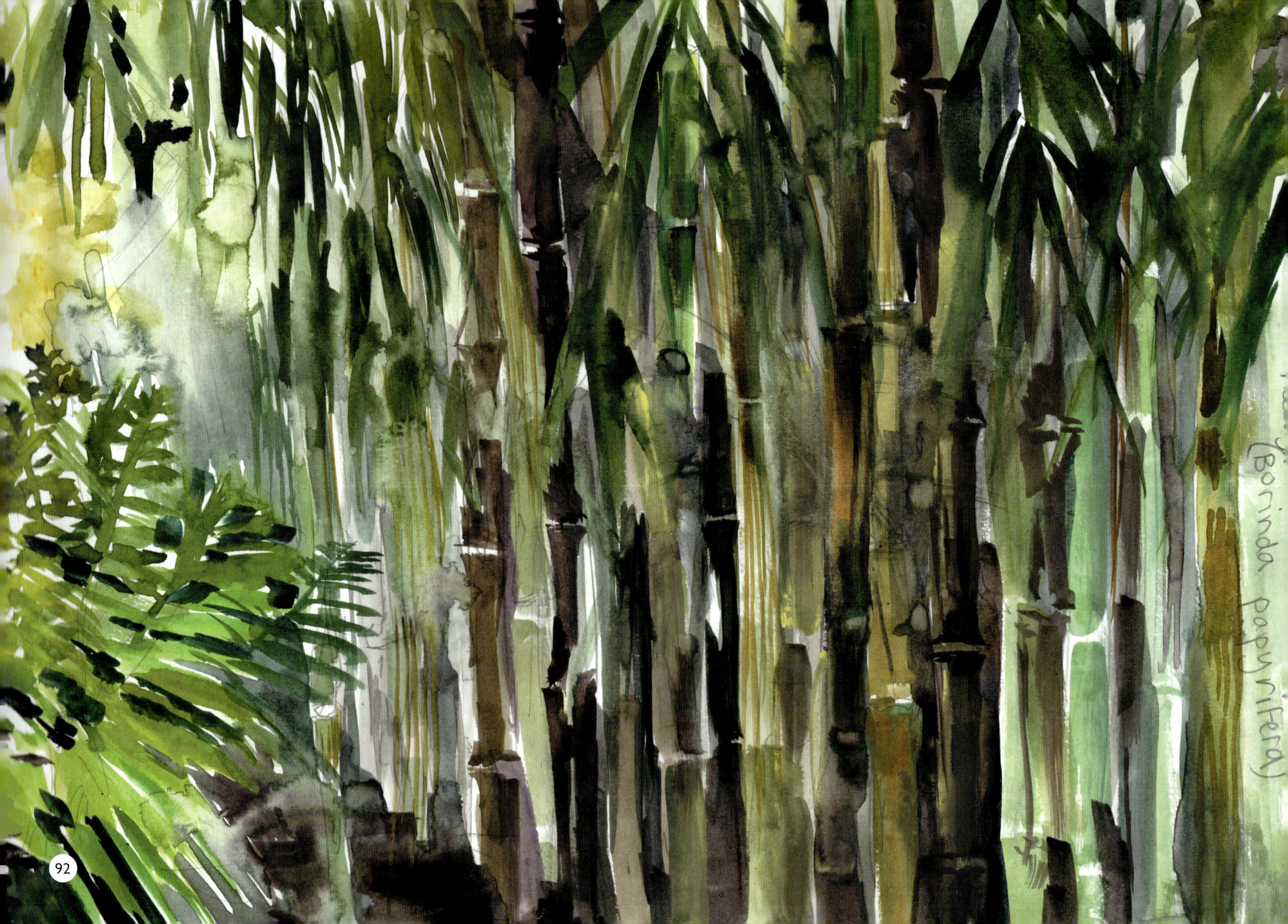

(Borinda papyrifera)

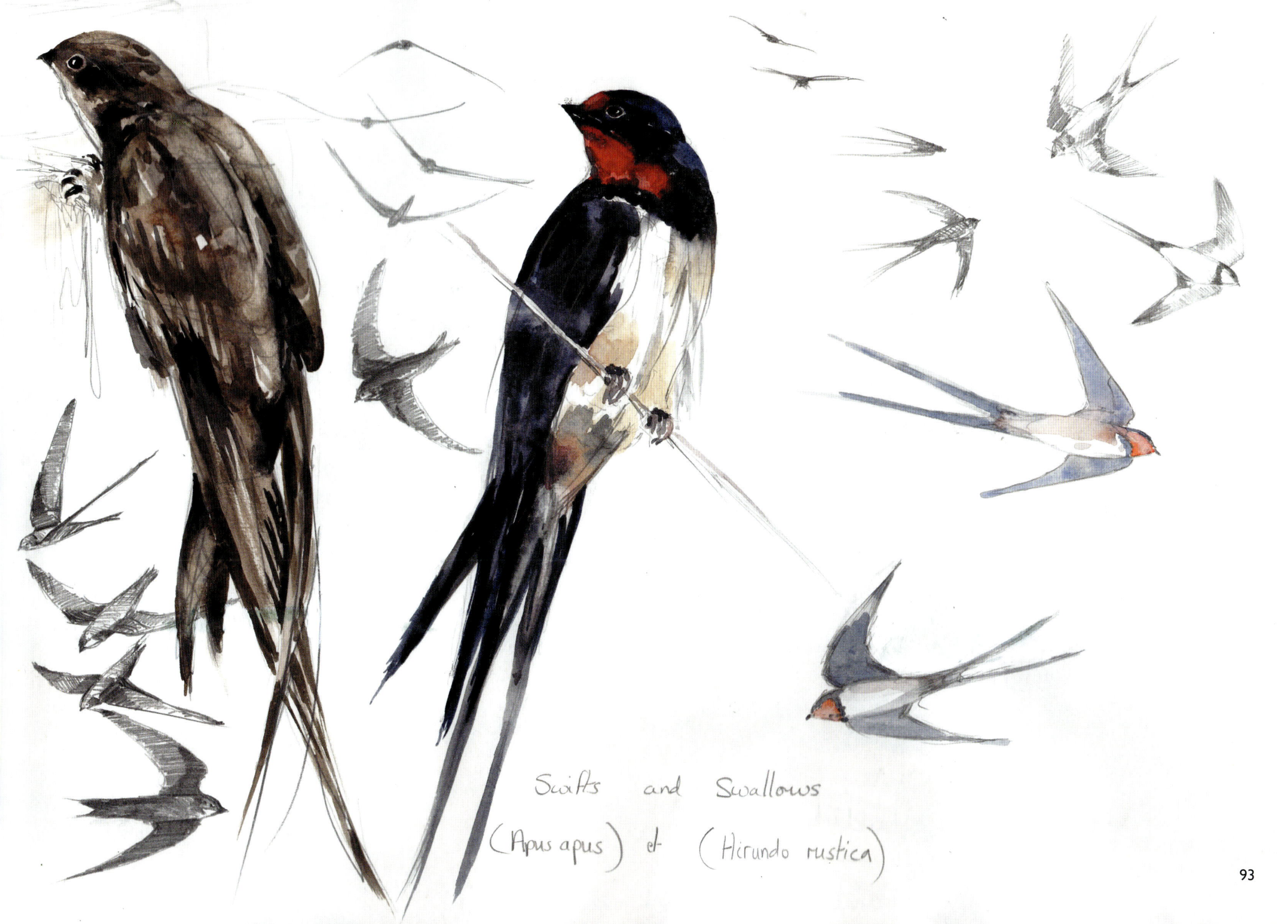

Swifts and Swallows
(Apus apus) et (Hirundo rustica)

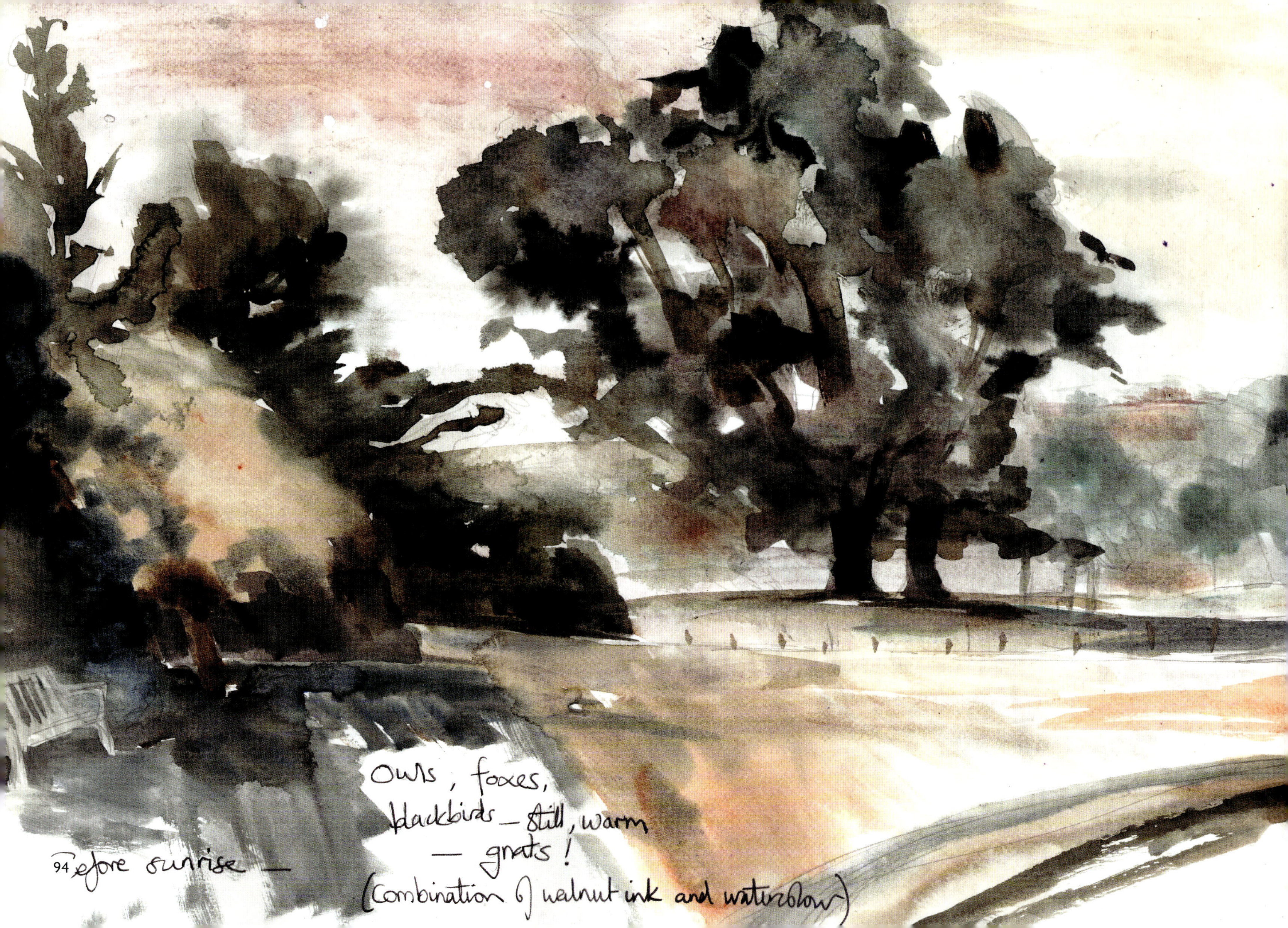
Owls, foxes,
blackbirds – still, warm
– gnats!
(Combination of walnut ink and watercolour)
94 Before sunrise –

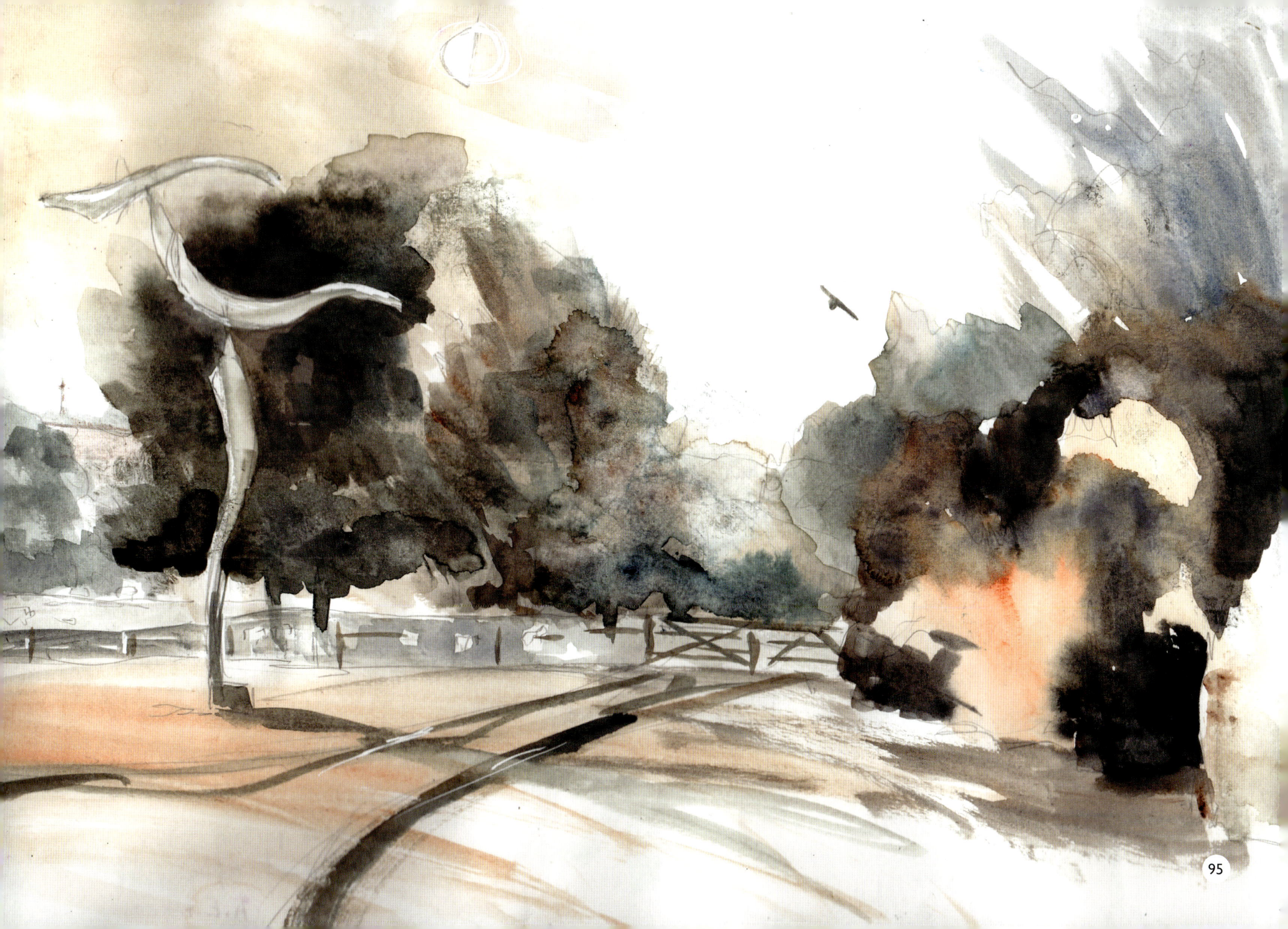

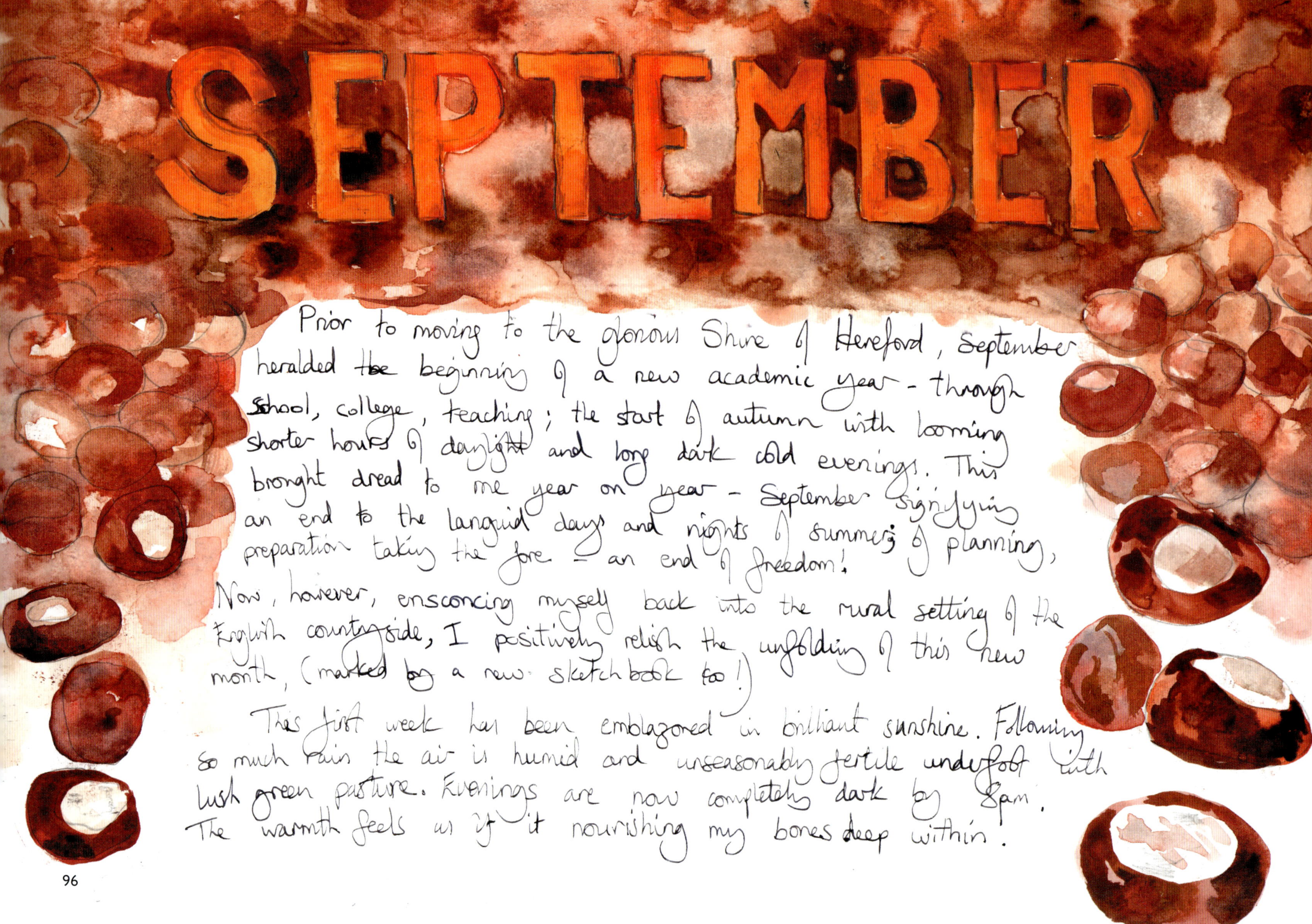

SEPTEMBER

Prior to moving to the glorious Shire of Hereford, September heralded the beginning of a new academic year — through school, college, teaching; the start of autumn with looming shorter hours of daylight and long dark cold evenings. This brought dread to me year on year — September signifying an end to the languid days and nights of summer; of planning, preparation taking the fore — an end of freedom!

Now, however, ensconcing myself back into the rural setting of the English countryside, I positively relish the unfolding of this new month, (marked by a new sketchbook too!)

This first week has been emblazoned in brilliant sunshine. Following so much rain the air is humid and unseasonably fertile underfoot with lush green pasture. Evenings are now completely dark by 8pm. The warmth feels as if it nourishing my bones deep within.

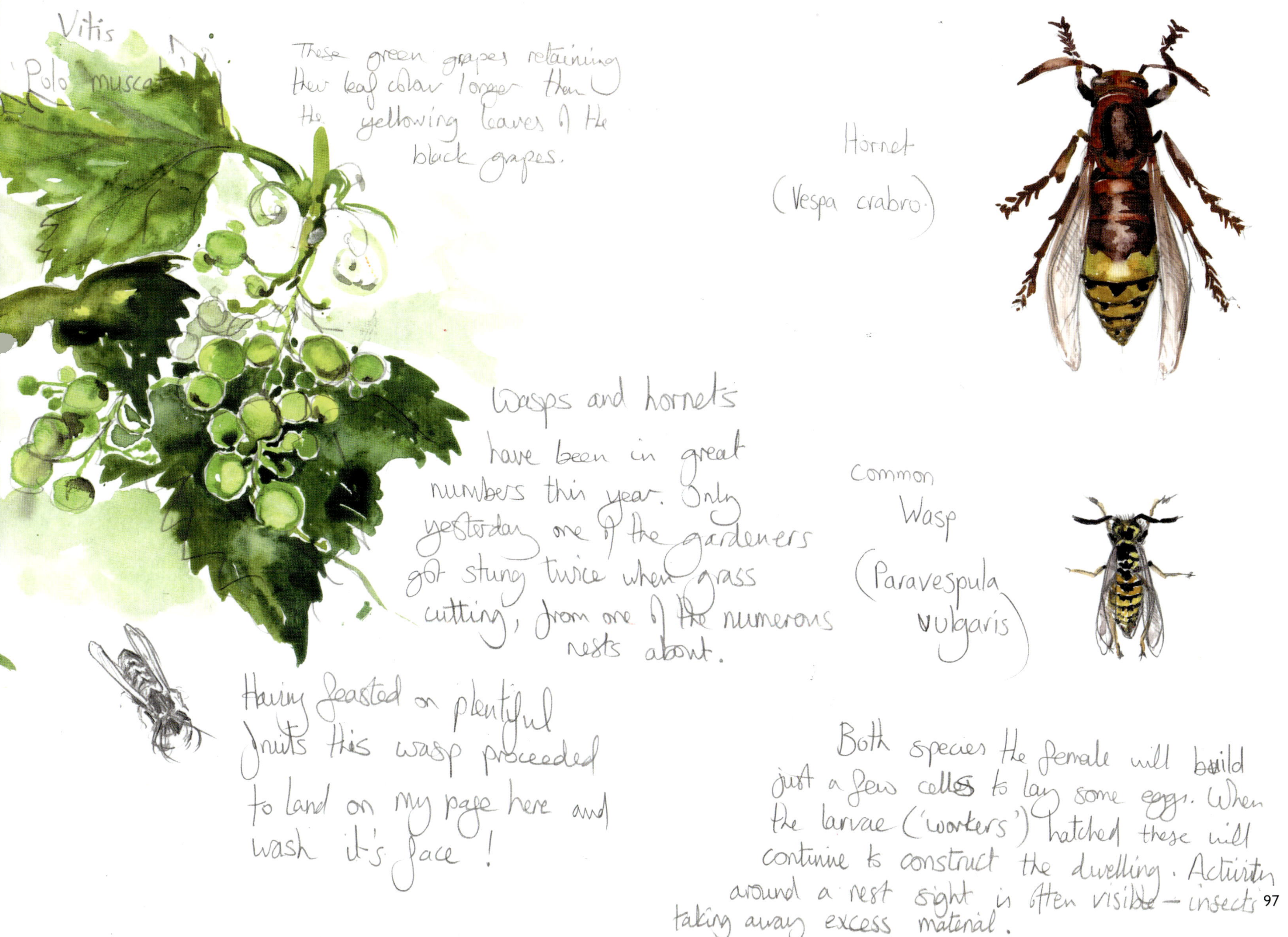

Vitis
'Polo muscat'

These green grapes retaining
their leaf colour longer than
the yellowing leaves of the
black grapes.

Hornet
(Vespa crabro.)

Wasps and hornets
have been in great
numbers this year. Only
yesterday one of the gardeners
got stung twice when grass
cutting, from one of the numerous
nests about.

Common
Wasp
(Paravespula
vulgaris)

Having feasted on plentiful
fruits this wasp proceeded
to land on my page here and
wash it's face!

Both species the female will build
just a few cells to lay some eggs. When
the larvae ('workers') hatched these will
continue to construct the dwelling. Activity
around a nest sight is often visible — insects
taking away excess material.

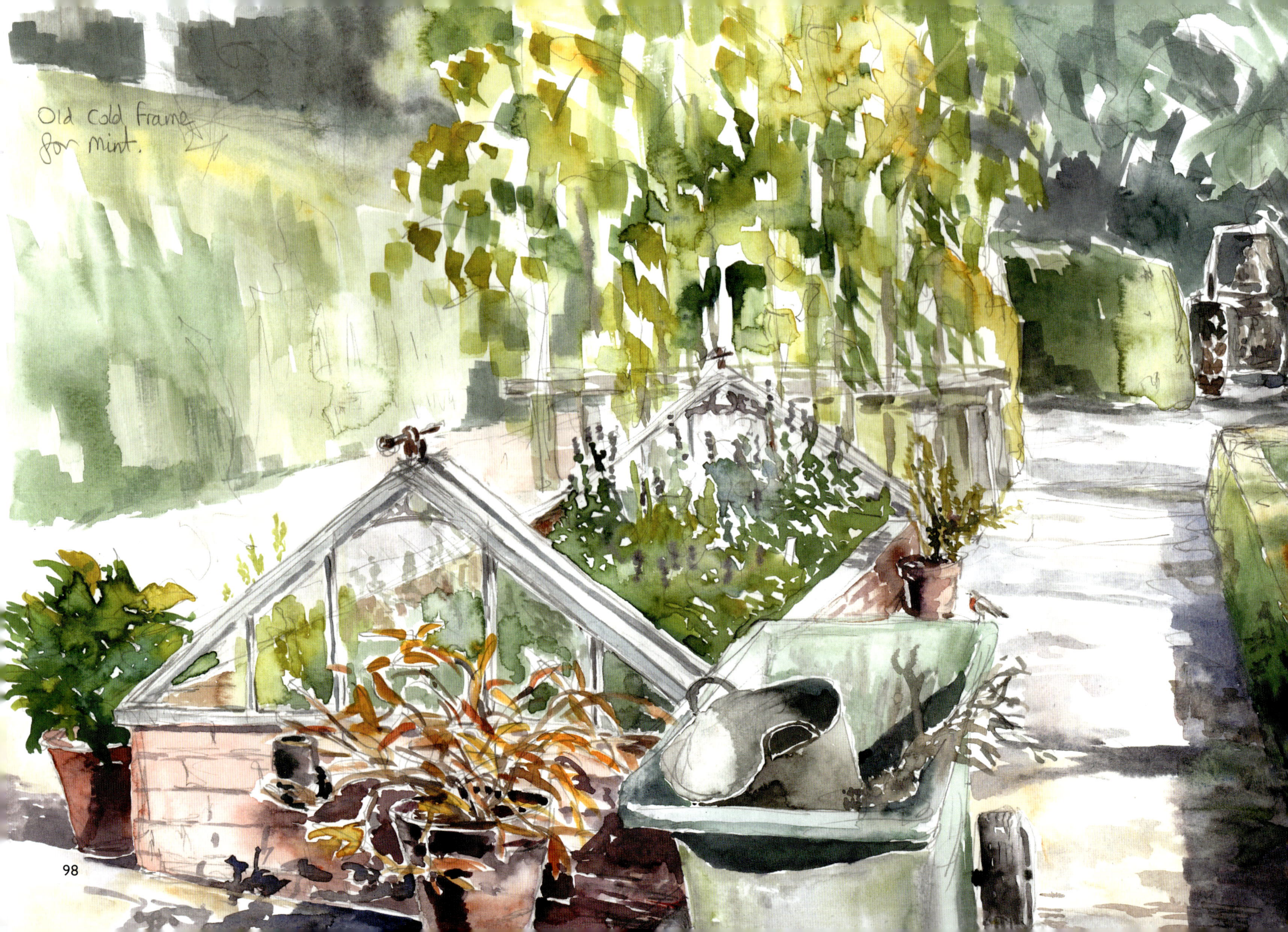
Old cold frame
for mint.

On my way to the Croft I had to pause to witness the scene — these insects feasting on over-ripe fallen pears in the kitchen garden. The wasps and butterflies sharing the same table without agression from the wasps. When flies or wasps came near the butterflies they simply flapped their wings a bit ... (who knows, perhaps they were quietly muttering "Back off"!)

Though I imagine, in the hot sun the potent pear juice had made them quite inebriated.

Wasps will soon be dying off. Apart from the queen, the others do not survive the winter. Red Admirals will begin their mass exodus to Southern shores of the continent, for the winter — What a sight that must be!

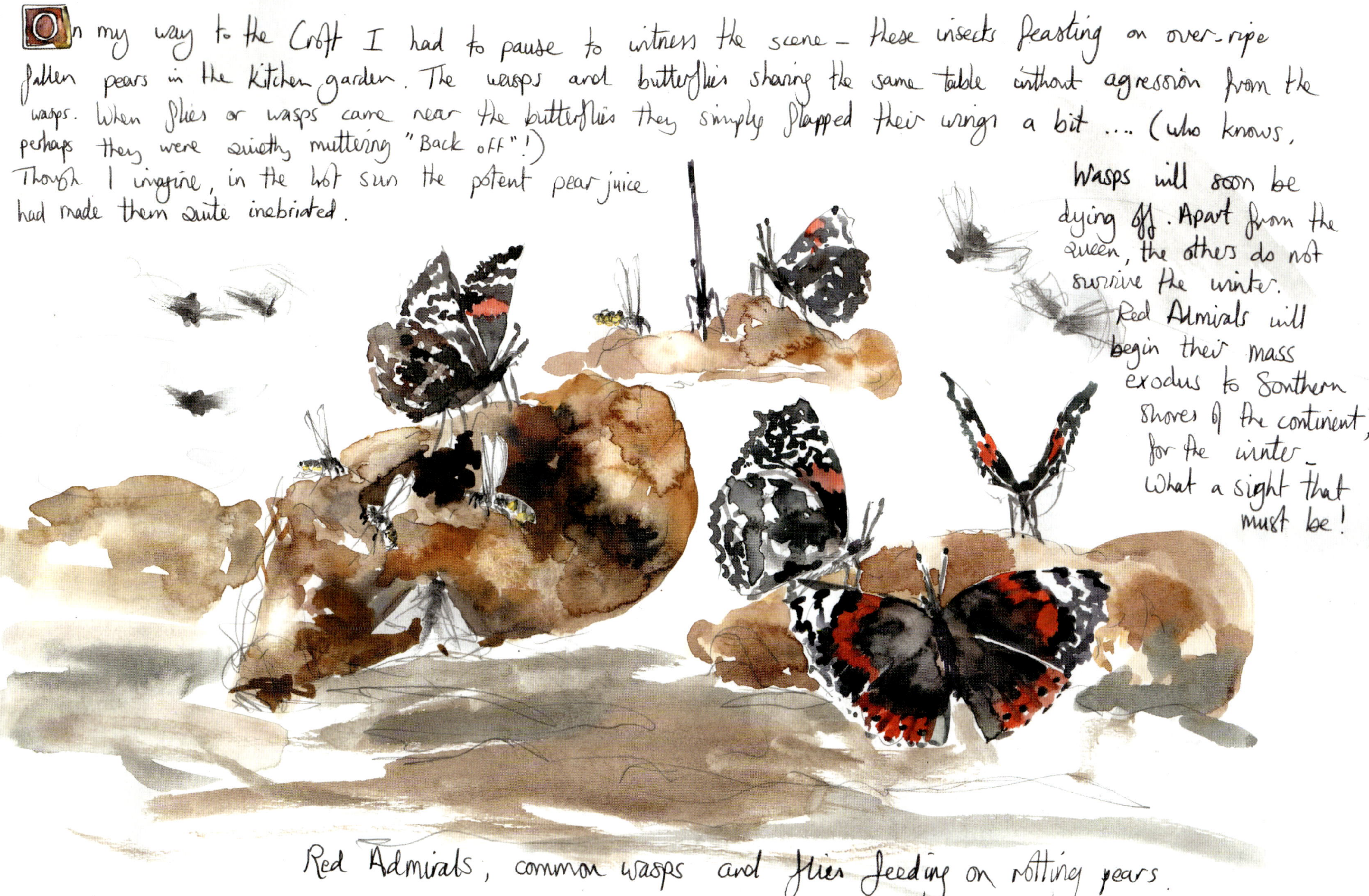

Red Admirals, common wasps and flies feeding on rotting pears.

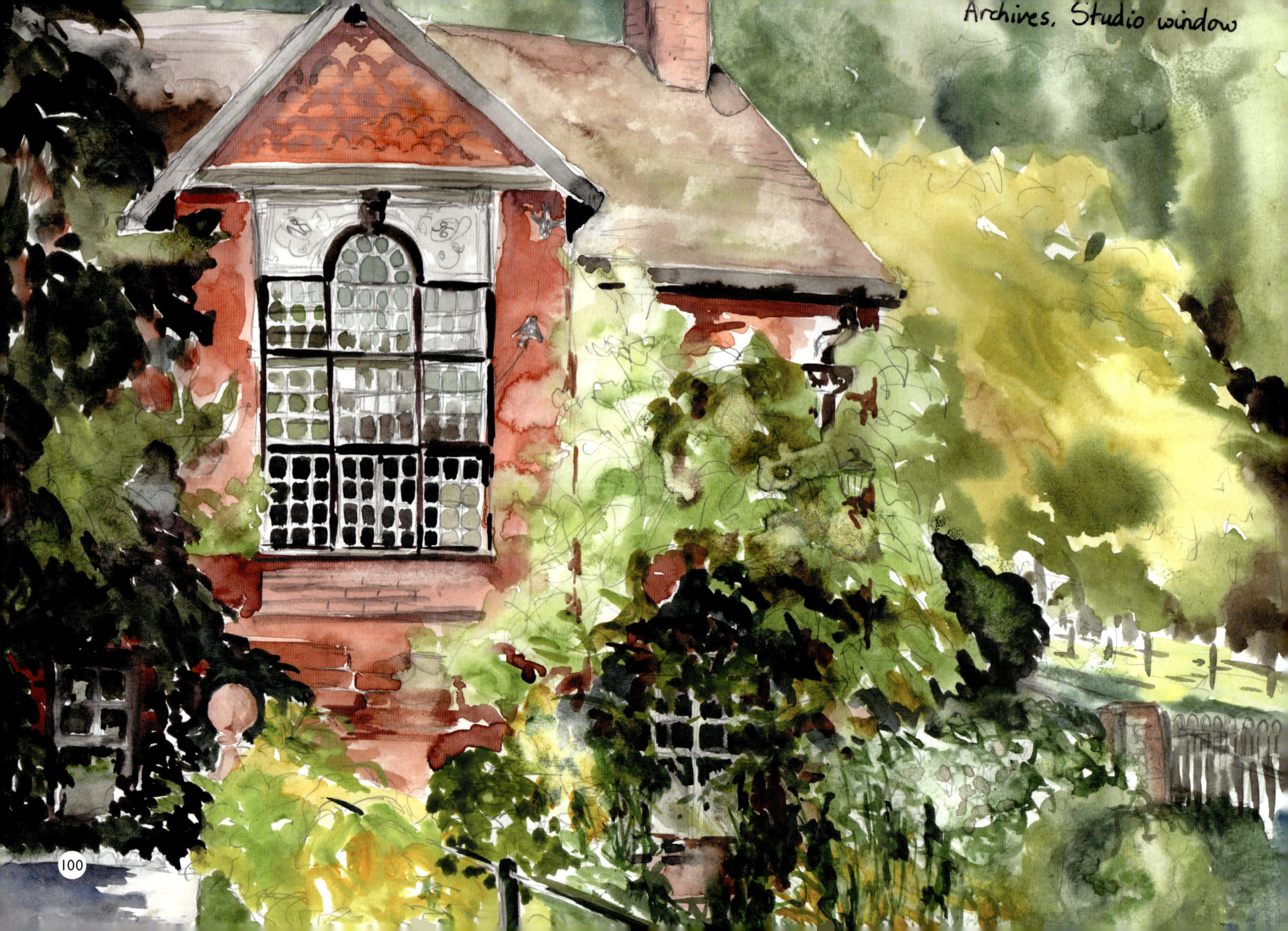

Archives, Studio window

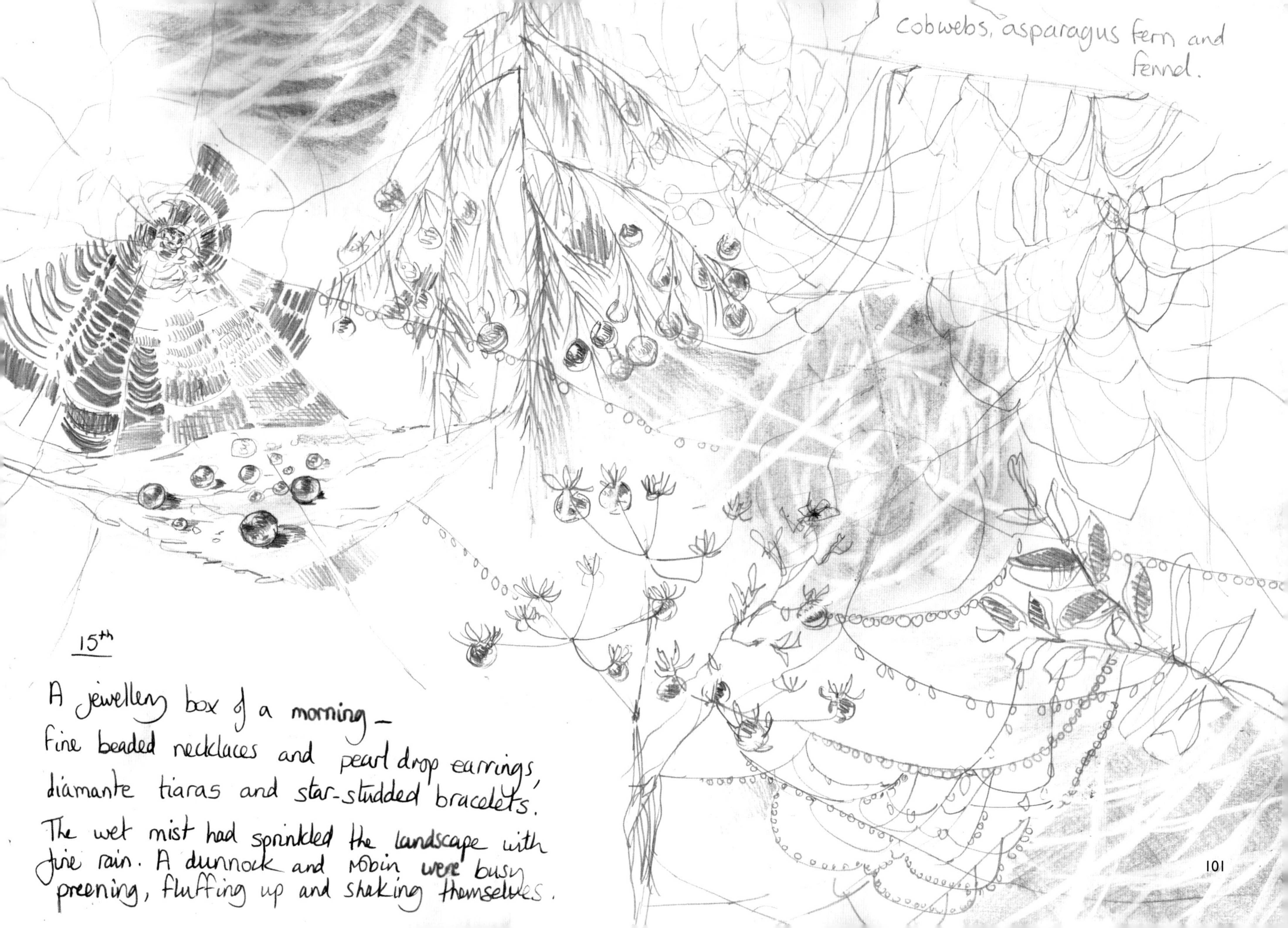

15ᵗʰ

A jewellery box of a morning —
Fine beaded necklaces and pearl drop earrings,
diamante tiaras and star-studded 'bracelets'.
The wet mist had sprinkled the landscape with
fine rain. A dunnock and robin were busy
preening, fluffing up and shaking themselves.

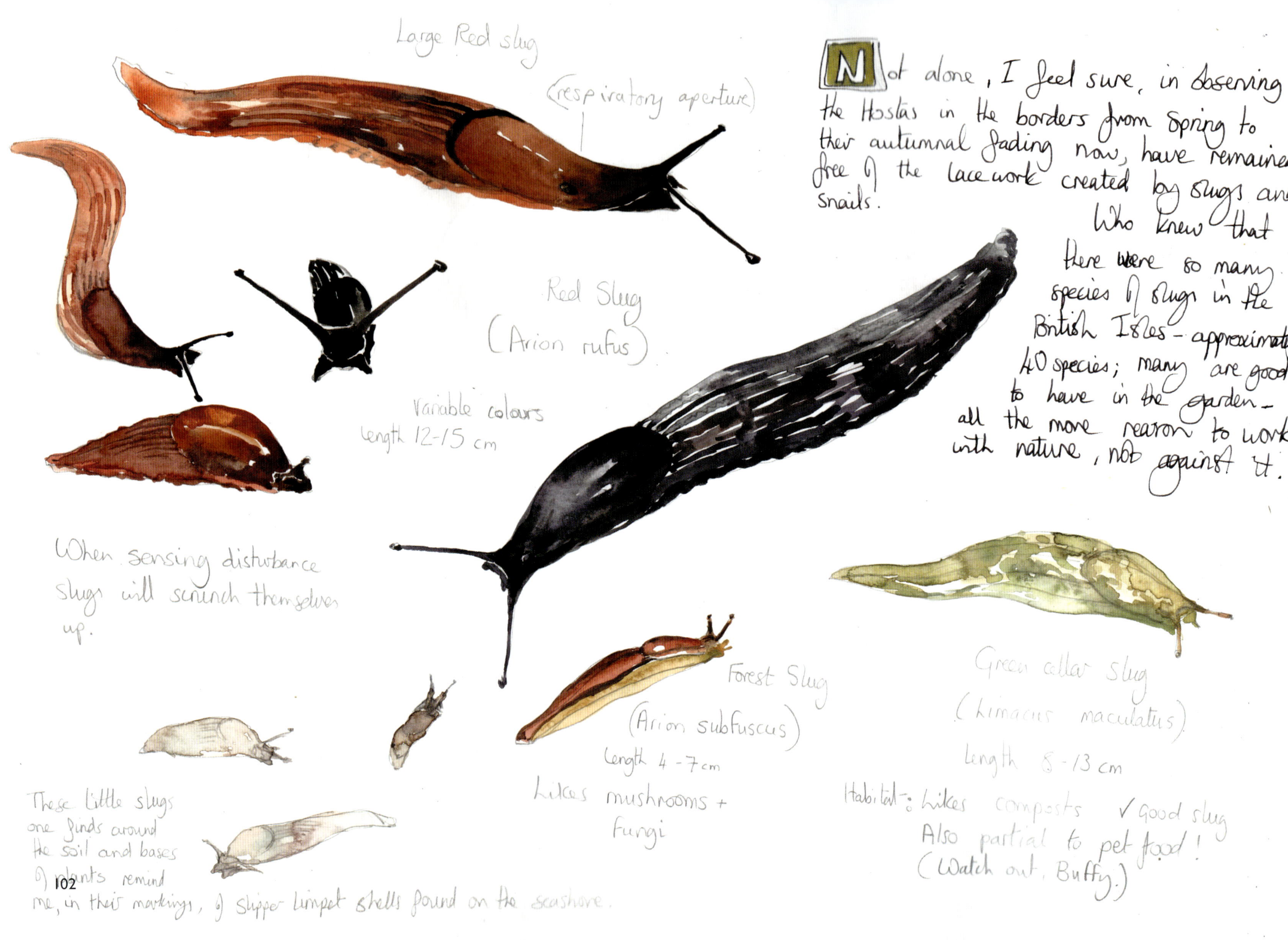

Large Red slug
(respiratory aperture)
Not alone, I feel sure, in observing the Hostas in the borders from spring to their autumnal fading now, have remained free of the lacework created by slugs and snails.
Who knew that there were so many species of slugs in the British Isles - approximately 40 species; many are good to have in the garden - all the more reason to work with nature, not against it.
Red Slug
(Arion rufus)
Variable colours
Length 12-15 cm
When sensing disturbance slugs will scrunch themselves up.
These little slugs one finds around the soil and bases of plants remind me, in their markings, of Slipper Limpet shells found on the seashore.
102
Forest Slug
(Arion subfuscus)
Length 4 - 7 cm
Likes mushrooms + Fungi
Green cellar slug
(Limacus maculatus)
Length 8 - 13 cm
Habitat: Likes composts ✓ Good slug
Also partial to pet food!
(Watch out, Buffy.)

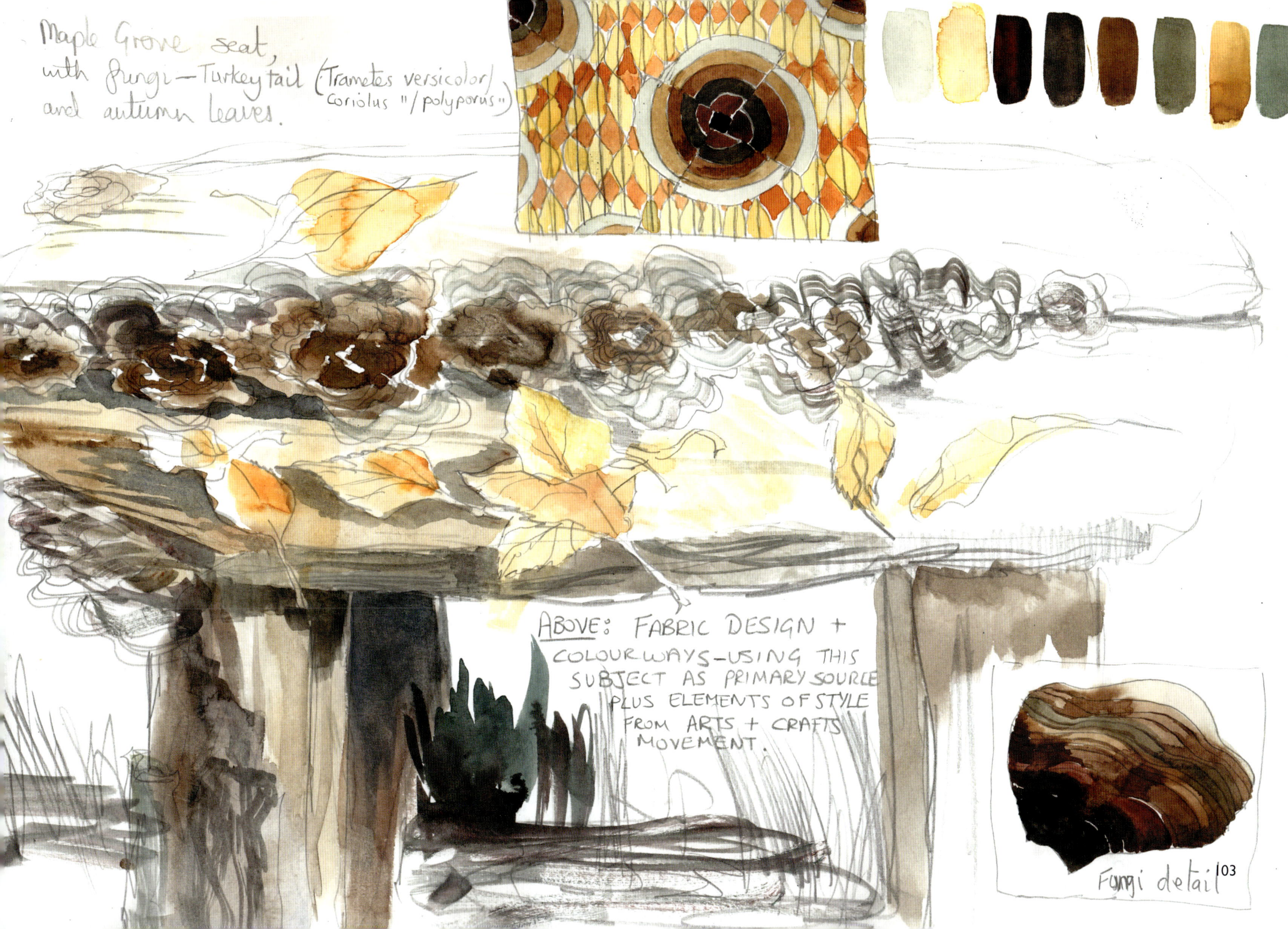

Maple Grove seat,
with fungi — Turkey tail (Trametes versicolor/
Coriolus "/polyporus")
and autumn leaves.

ABOVE: FABRIC DESIGN +
COLOURWAYS - USING THIS
SUBJECT AS PRIMARY SOURCE
PLUS ELEMENTS OF STYLE
FROM ARTS + CRAFTS
MOVEMENT.

Fungi detail
103

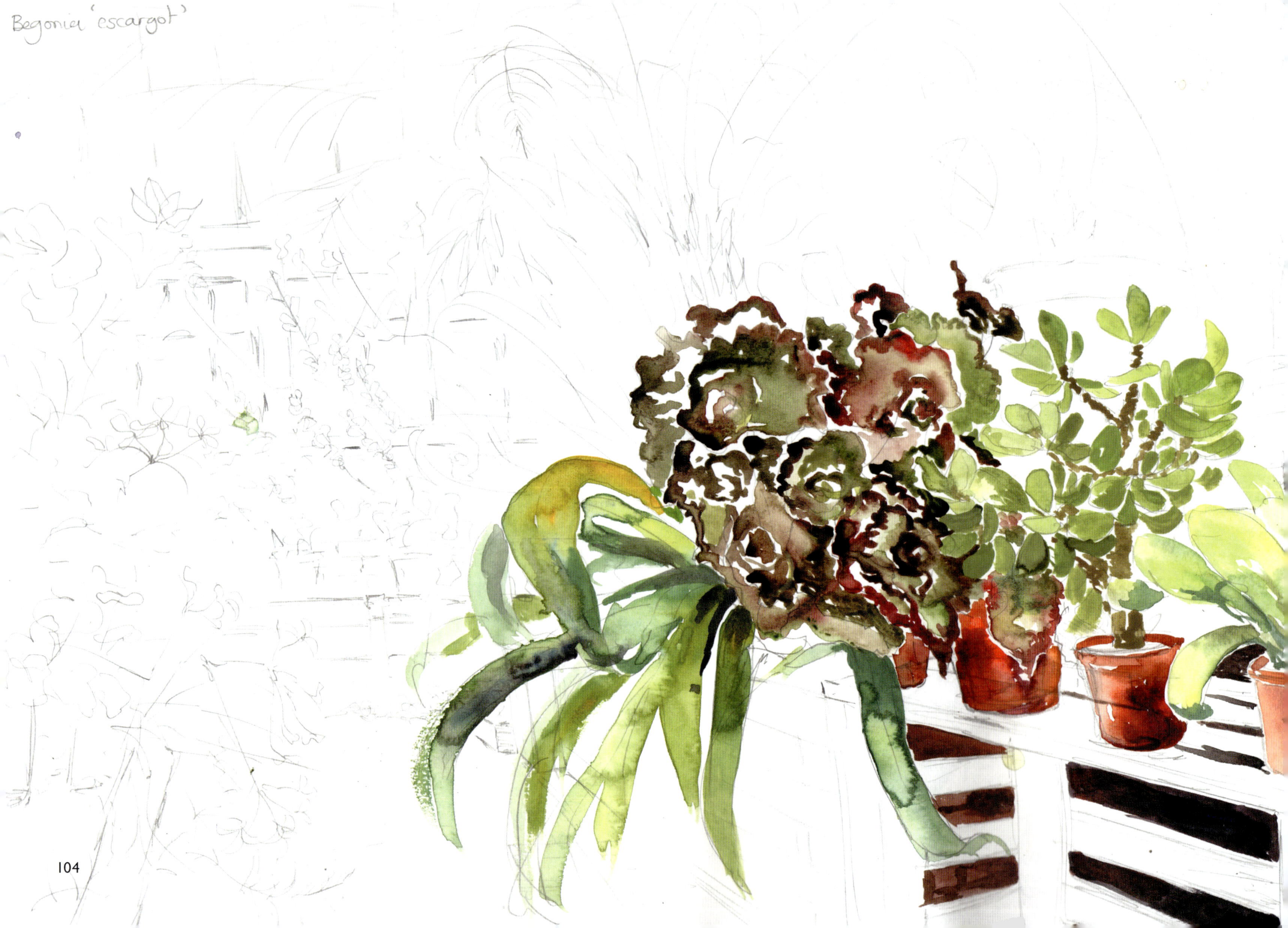
Begonia 'escargot'

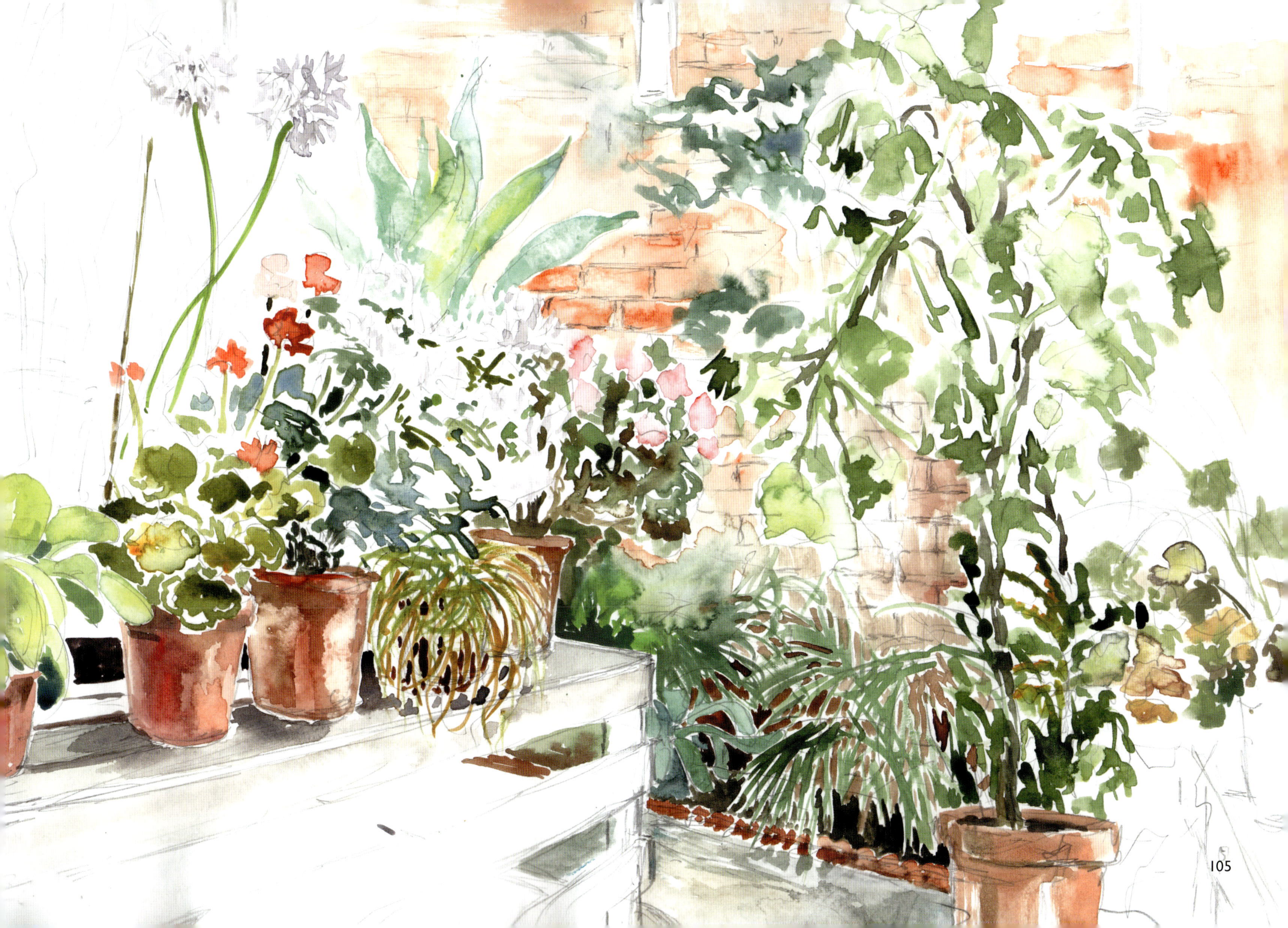

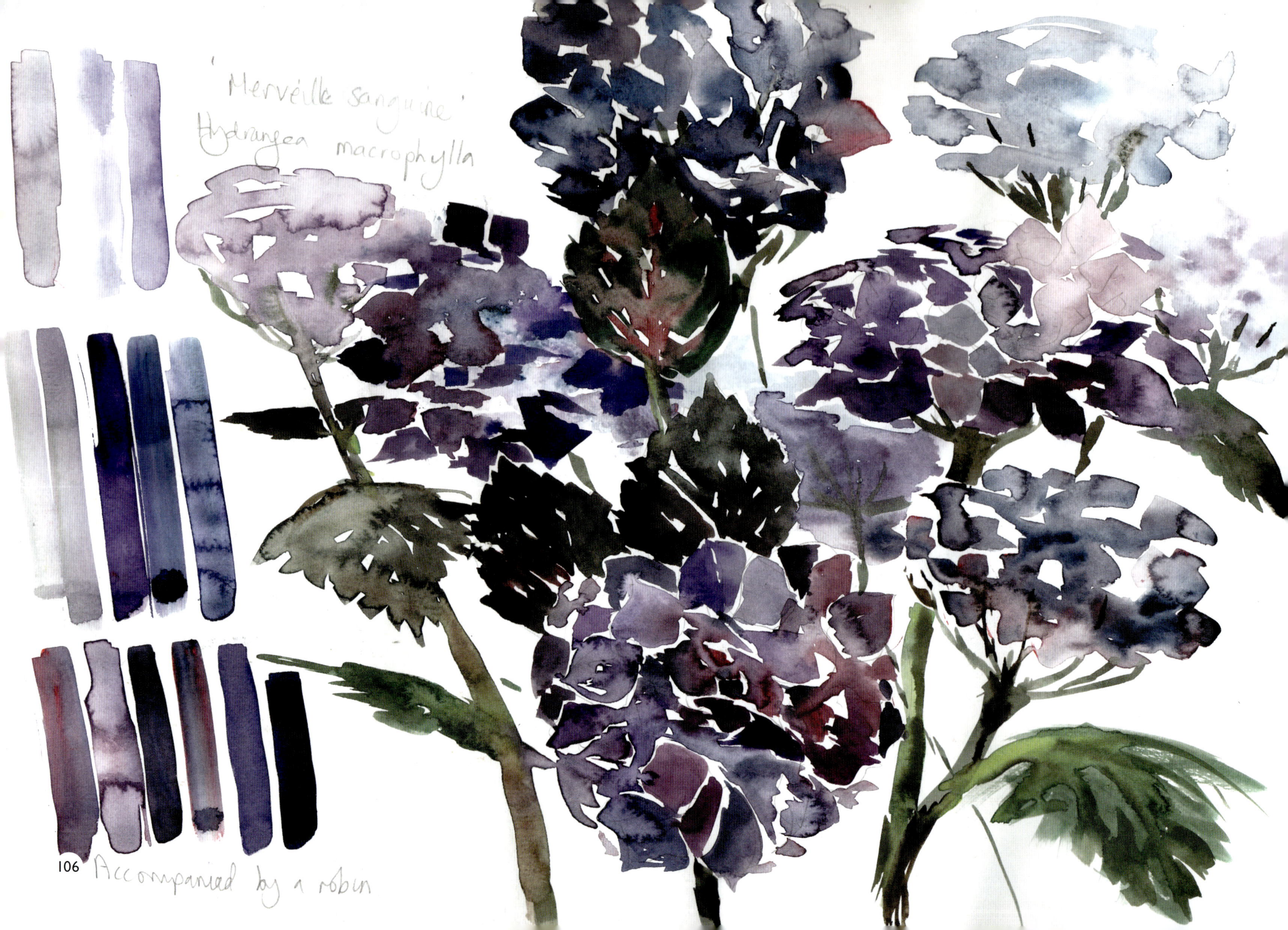
'Merveille sanguine'
Hydrangea macrophylla
106 Accompanied by a robin

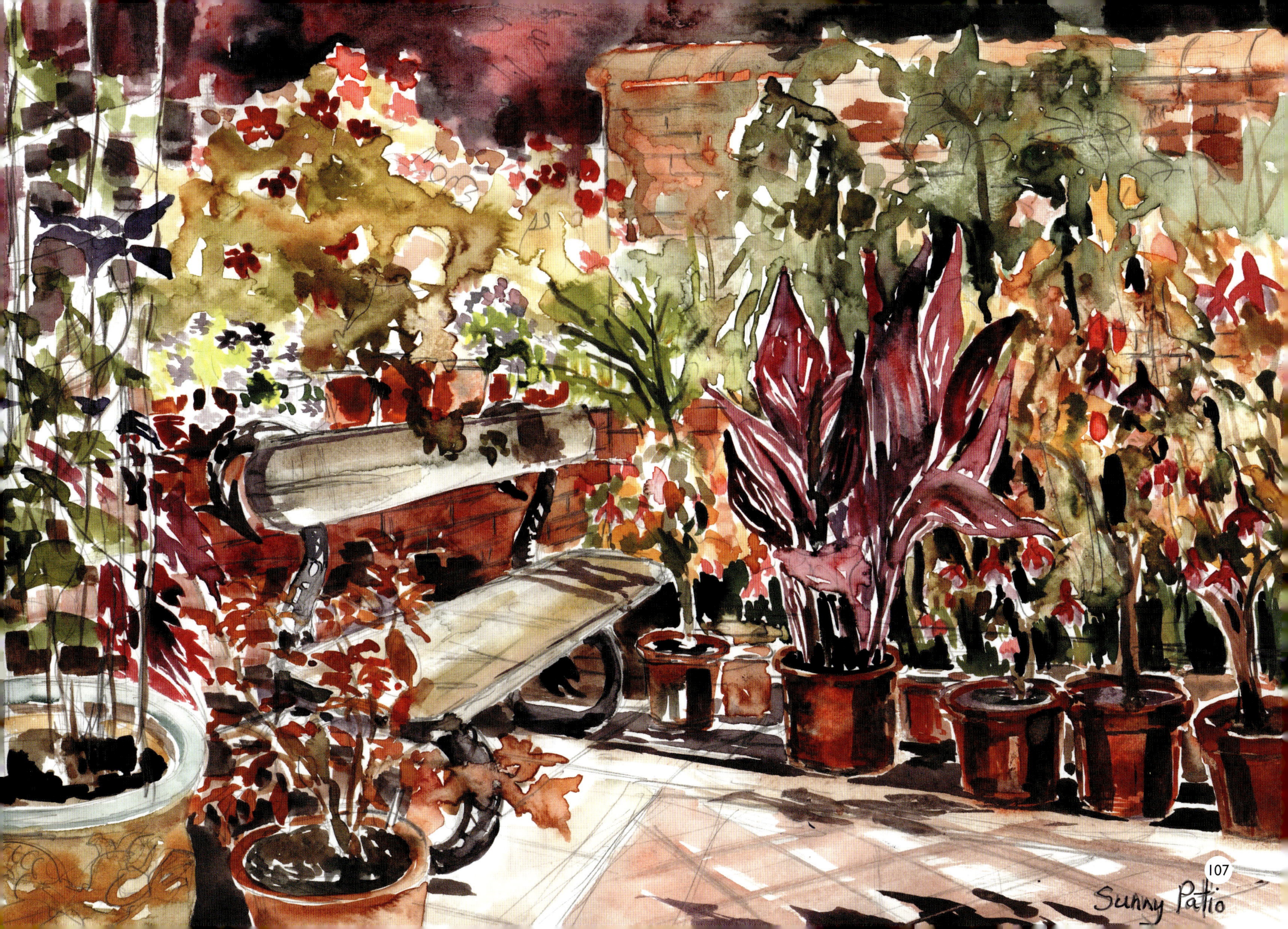

Sunny Patio

OCTOBER

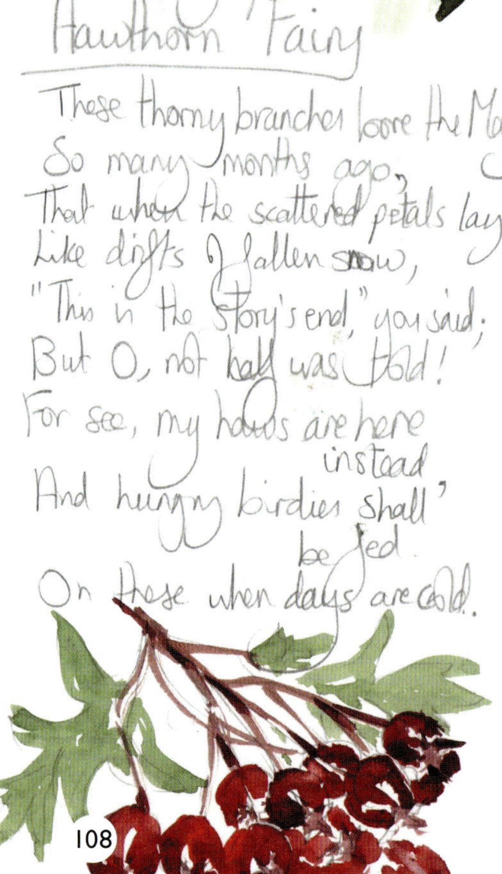

The gardens seem momentarily suspended —
in flux betwixt summer and autumn —
summer not wanting to relinquish it's
placid greens to the fiery reds of autumn.

In the kitchen garden areas of the vegetable
garden have been cleared. Potatoes have been
dug up and stored. Runner beans earthed up,
the spent foliage transported to the compost bins
by wheelbarrow and then taken by tractor and
trailor up the lane to the main composting/
bonfire area.

I have noticed many butterflies in the kitchen garden
particularly, and around the sunny terrace area. I
suspect they are feasting on late flowering plants'
nectar as well as fruits — sugars from apples and pears.
Some species shall hibernate until Spring, some will fly to warmer
climes, others will perish.

108

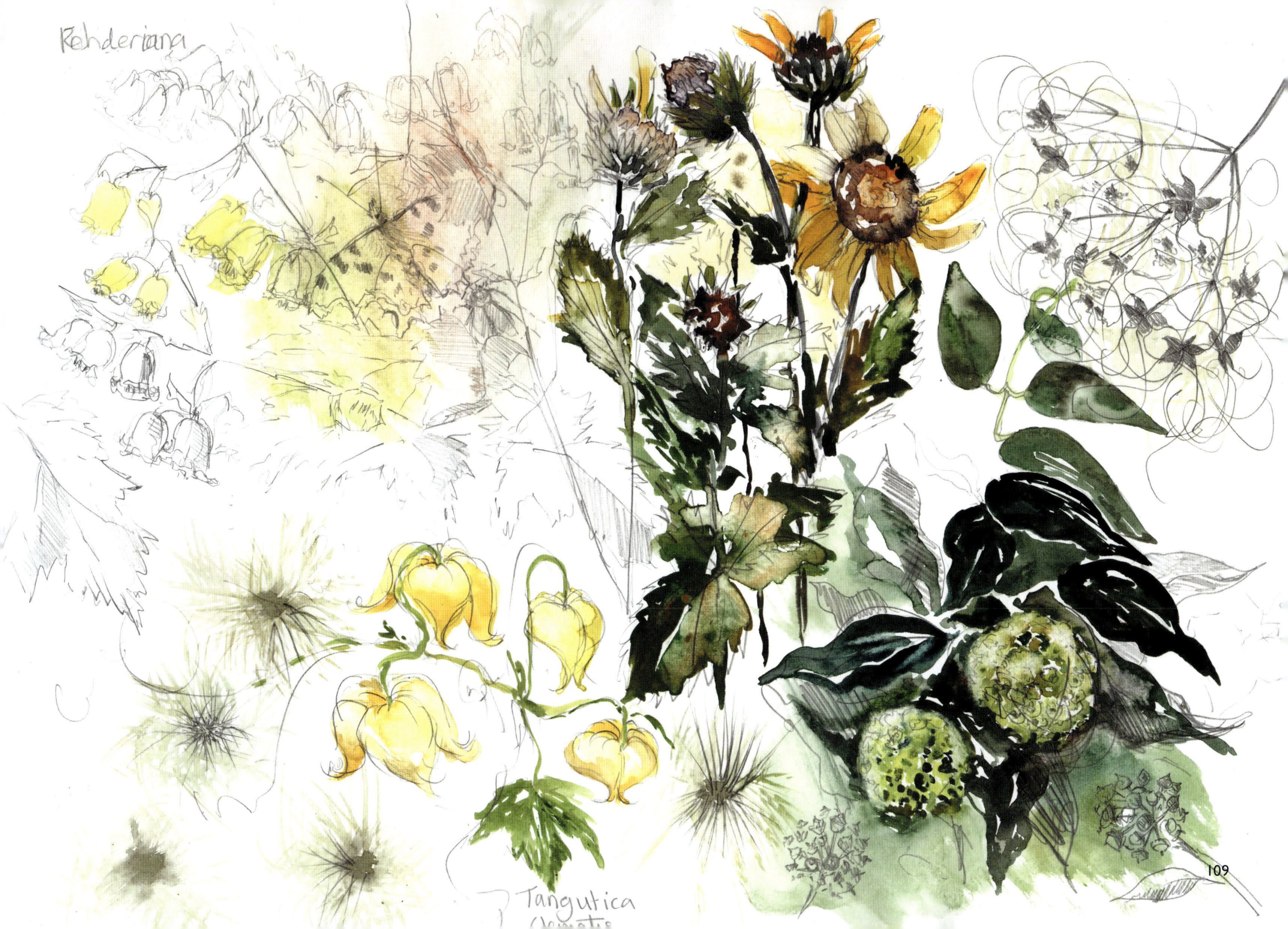
Rehderiana
Tangutica
Clematis
109

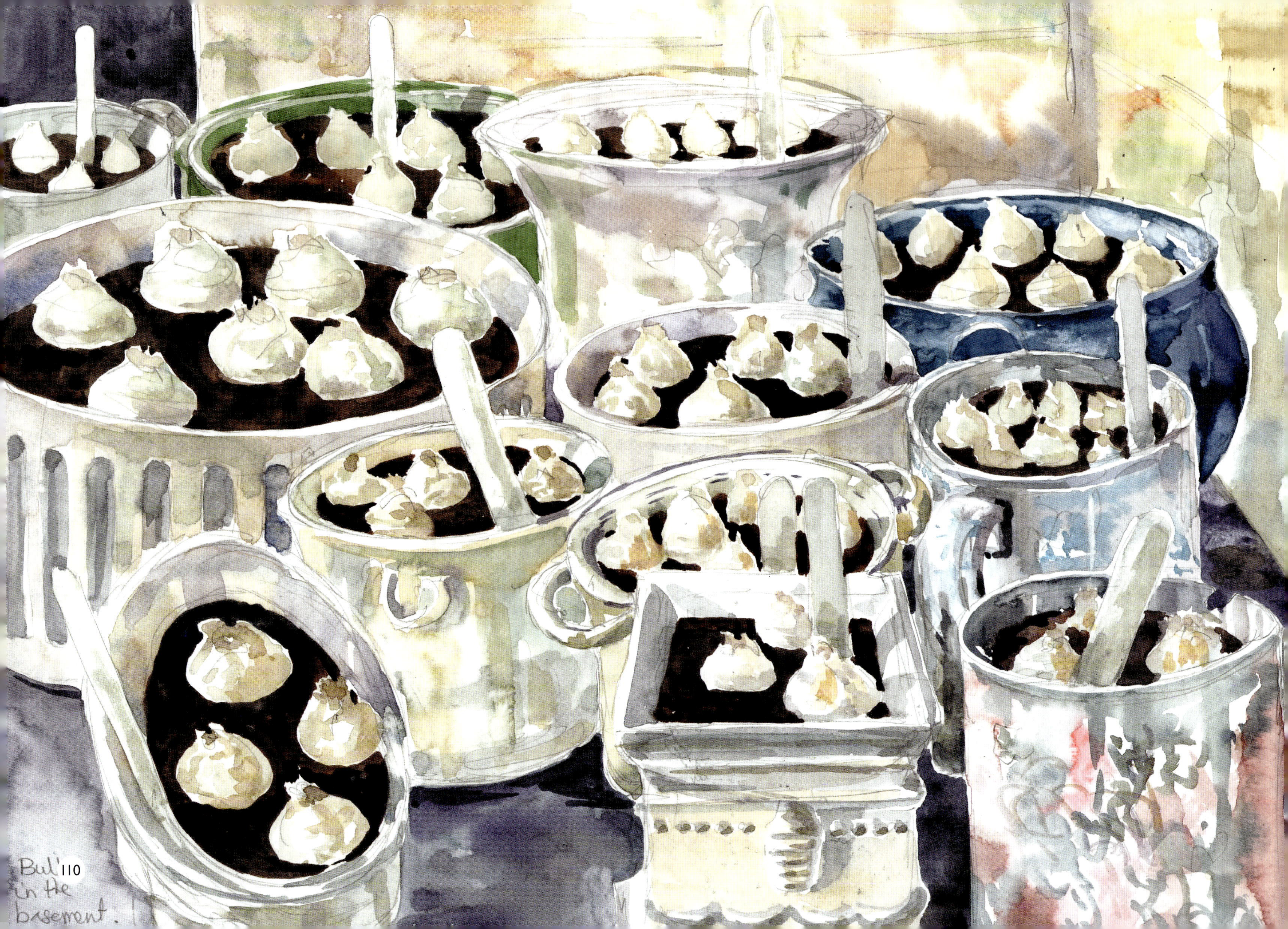
Bul '110
in the
basement.

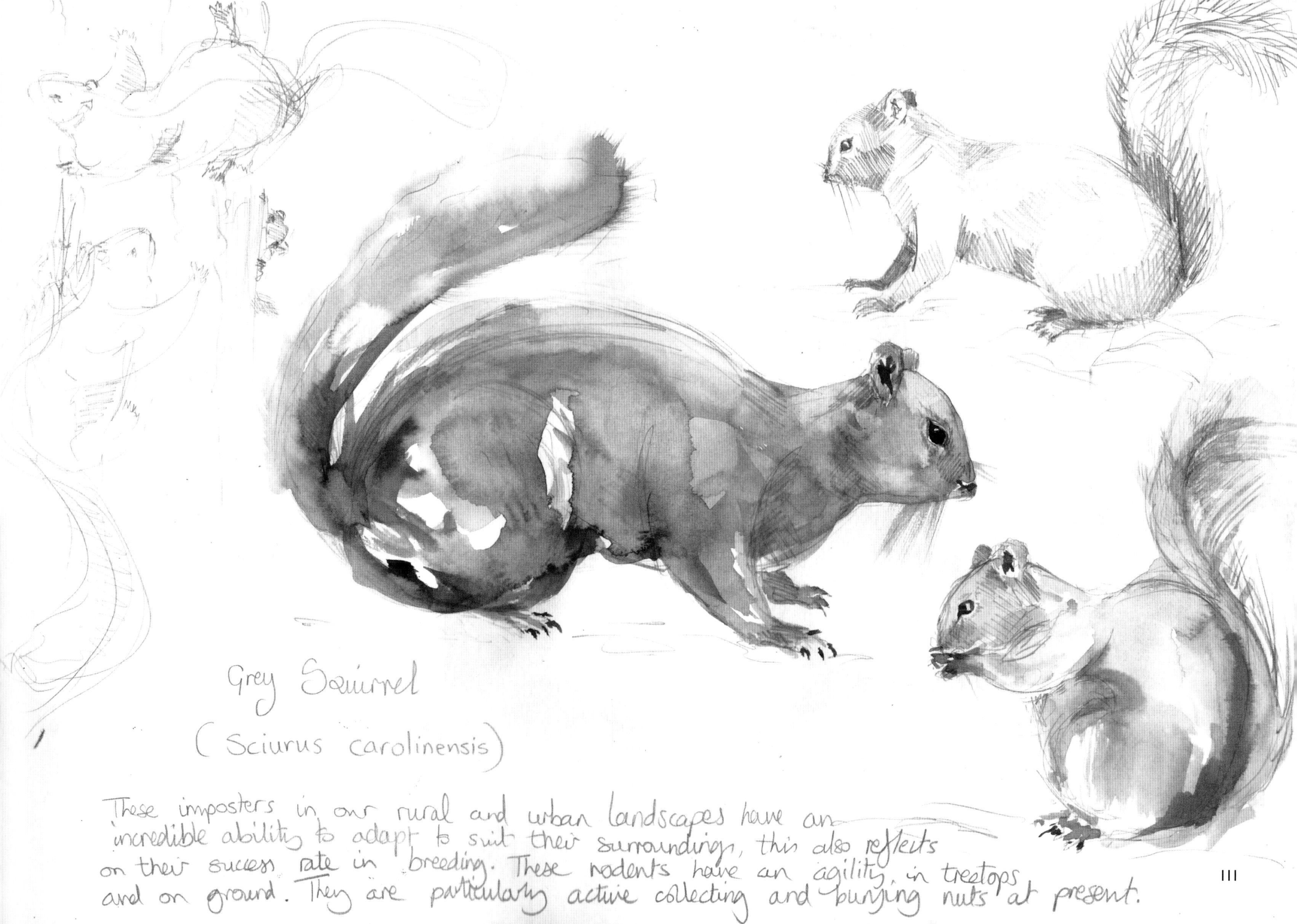
Grey Squirrel

(Sciurus carolinensis)

These imposters in our rural and urban landscapes have an
incredible ability to adapt to suit their surroundings, this also reflects
on their success rate in breeding. These rodents have an agility in treetops
and on ground. They are particularly active collecting and burying nuts at present.

111

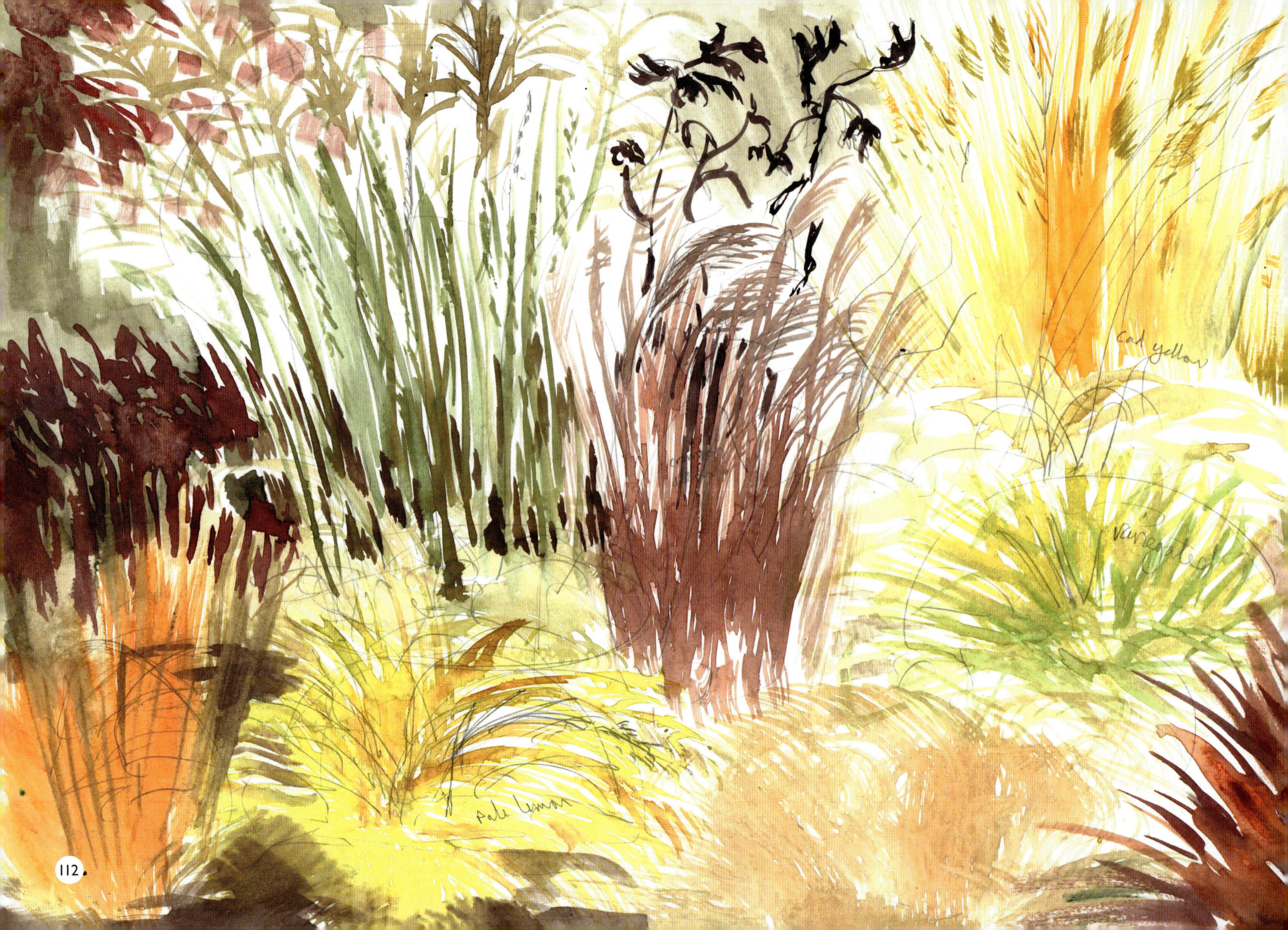
Cal yellow
variegated
Pale Lemon

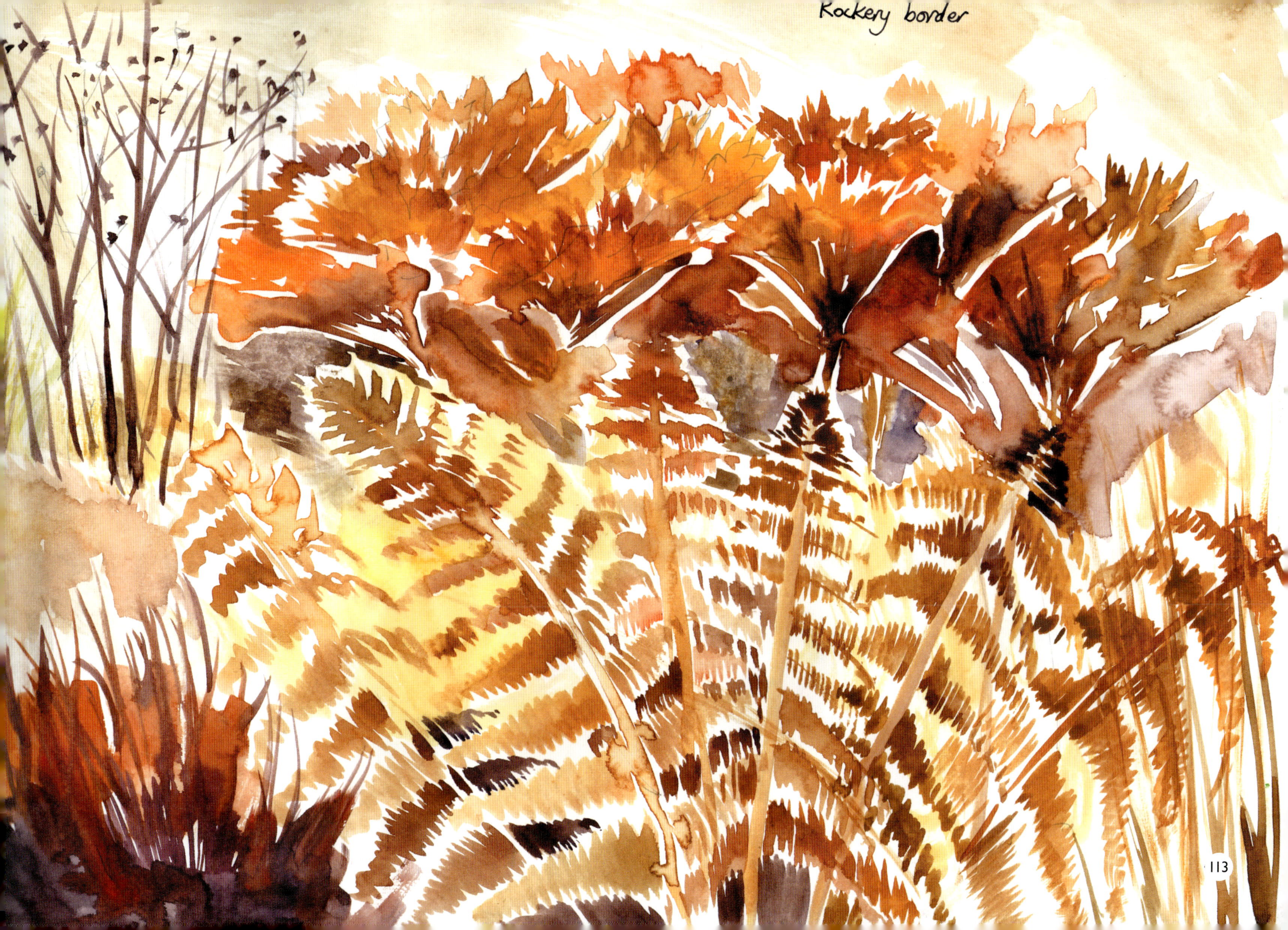
Rockery border

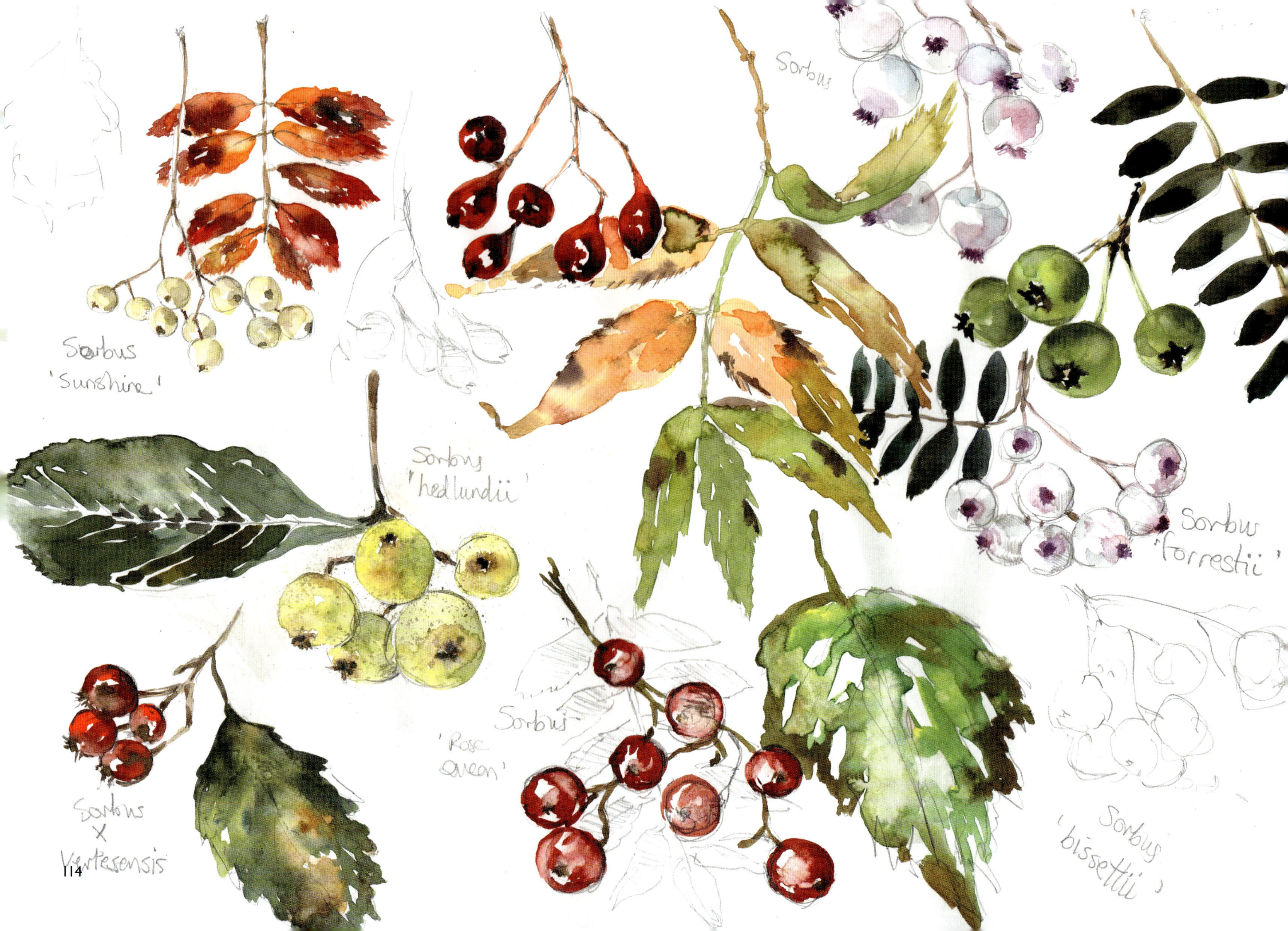

Sorbus
Sorbus 'sunshine'
Sorbus 'hedlundii'
Sorbus 'forrestii'
Sorbus 'Rose Queen'
Sorbus x vilmorinensis
Sorbus 'bissettii'
114

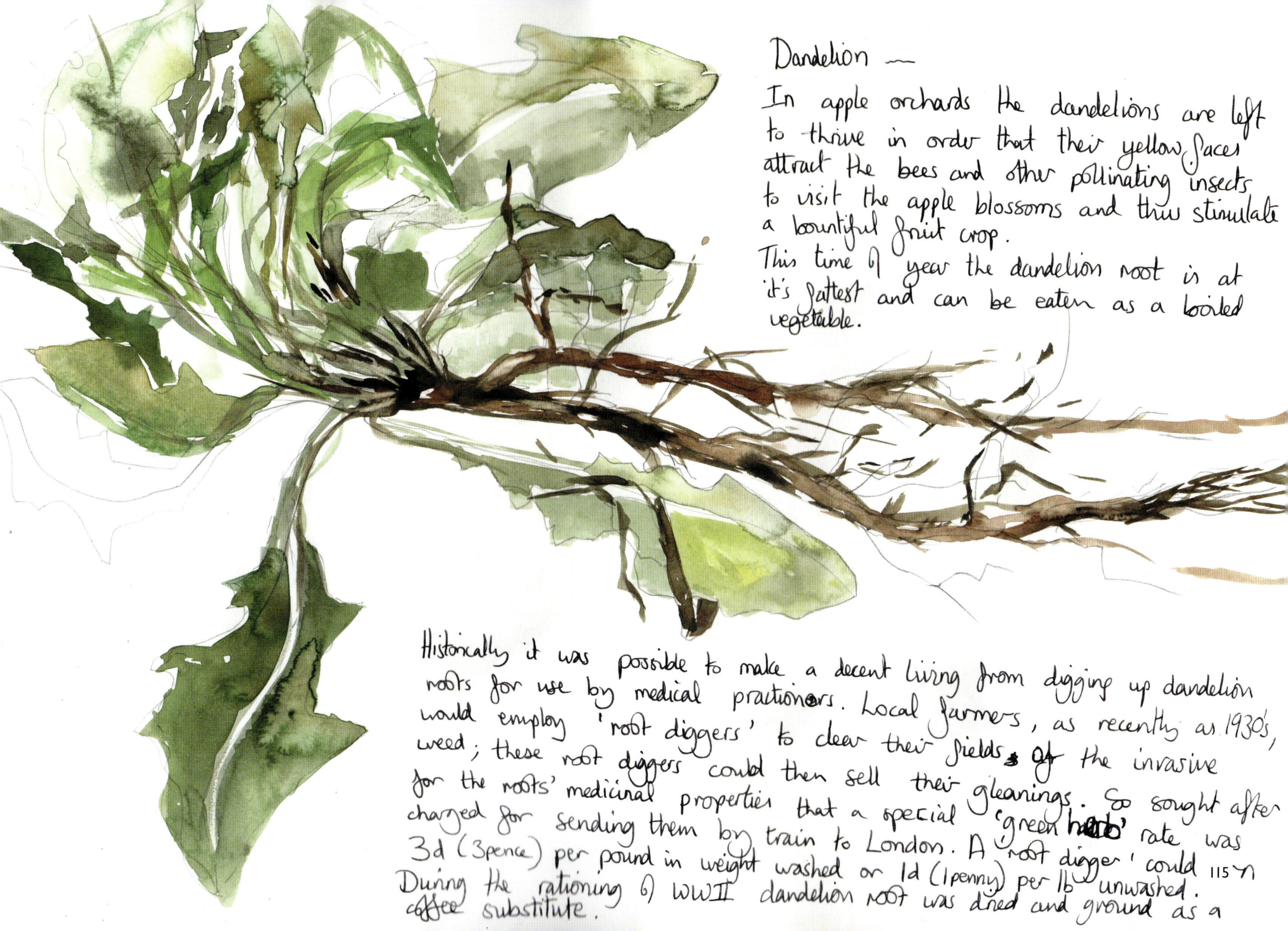

Dandelion —

In apple orchards the dandelions are left to thrive in order that their yellow faces attract the bees and other pollinating insects to visit the apple blossoms and thus stimulate a bountiful fruit crop.

This time of year the dandelion root is at it's fattest and can be eaten as a boiled vegetable.

Historically it was possible to make a decent living from digging up dandelion roots for use by medical practioners. Local farmers, as recently as 1930's, would employ 'root diggers' to clear their fields of the invasive weed; these root diggers could then sell their gleanings. So sought after for the roots' medicinal properties that a special 'green herb' rate was charged for sending them by train to London. A 'root digger' could 115n 3d (3pence) per pound in weight washed or 1d (1penny) per lb unwashed. During the rationing of WWII dandelion root was dried and ground as a coffee substitute.

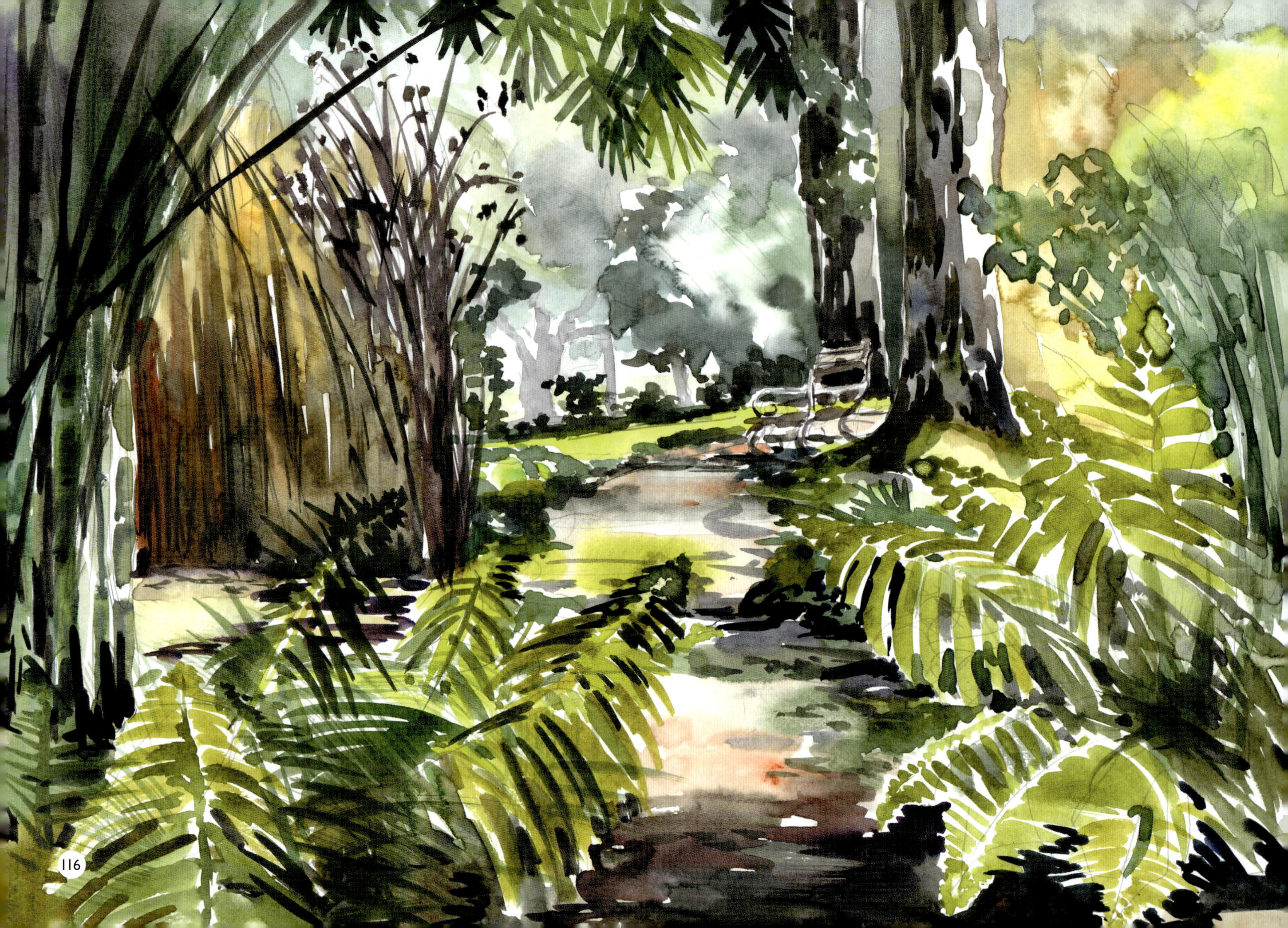

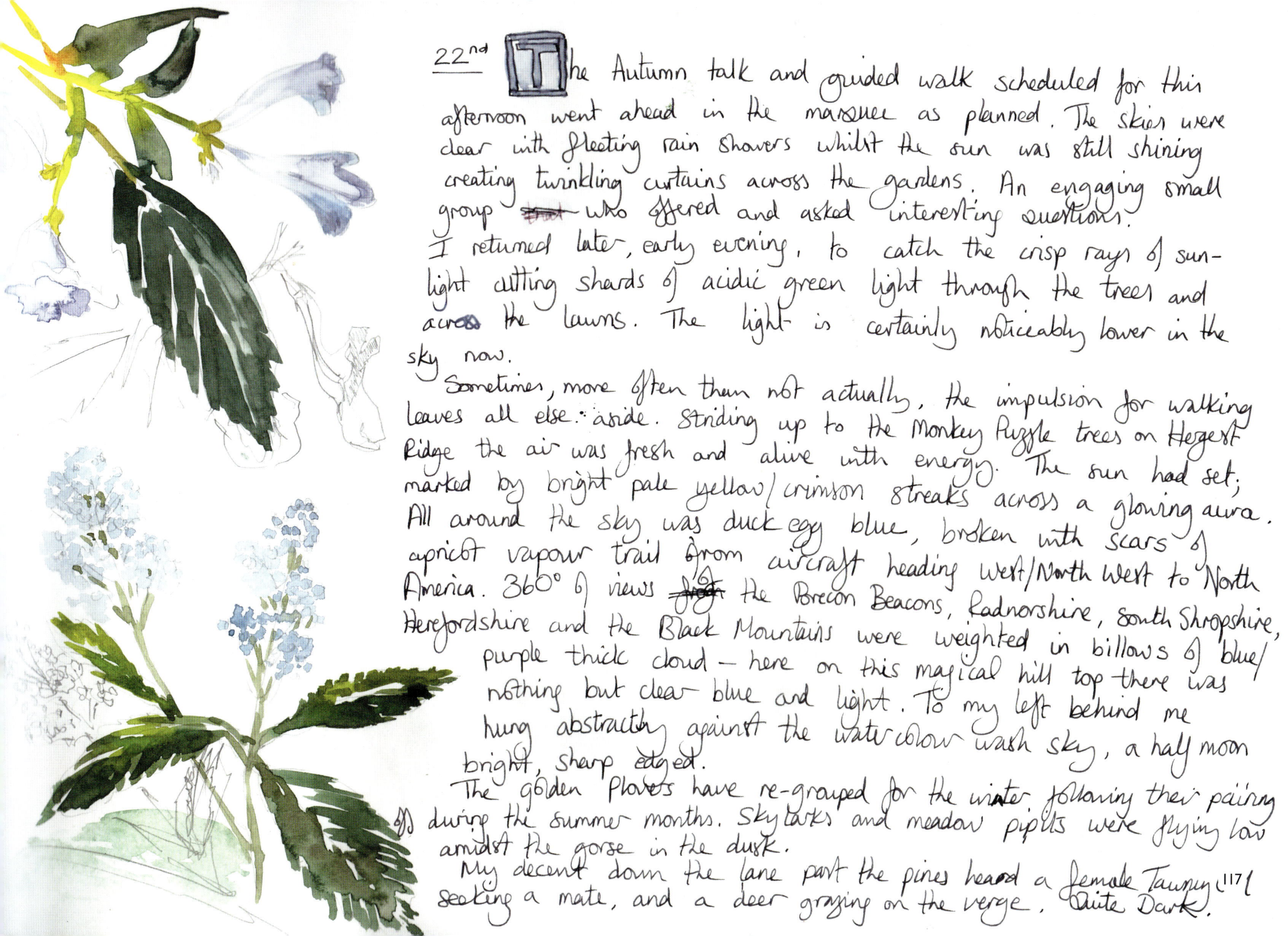

22nd The Autumn talk and guided walk scheduled for this afternoon went ahead in the marquee as planned. The skies were clear with fleeting rain showers whilst the sun was still shining creating twinkling curtains across the gardens. An engaging small group who offered and asked interesting questions.

I returned later, early evening, to catch the crisp rays of sunlight cutting shards of acidic green light through the trees and across the lawns. The light is certainly noticeably lower in the sky now.

Sometimes, more often than not actually, the impulsion for walking leaves all else aside. Striding up to the Monkey Puzzle trees on Hegdof Ridge the air was fresh and alive with energy. The sun had set; marked by bright pale yellow/crimson streaks across a glowing aura. All around the sky was duck egg blue, broken with scars of apricot vapour trail from aircraft heading West/North West to North America. 360° of views the Brecon Beacons, Radnorshire, South Shropshire, Herefordshire and the Black Mountains were weighted in billows of blue/purple thick cloud — here on this magical hill top there was nothing but clear blue and light. To my left behind me hung abstractly against the watercolour wash sky, a half moon bright, sharp edged.

The golden plovers have re-grouped for the winter following their pairing off during the summer months. Skylarks and meadow pipits were flying low amidst the gorse in the dusk.

My decent down the lane past the pines heard a female Tawny[117] seeking a mate, and a deer grazing on the verge. Quite Dark.

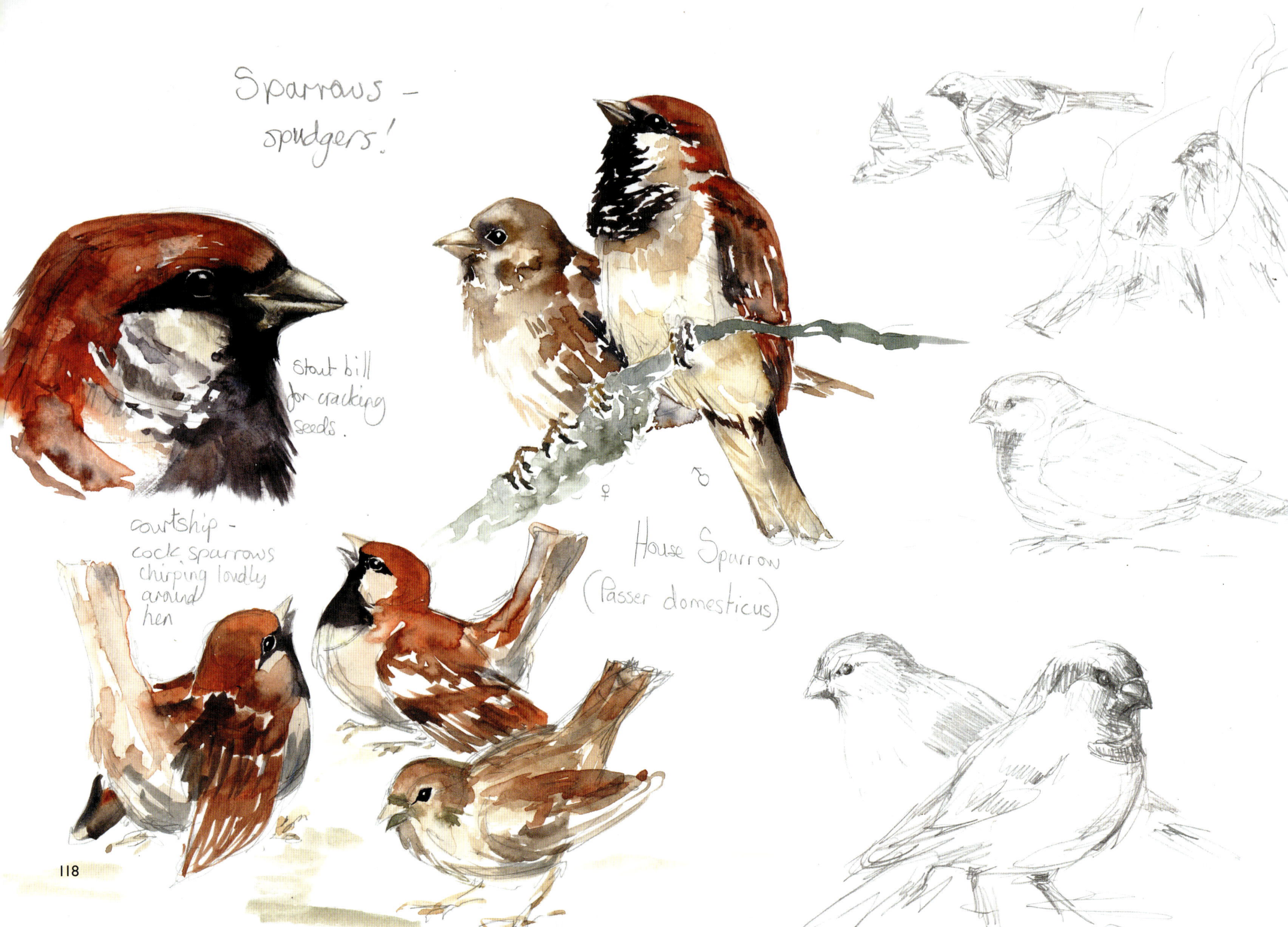

Sparrows -
spudgers!
Stout bill for cracking seeds.
courtship - cock sparrows chirping loudly around hen
House Sparrow
(Passer domesticus)
♀
♂
118

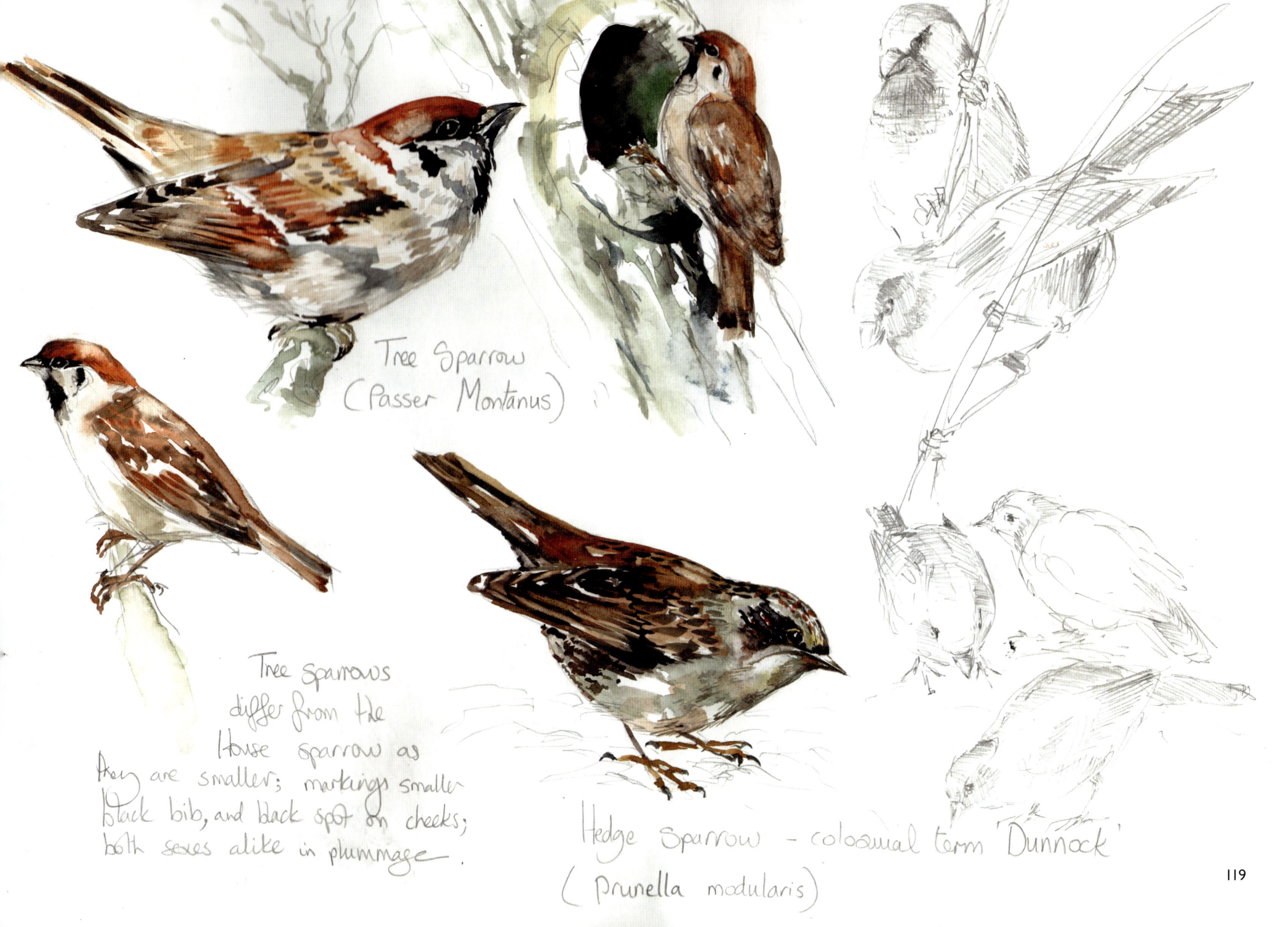

Tree Sparrow
(Passer Montanus)

Tree sparrows
differ from the
House sparrow as
they are smaller; markings smaller
black bib, and black spot on cheeks;
both sexes alike in plumage.

Hedge Sparrow - coloquial term 'Dunnock'
(Prunella modularis)

119

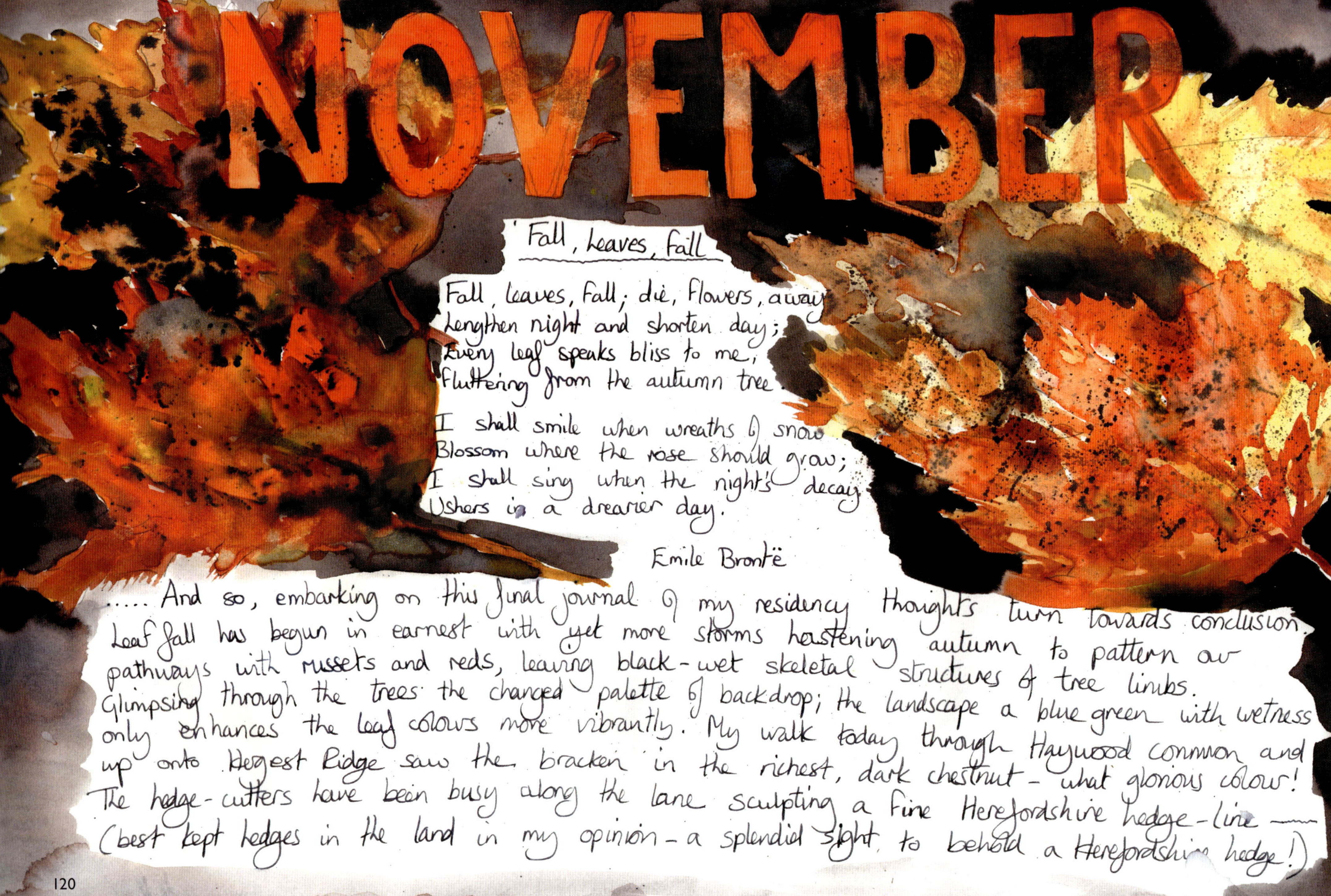

..... And so, embarking on this final journal of my residency thoughts turn towards conclusion. Leaf fall has begun in earnest with yet more storms hastening autumn to pattern our pathways with russets and reds, leaving black-wet skeletal structures of tree limbs. Glimpsing through the trees the changed palette of backdrop; the landscape a blue-green with wetness only enhances the leaf colours more vibrantly. My walk today through Haywood Common and up onto Hergest Ridge saw the bracken in the richest, dark chestnut — what glorious colour! The hedge-cutters have been busy along the lane sculpting a fine Herefordshire hedge-line ——— (best kept hedges in the land in my opinion — a splendid sight to behold a Herefordshire hedge!)

120

As the month of November has begun so too has autumn. The deluge of storms and subsequent heavy rain and strong winds have prompted a dramatic change in leaf colour and fall. Early morn today, the sun low in the sky, was casting beams of bright colours through the trees; rust reds, burnt orange, mustard yellows, golden greens through dark umber. Maple Grove is completely saturated making walking treacherous if not rather hilarious! The winter migrant birds are arriving; several fieldfares were squawking about in the tree tops, on the uppermost tips of fir trees, and a flock of crows, sizeable in numbers, was migrating from their roost on Castle Hill towards farmland feeding around Lower Hergest.

The brilliance of saturated colour was making me halt at every step, absorbing the beauty of the surroundings. Walking back down the wet lane of Ridgebourne, rivulets of water running down the gulleys either side, the sun catching the lane is blinding light. The previously smouldering bonfire in the composting area after all the rain, now only remains an acrid lingering smell as I walk past.

Now is the time for burning leaves

Now is the time for burning leaves,
They go to the fire; the nostril pricks with smoke
Wandering slowly into a weeping mist.
Brittle and blotched, ragged and rotten sheaves!
A flame seizes the smouldering ruin and bites
On stubborn stalks that crackle as they resist.

The last hollyhock's fallen tower is dust;
All the spices of June are a bitter reek,
All the extravagant riches spent and mean.
All burns! The reddest rose is a ghost;
Sparks whirl up, to expire in the mist; the wild
Fingers of fire are making corruption clean.

Now is the time for stripping the spirit bare,
Time for the burning of days ended and done,
Idle solace of things that have gone before:
Rootless hope and fruitless desire are there;
Let them go to the fire, with never a look behind.
The world that was ours is a world that is ours no more.

They will come again, the leaf and the flower, to arise
From squalor of rottenness into the old splendour,
And magical scents to a wondering memory bring;
The same glory, to shine upon different eyes.
Earth cares for her own ruins, naught for ours.
Nothing is certain, only the certain spring.
Laurence Binyon (1869-194...)

Archive Studio
122

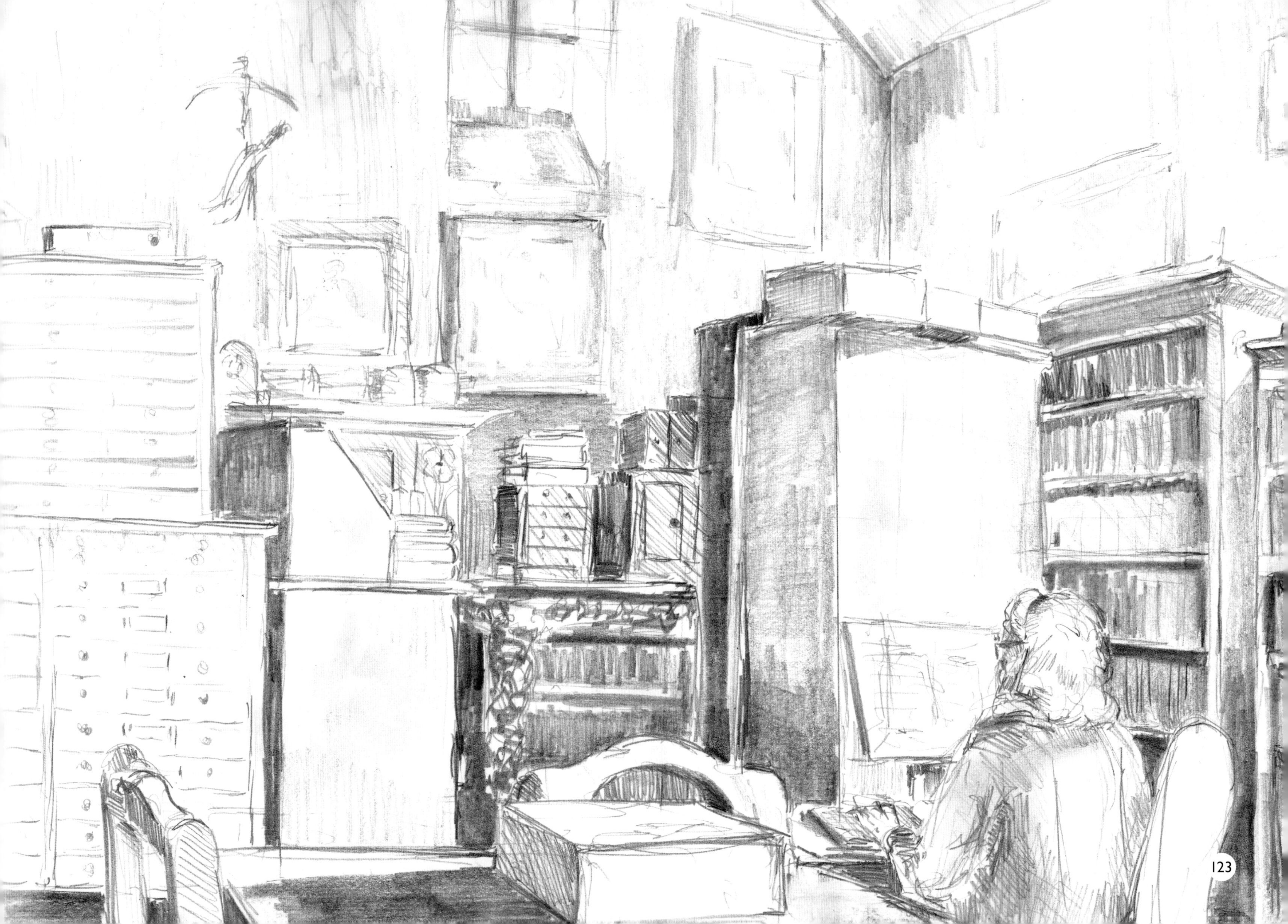

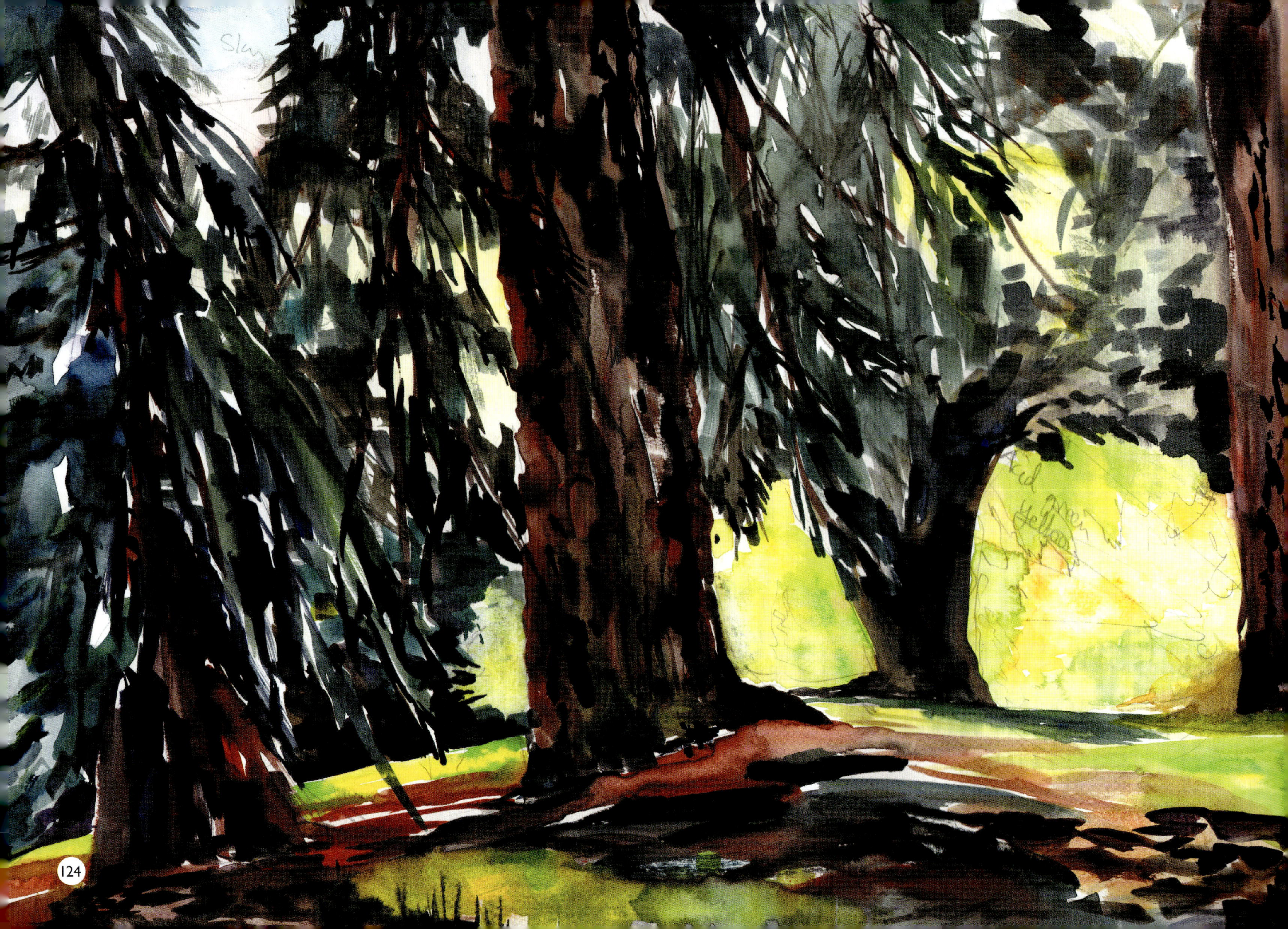
Sky
kid green
yellow

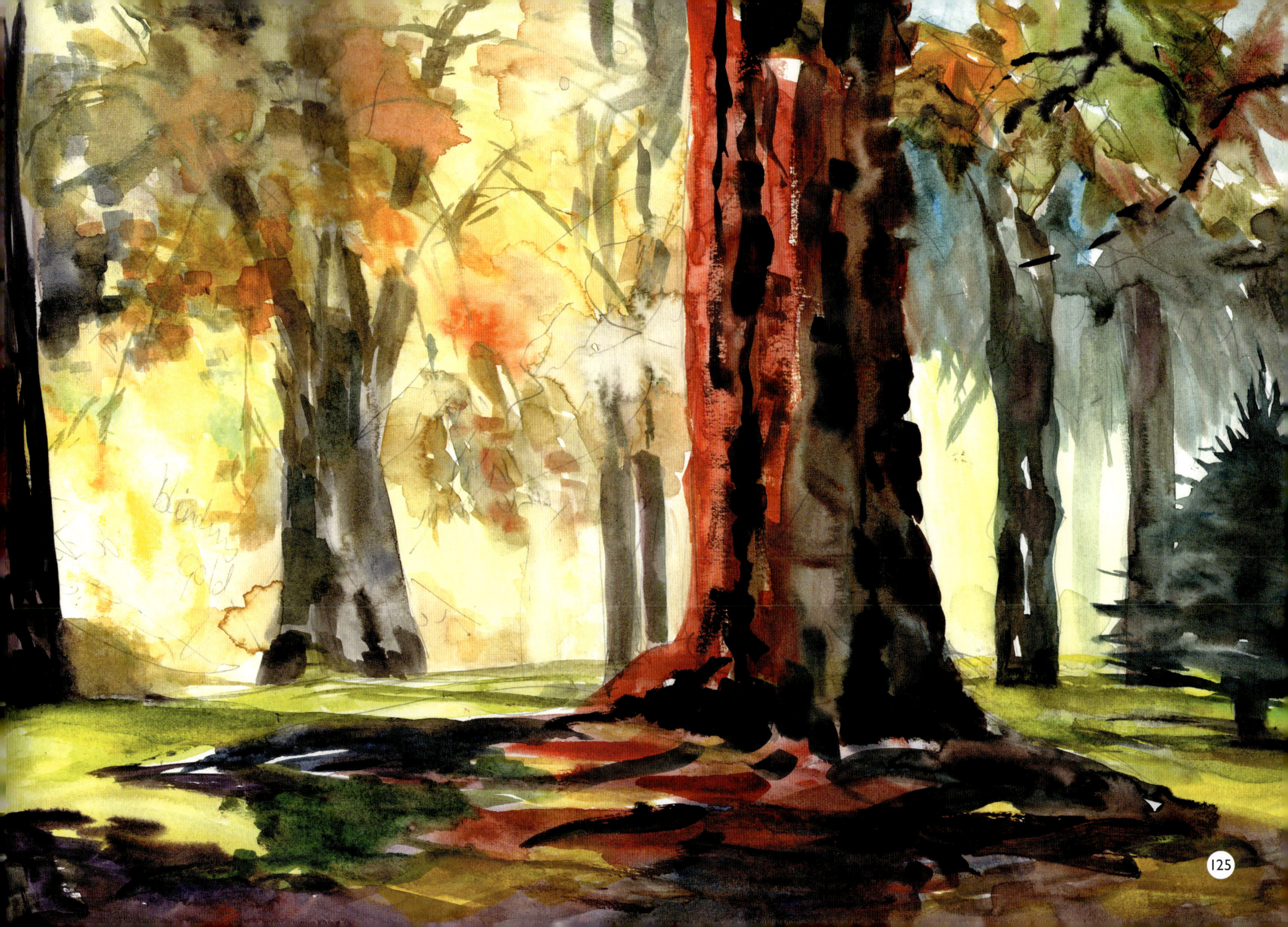
Blätter
gold

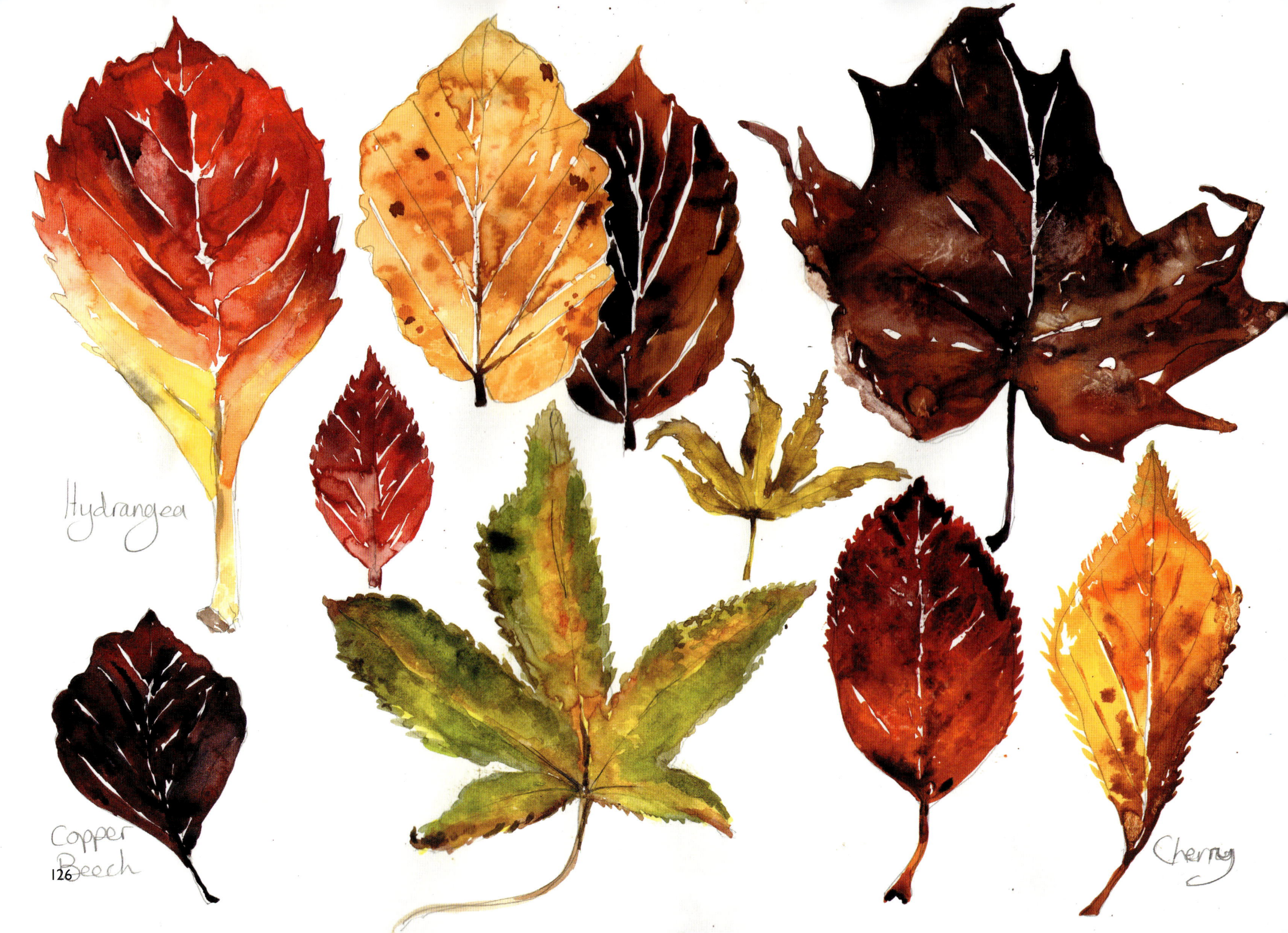

Hydrangea
Copper
Beech
126
Cherry

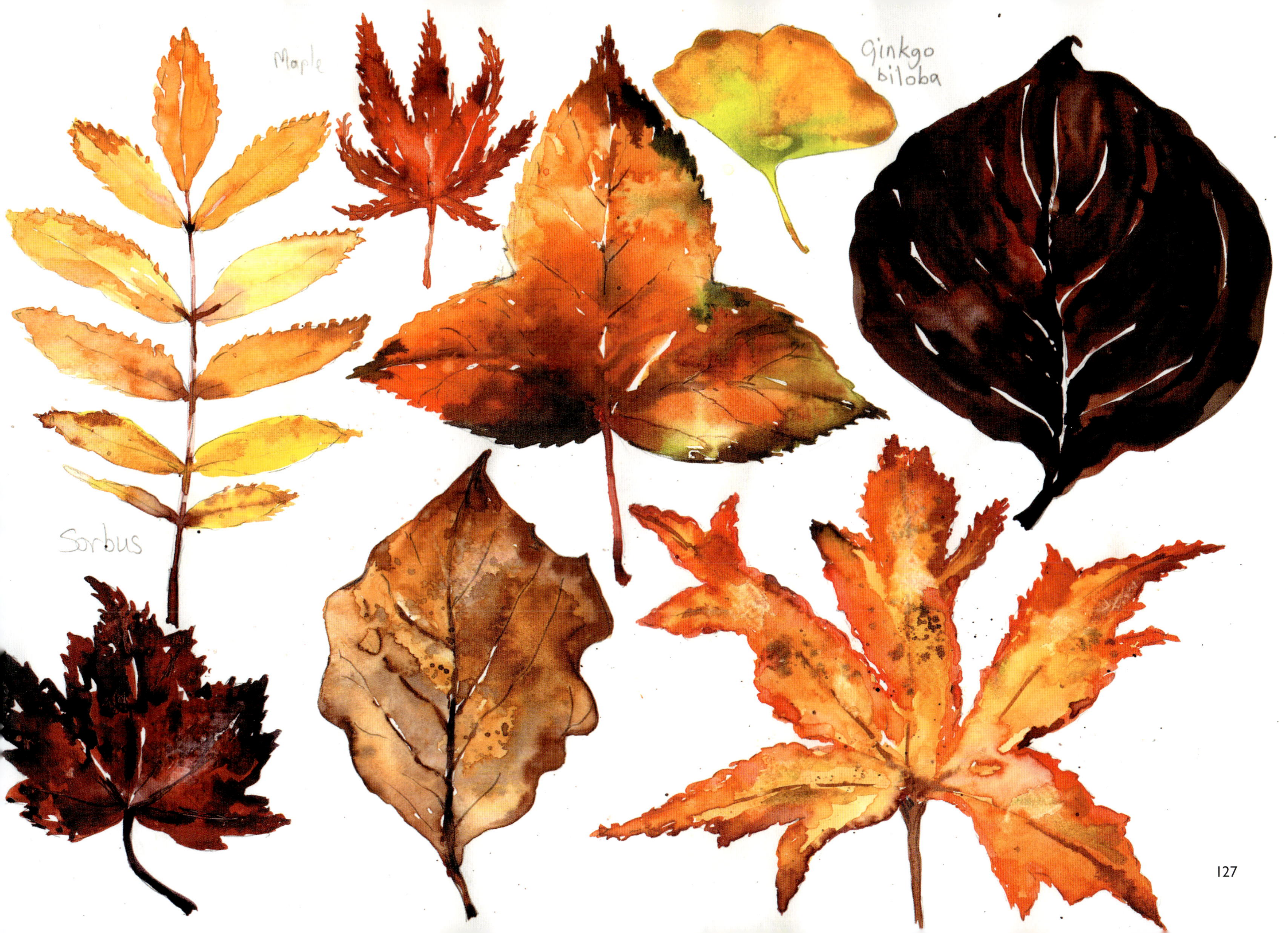

Maple
ginkgo biloba
Sorbus

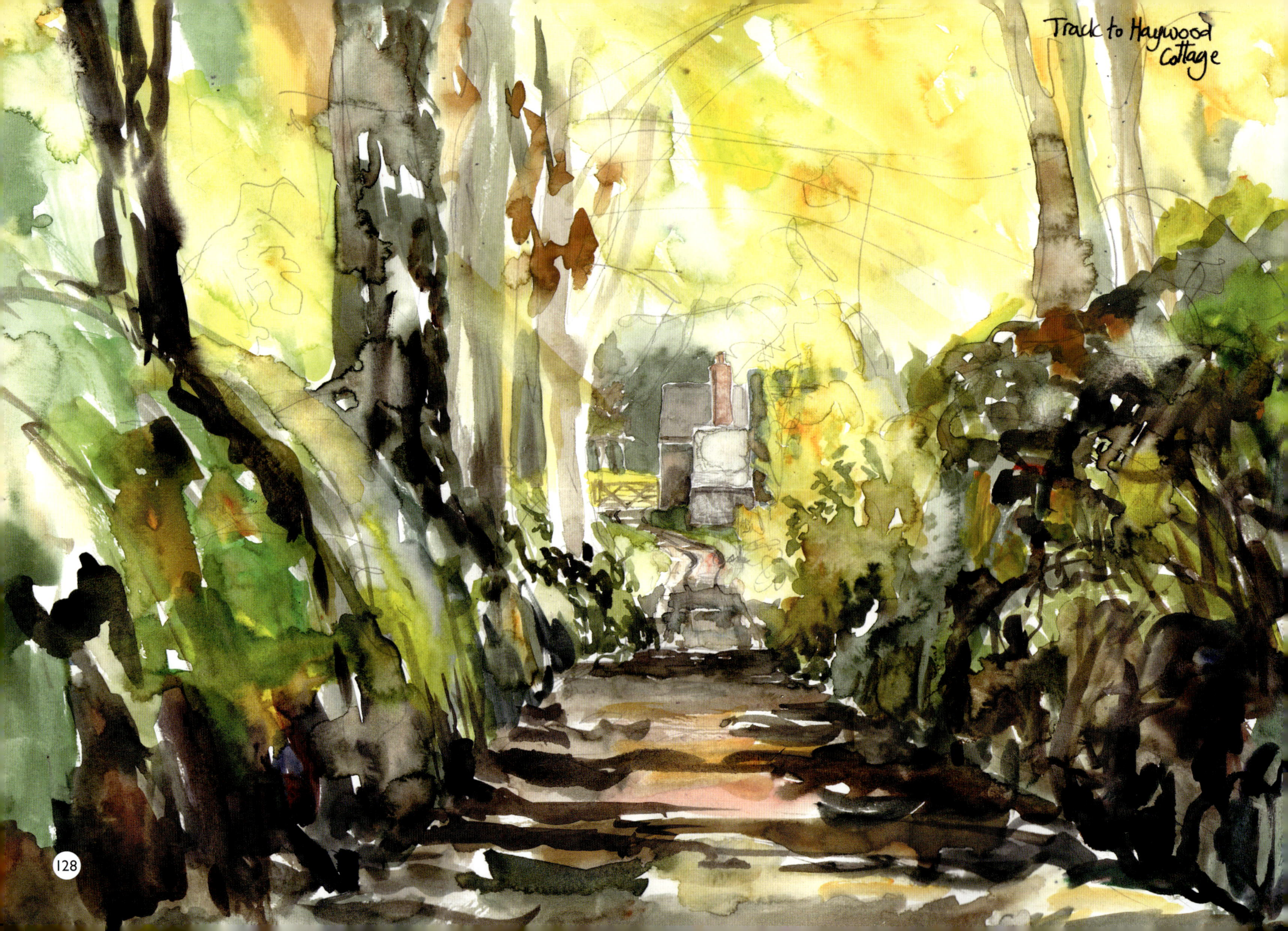
Track to Haywood Cottage

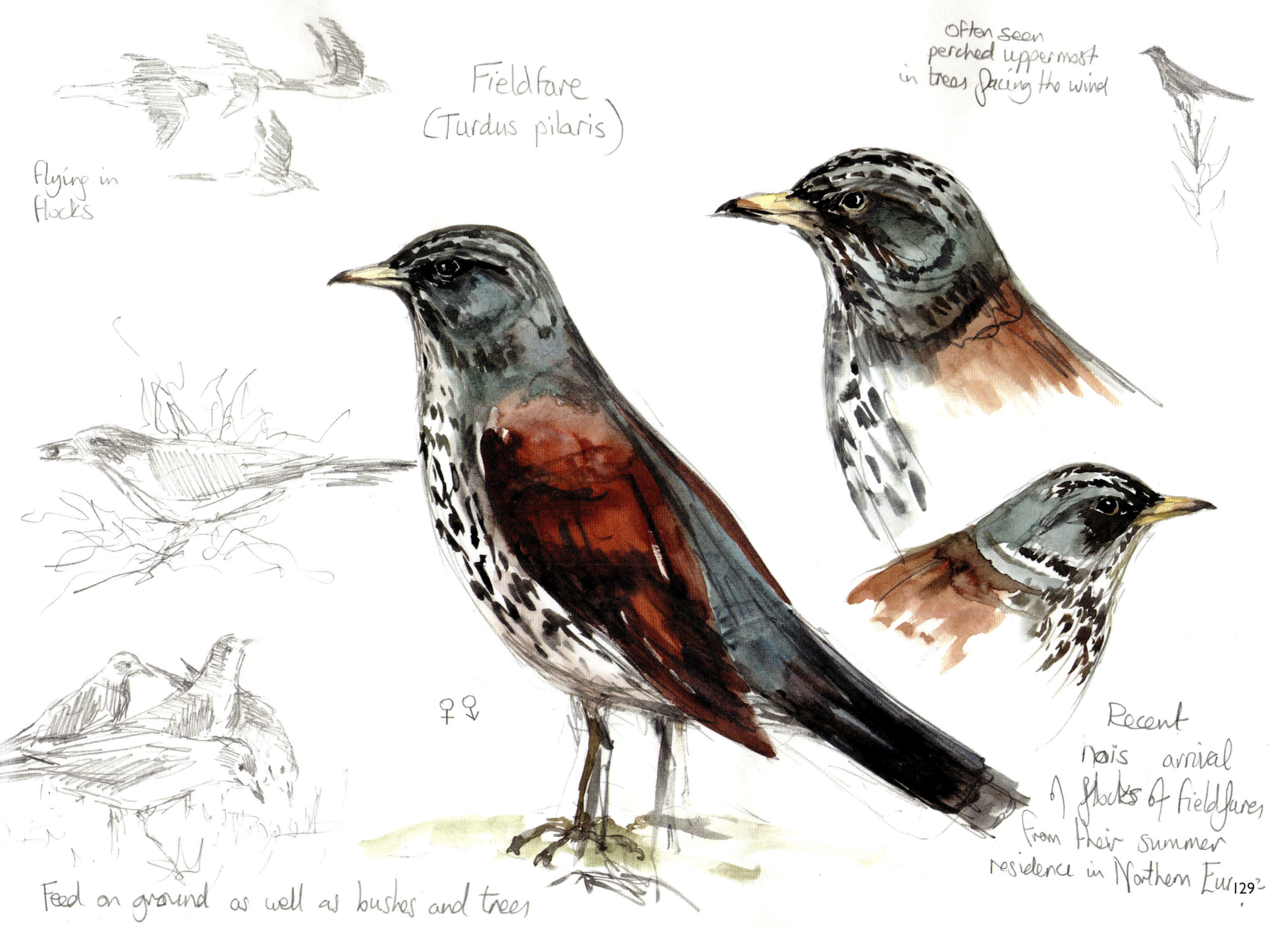

Fieldfare
(Turdus pilaris)
Flying in flocks
Often seen perched uppermost in trees facing the wind
♀♀
Recent noisy arrival of flocks of fieldfares from their summer residence in Northern Eur
Feed on ground as well as bushes and trees
129

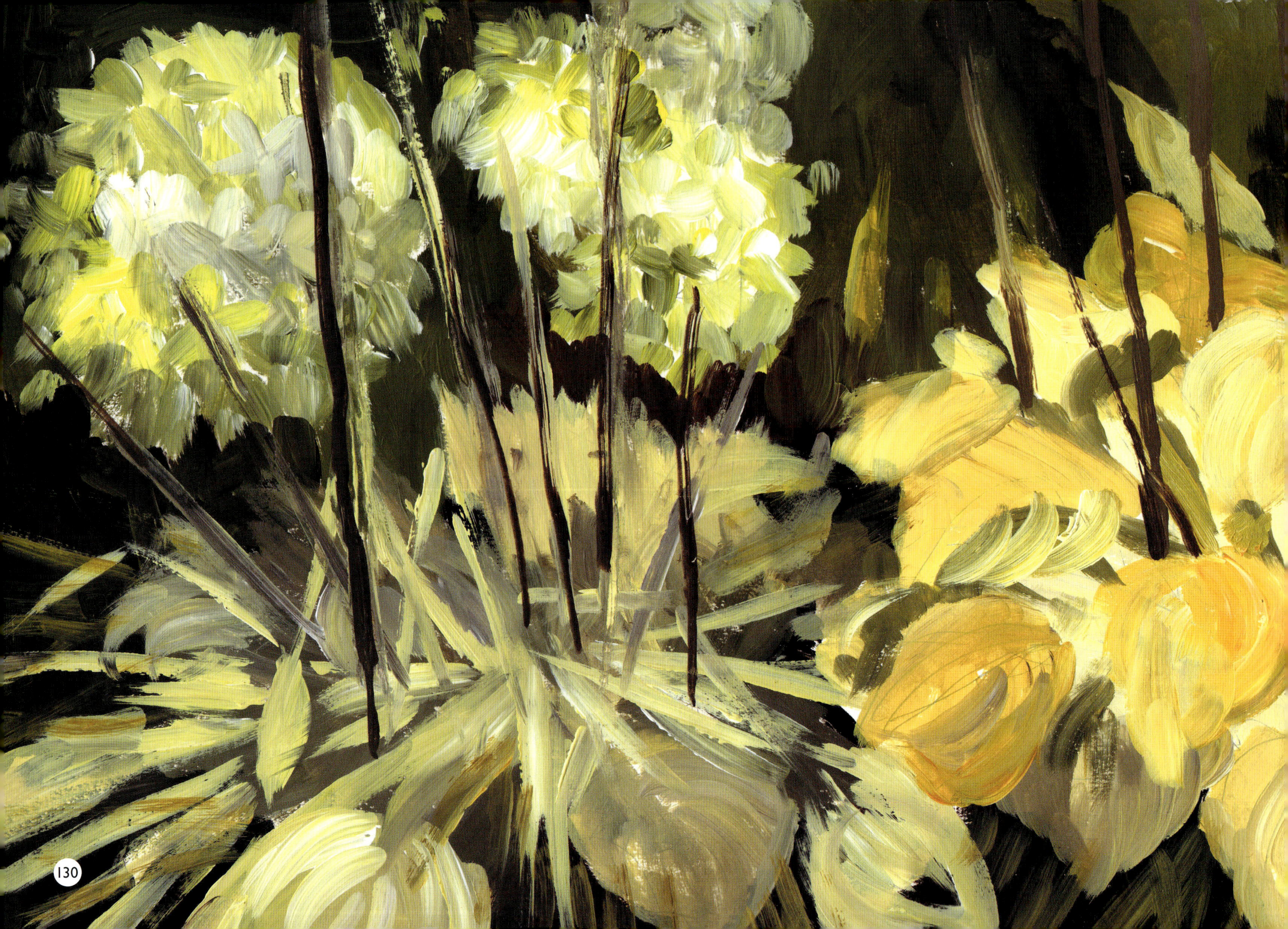

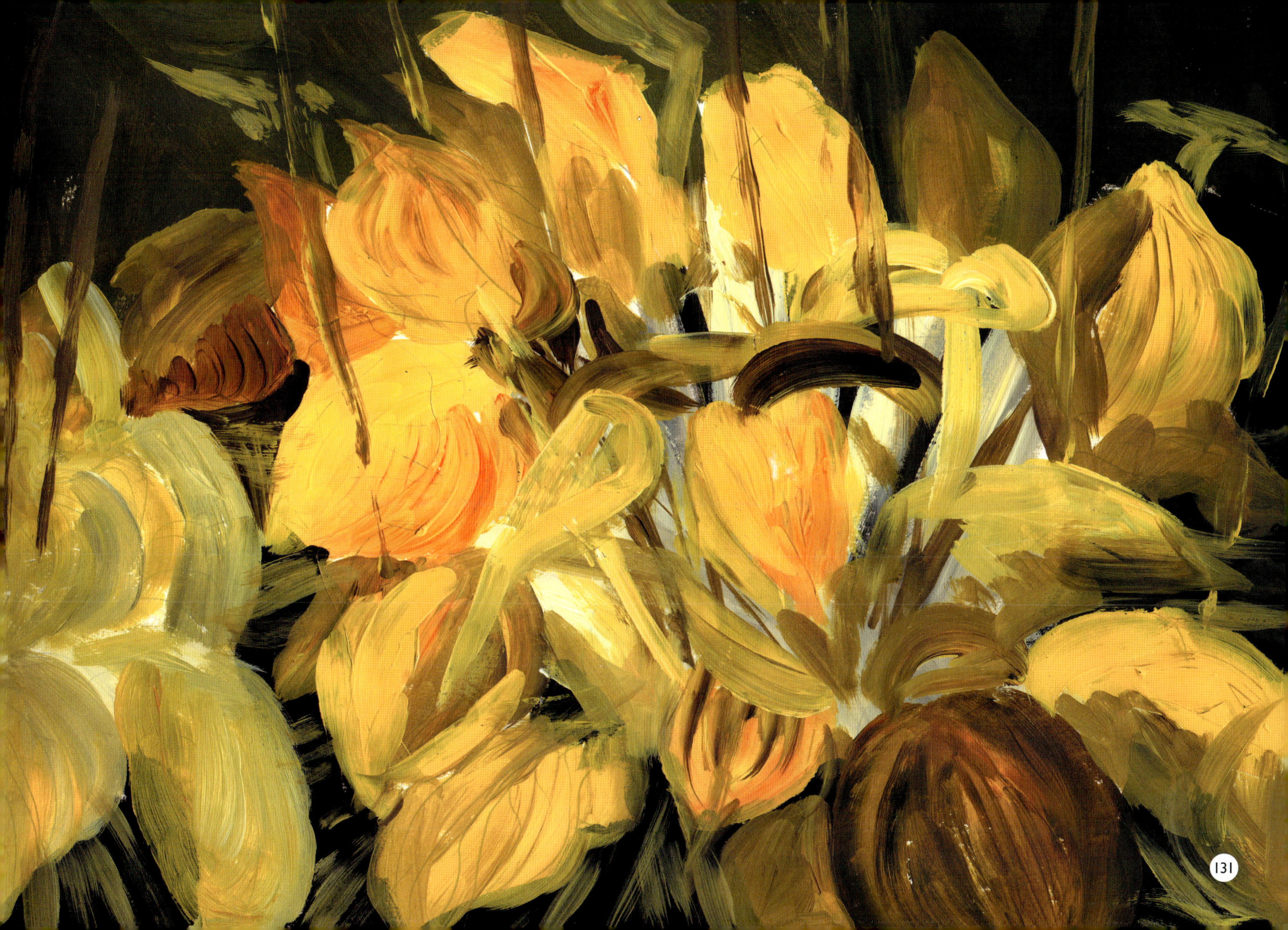

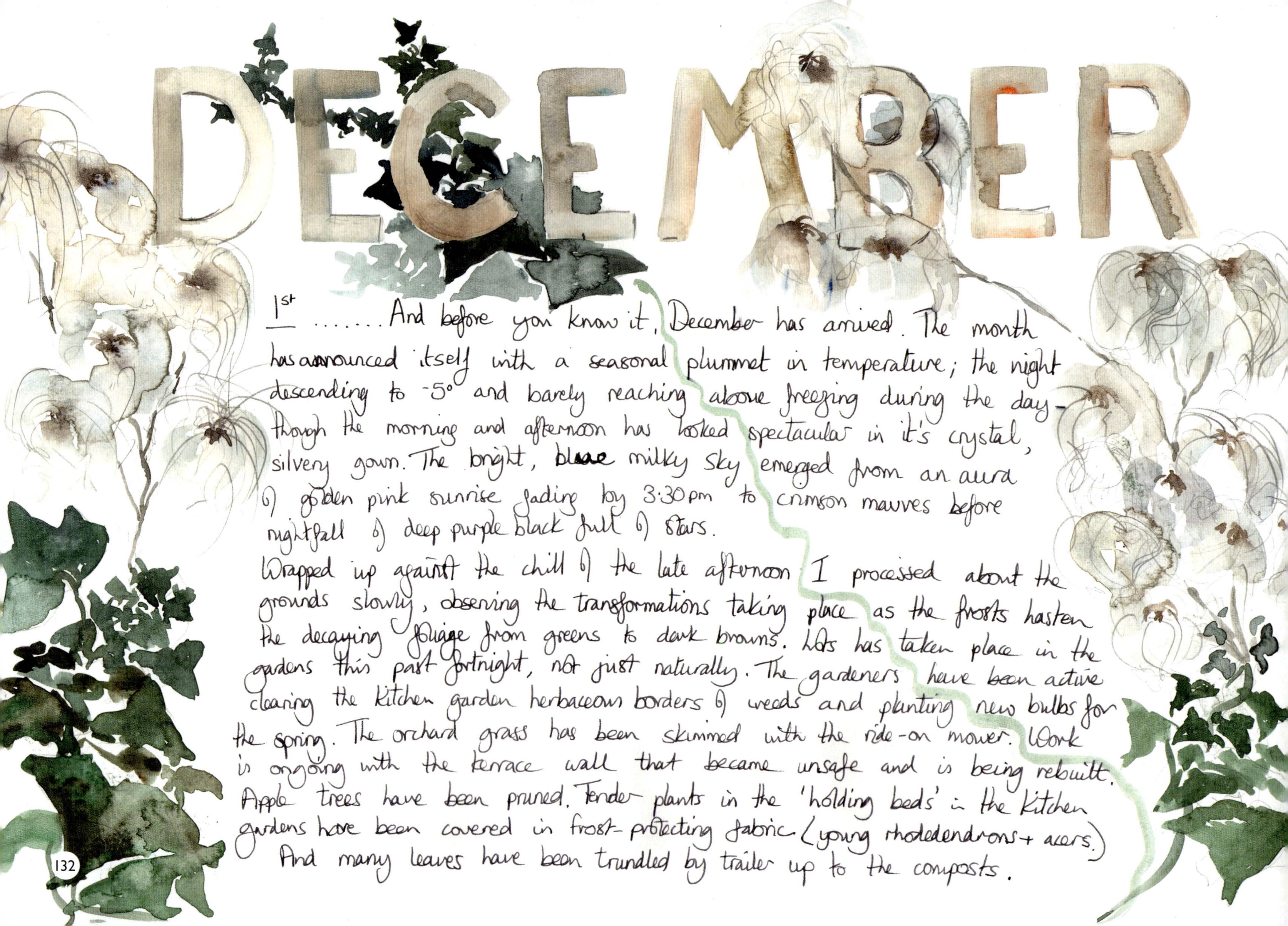

DECEMBER

<u>1st</u> .... And before you know it, December has arrived. The month has announced itself with a seasonal plummet in temperature; the night descending to -5° and barely reaching above freezing during the day — though the morning and afternoon has looked spectacular in it's crystal, silvery gown. The bright, blue milky sky emerged from an aura of golden pink sunrise fading by 3:30 pm to crimson mauves before nightfall & deep purple black full of stars.

Wrapped up against the chill of the late afternoon I processed about the grounds slowly, observing the transformations taking place as the frosts hasten the decaying foliage from greens to dark browns. Lots has taken place in the gardens this past fortnight, not just naturally. The gardeners have been active clearing the kitchen garden herbaceous borders of weeds and planting new bulbs for the spring. The orchard grass has been skimmed with the ride-on mower. Work is ongoing with the terrace wall that became unsafe and is being rebuilt. Apple trees have been pruned. Tender plants in the 'holding beds' in the kitchen gardens have been covered in frost-protecting fabric (young rhododendrons + acers.) And many leaves have been trundled by trailer up to the composts.

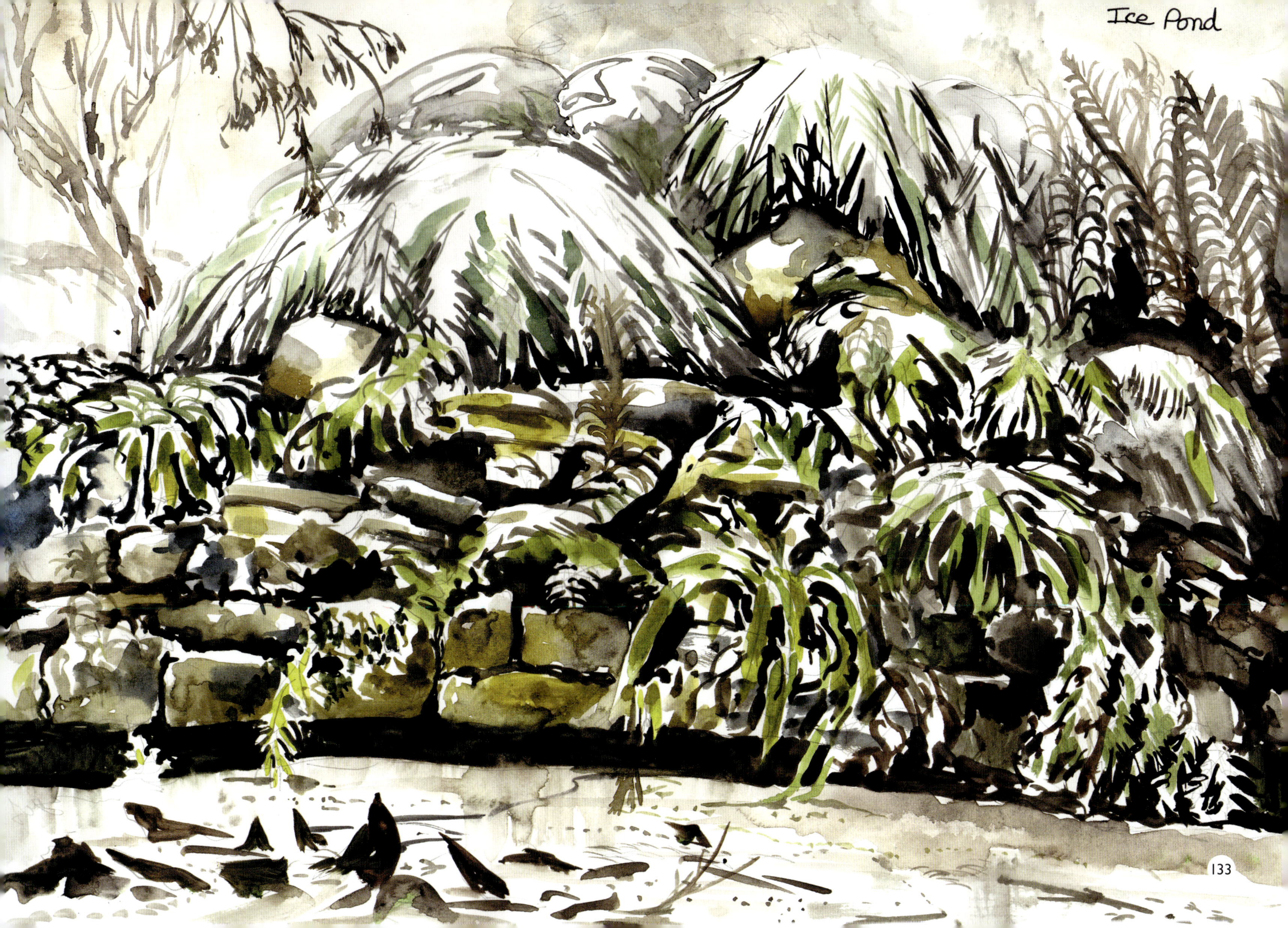
Ice Pond

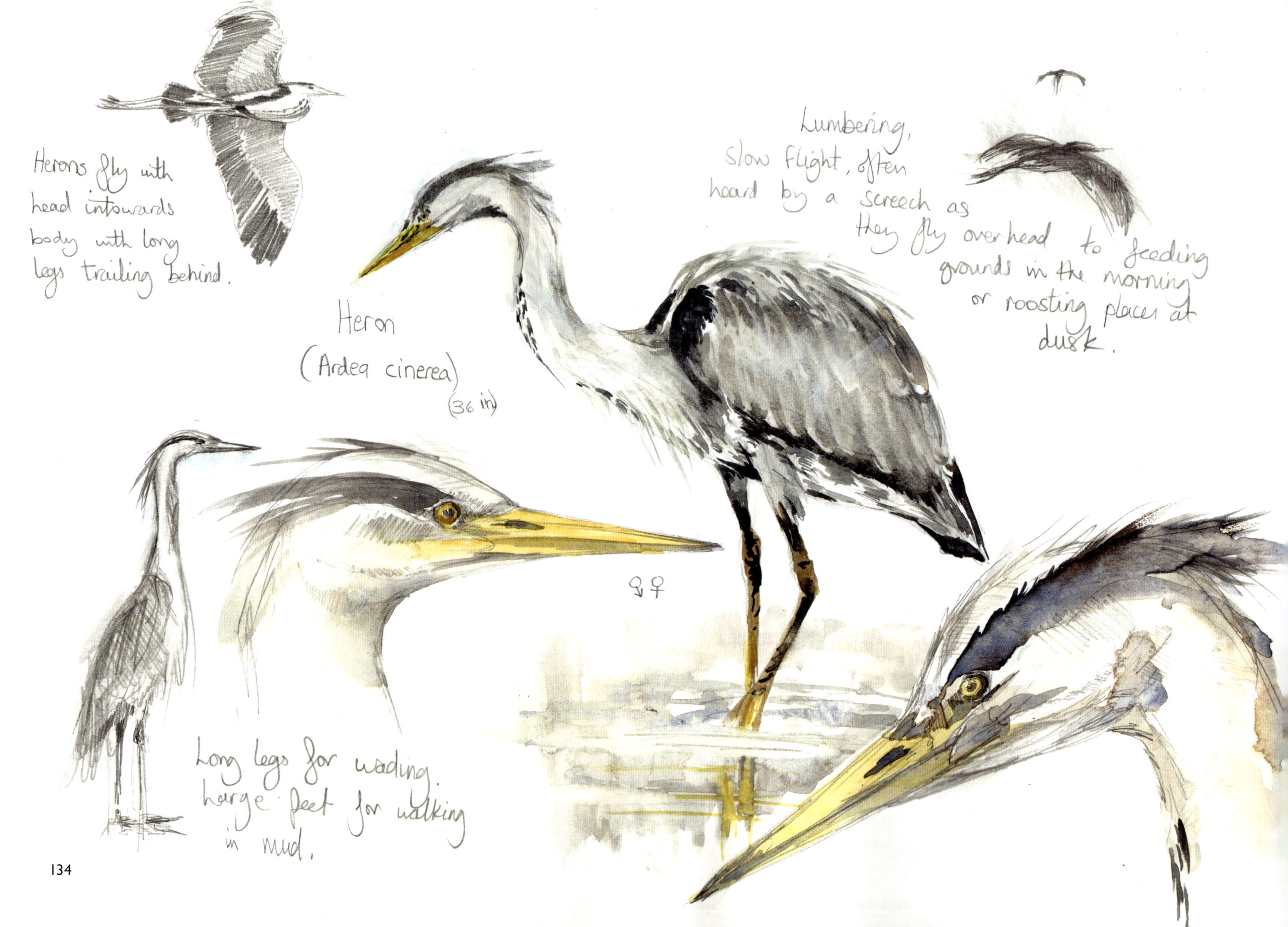

Herons fly with
head intowards
body with long
legs trailing behind.

Lumbering,
slow flight, often
heard by a screech as
they fly overhead to feeding
grounds in the morning
or roosting places at
dusk.

Heron
(Ardea cinerea)
(36 in)

Long legs for wading.
Large feet for walking
in mud.

134

Postscript

The context of Hergest Court today — obtaining 500 years post-Thomas Vaughan, various notaries resided there, and in 1912 The Manor of Hergest, 339 acres including Haywood Common and Park Wood, was purchased at auction by W.H. Banks. One hundred years ago to date, in 1923, a valuation was made of Hergest Court at £279. (I doubt that would even cover a week's scaffold hire at present!)

'Marcescence' — trees (deciduous) whose leaves wither but do not fall, usually falling once new growth pushes forth in spring.

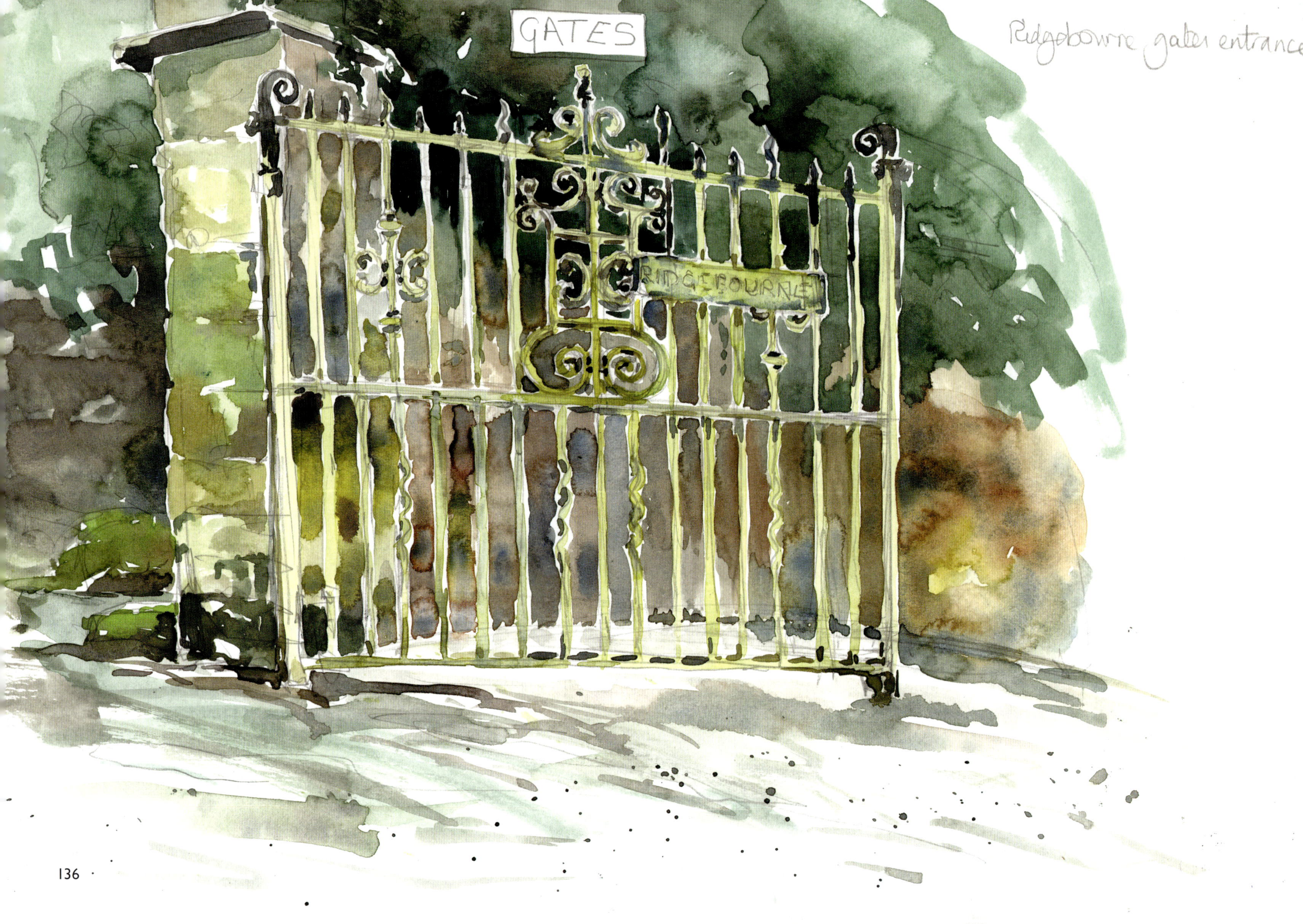

GATES
RIDGEBOURNE

Ridgebourne gates entrance

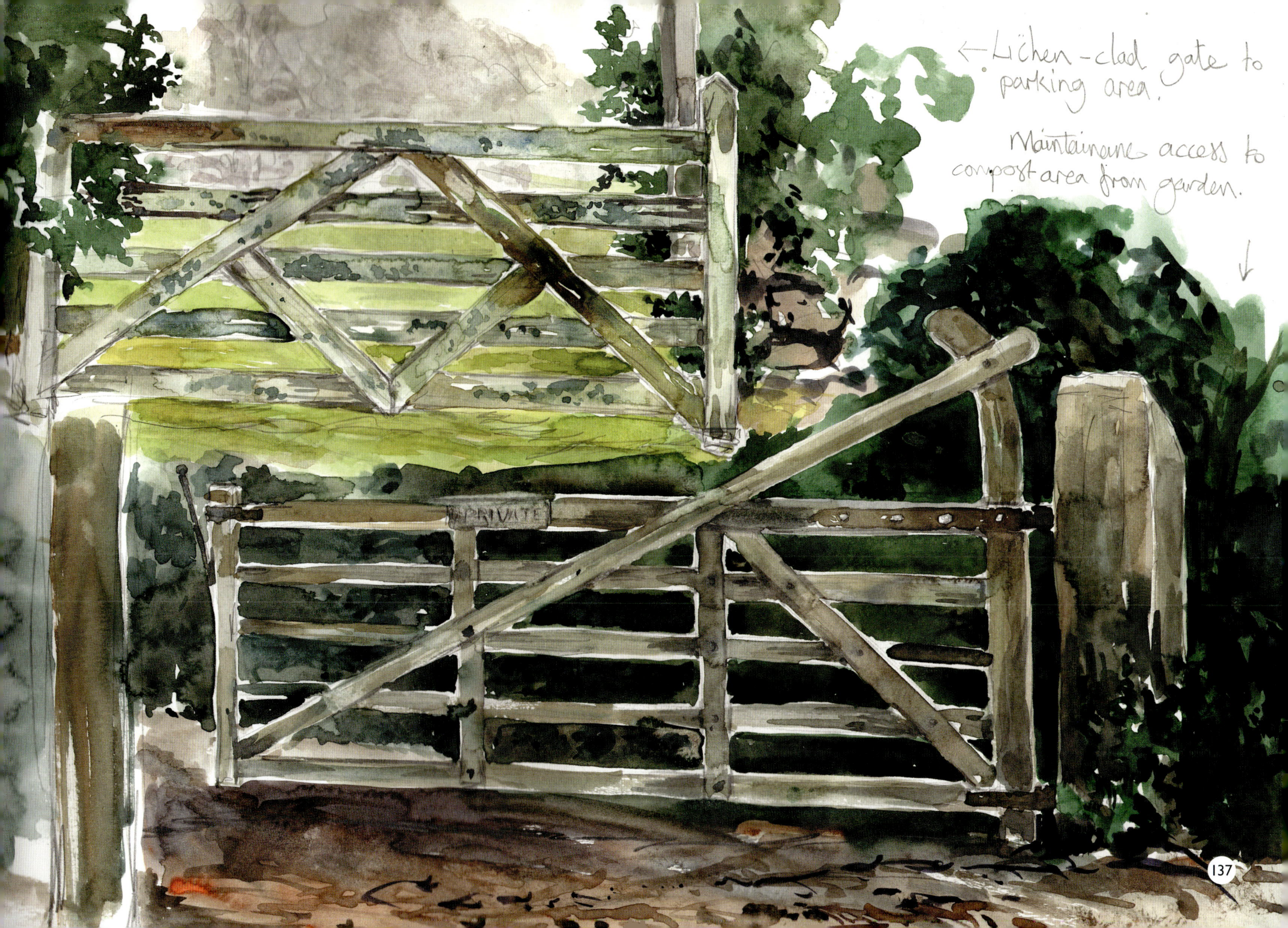

← Lichen-clad gate to parking area.

Maintainance access to compost area from garden.

PRIVATE

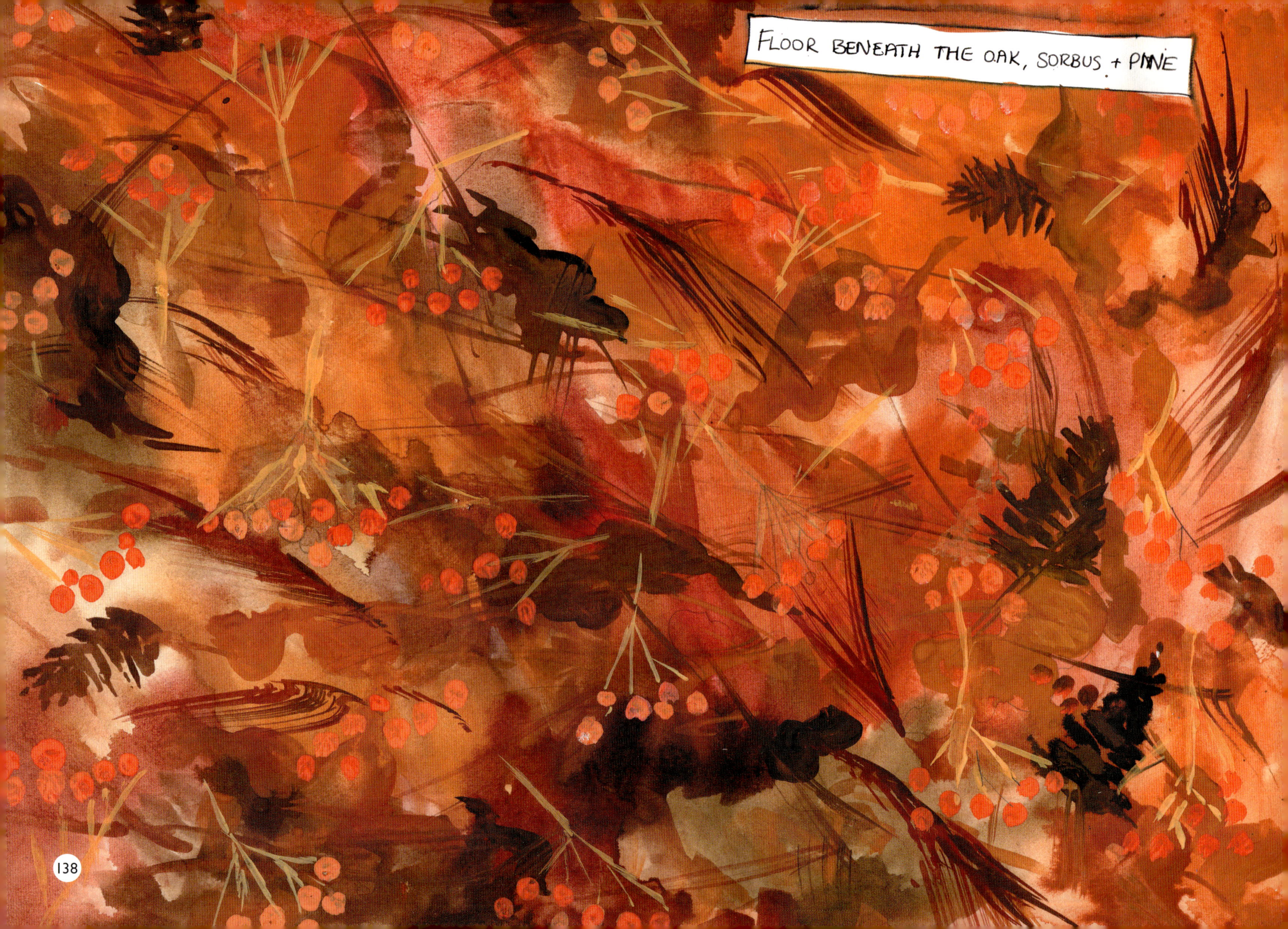
FLOOR BENEATH THE OAK, SORBUS + PINE

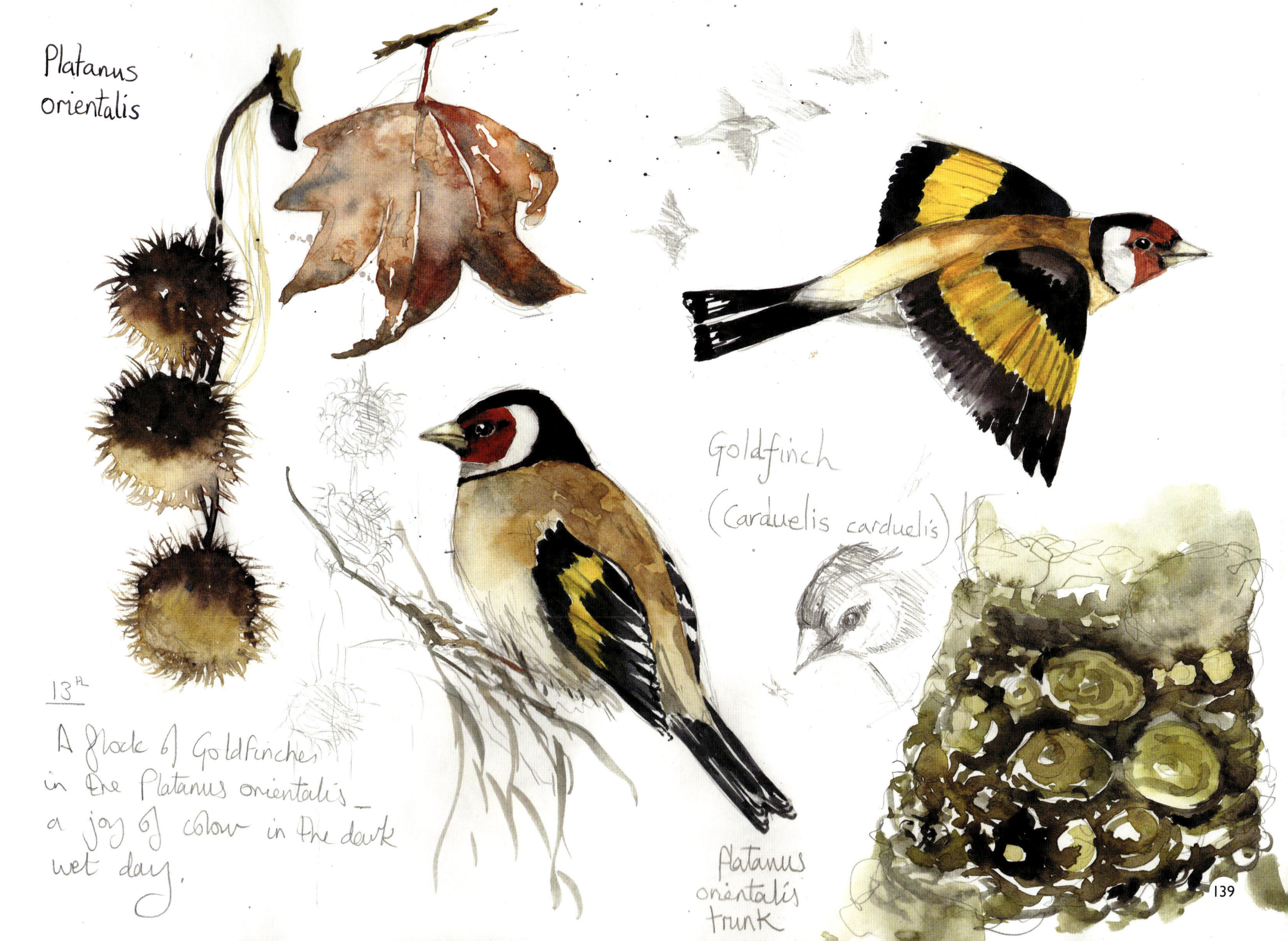

Platanus
orientalis

Goldfinch
(Carduelis carduelis)

13th
A flock of Goldfinches
in the Platanus orientalis —
a joy of colour in the dark
wet day.

Platanus
orientalis
trunk

139

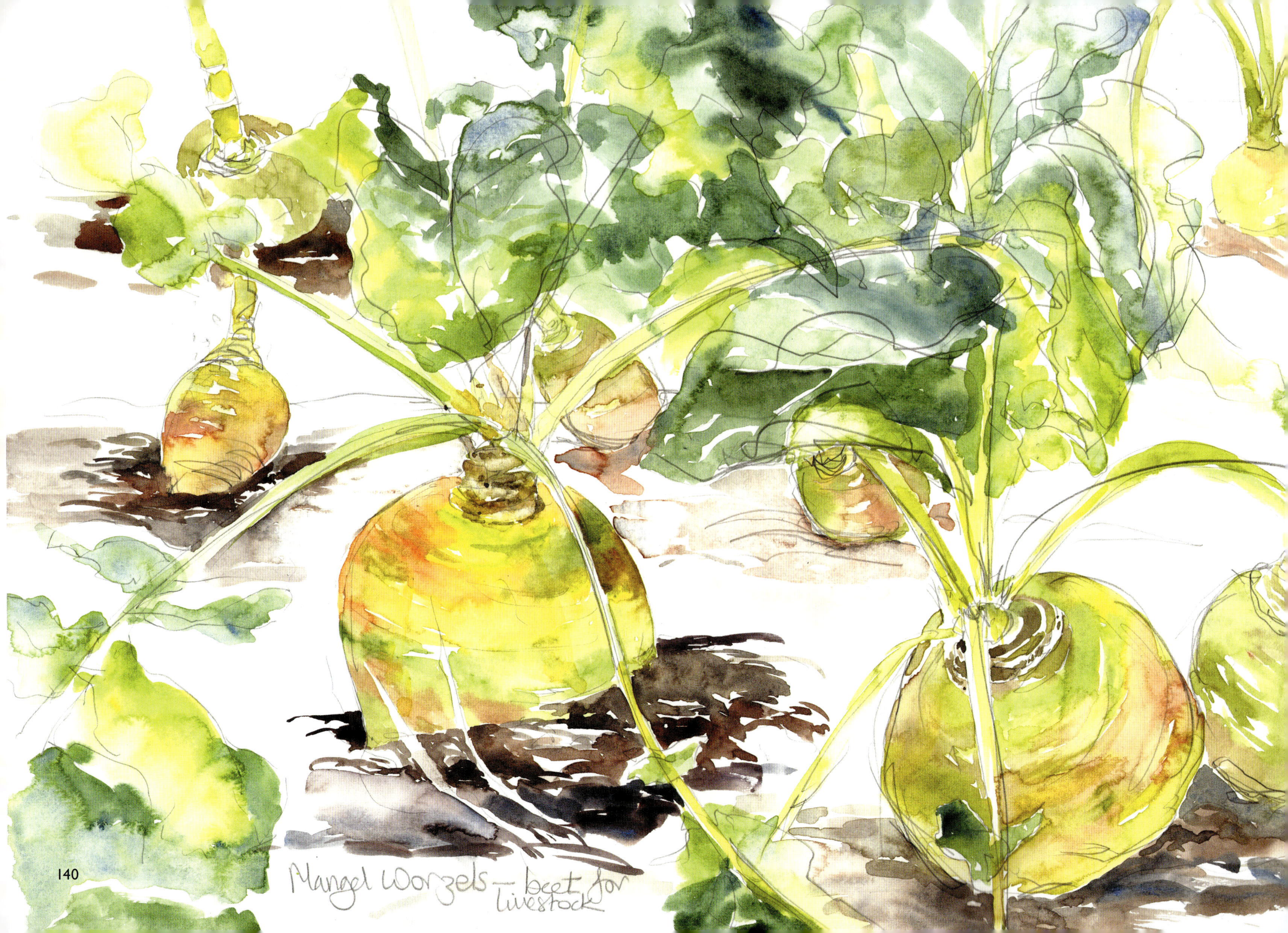

Mangel Worzels – beet for livestock

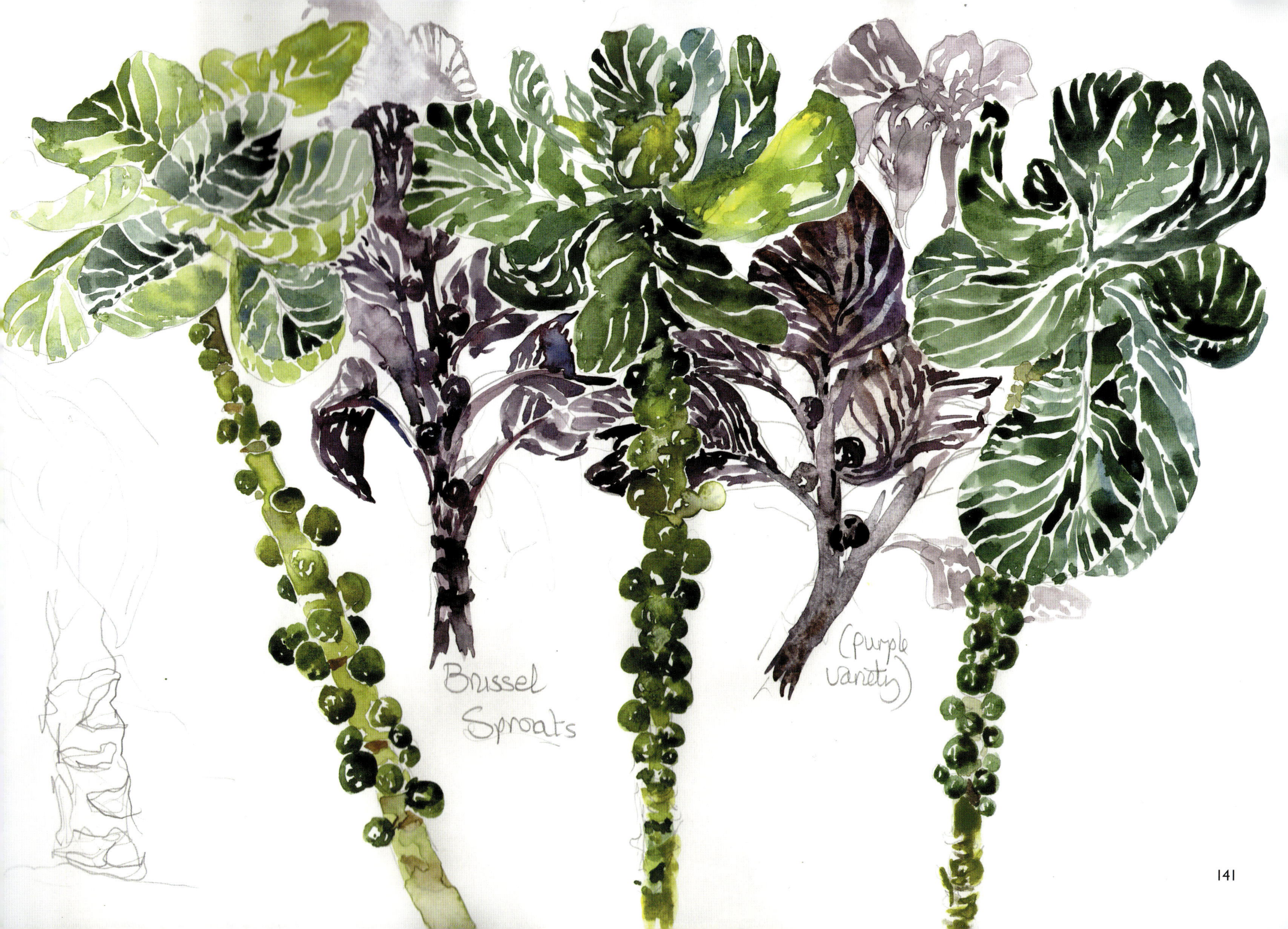

Brussel
Sprouts
(purple
variety)

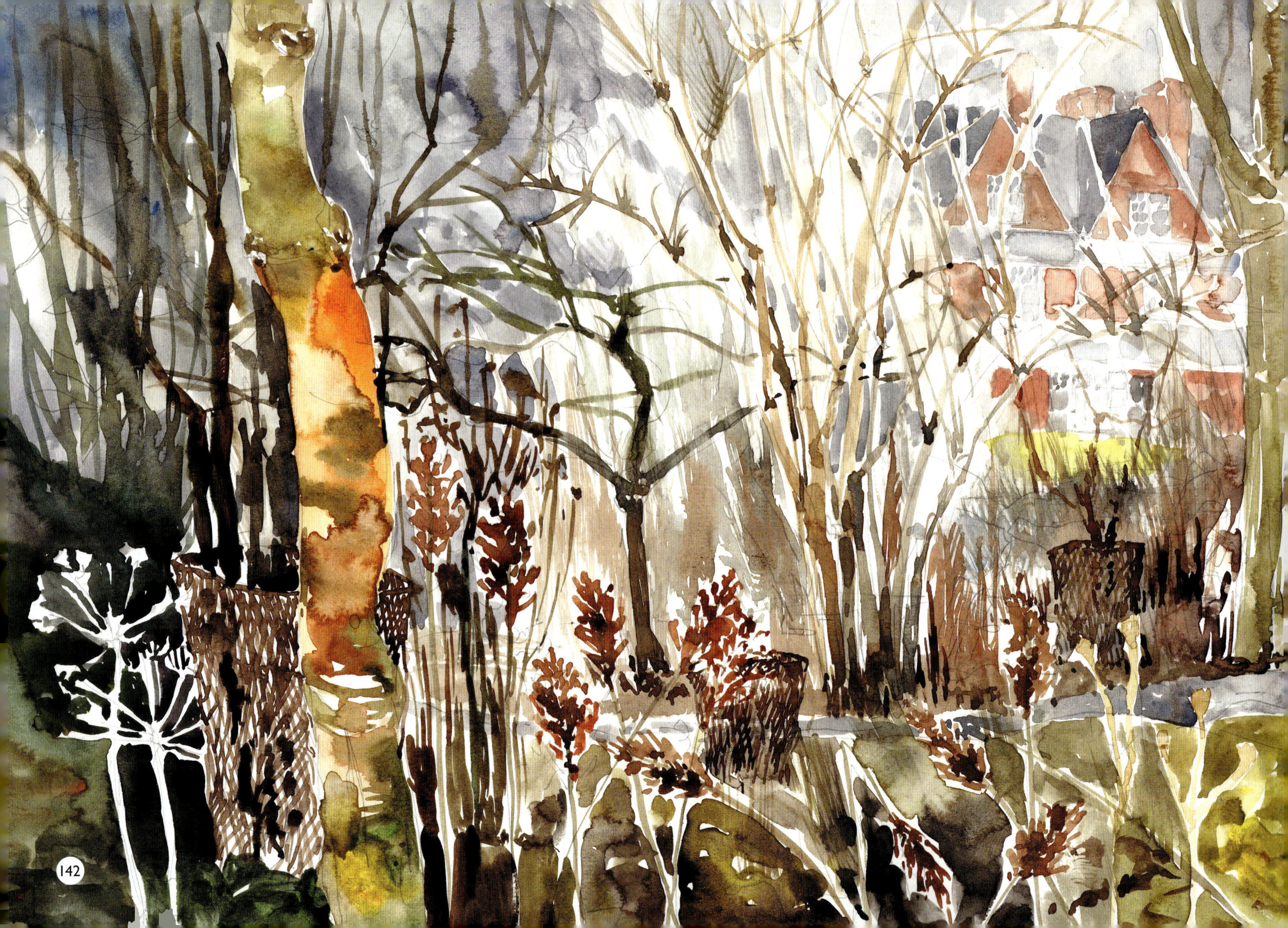

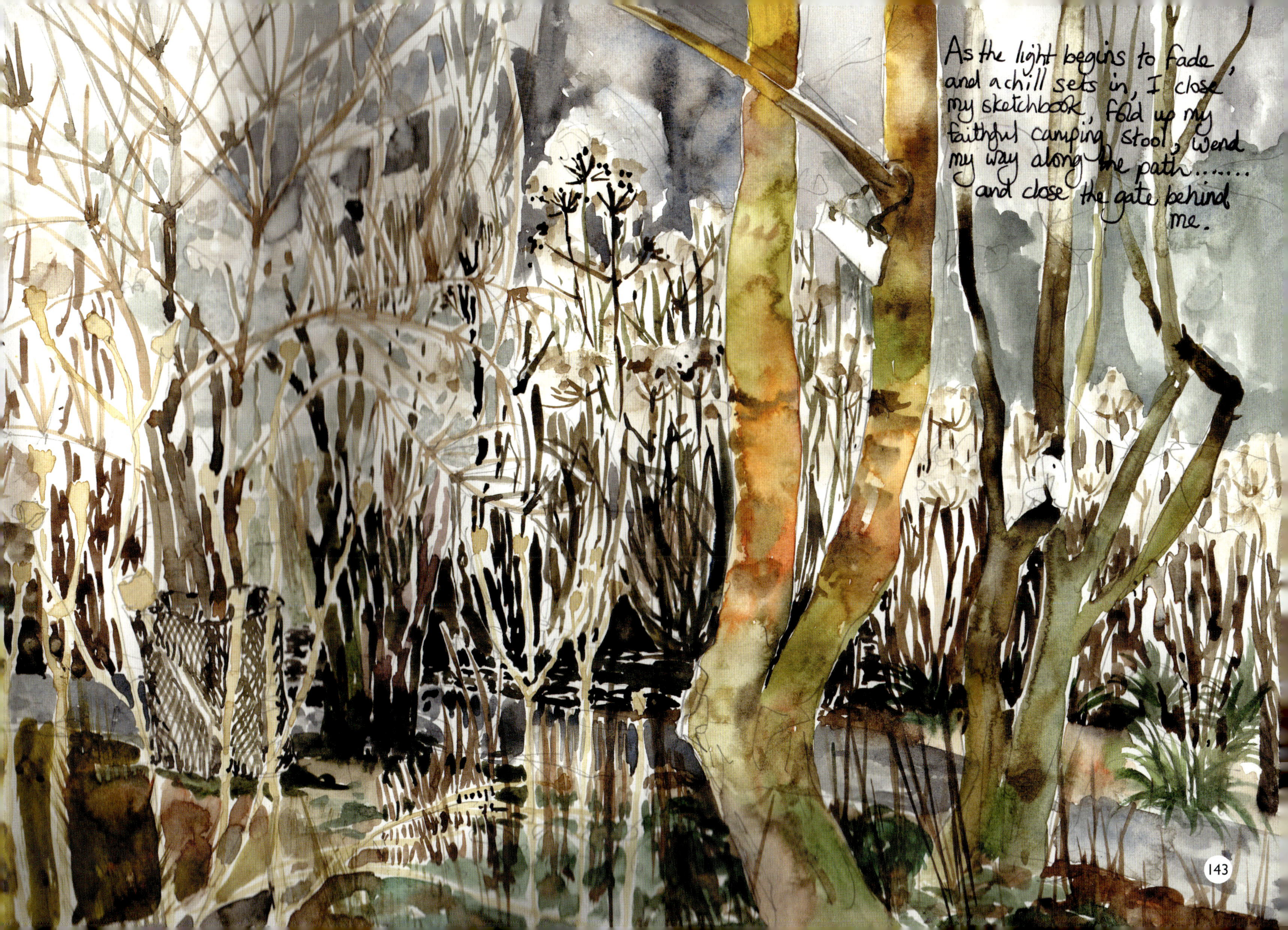
As the light begins to fade,
and a chill sets in, I close
my sketchbook, fold up my
faithful camping stool, wend
my way along the path........
and close the gate behind
me.

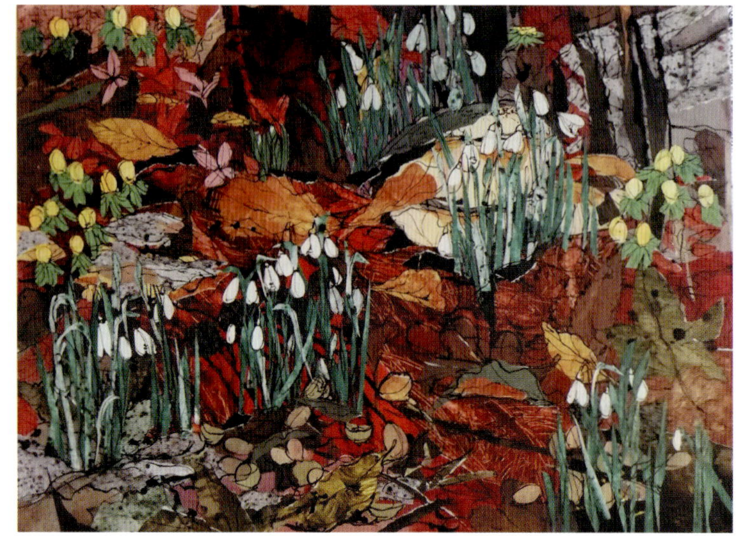

January Snowdrops and winter aconites

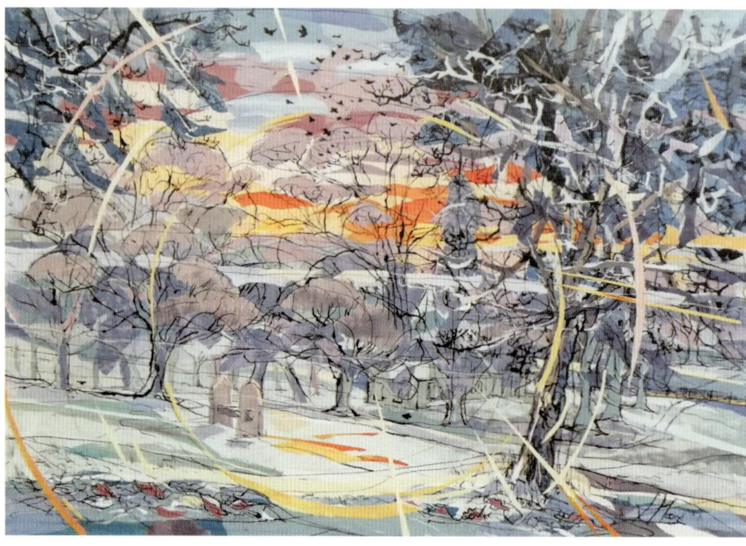

January Sunrise through frosty mist

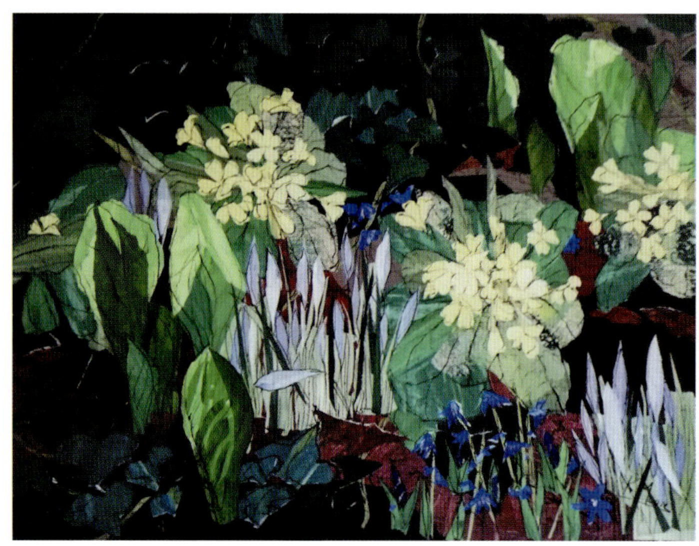

February Early Spring border

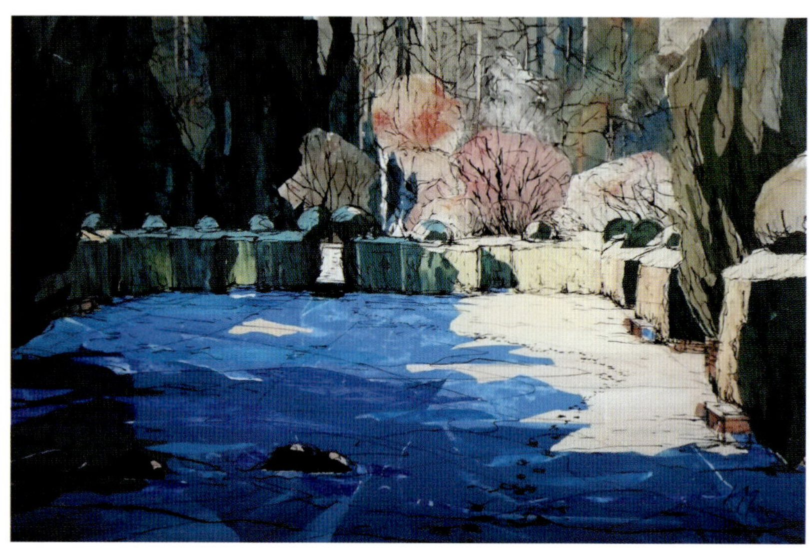

February Croquet lawn in snow

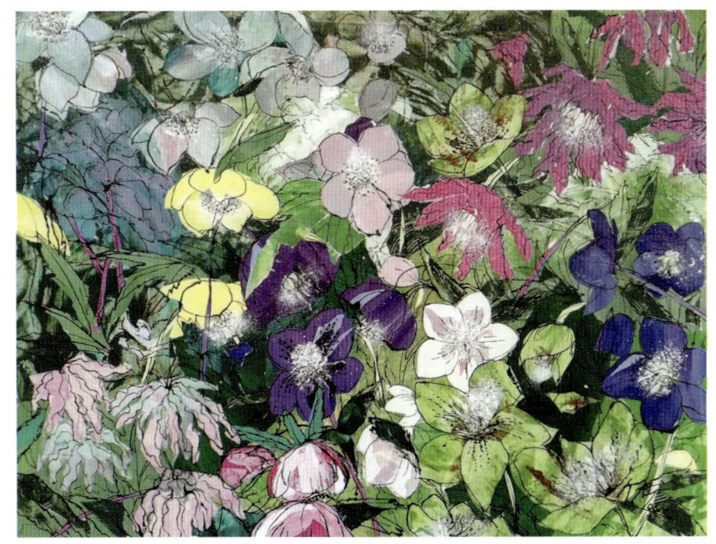

March Spring border

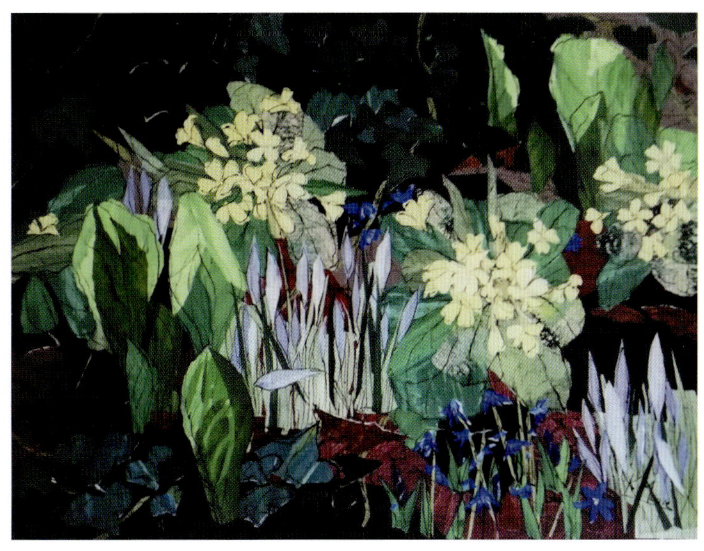

March Hellebores

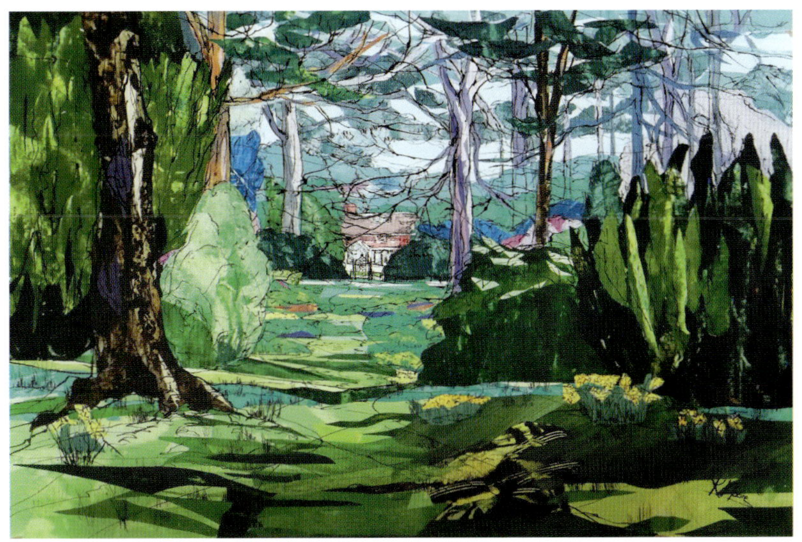

April Woodland with daffodils

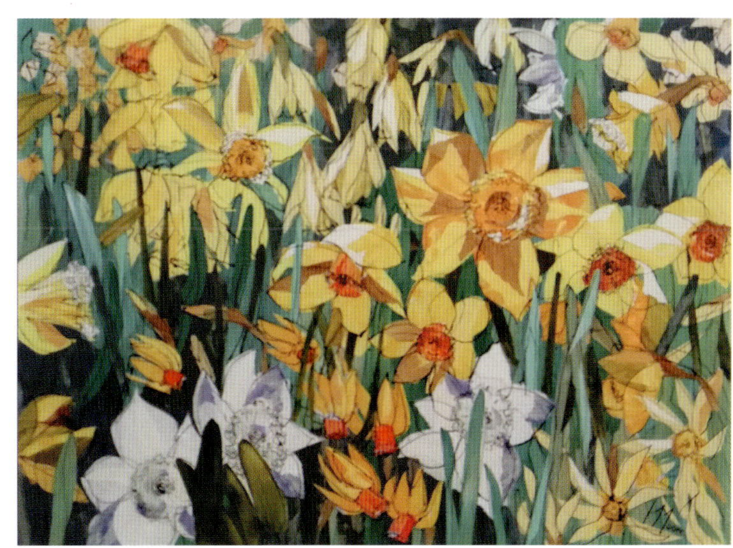

April Daffodils

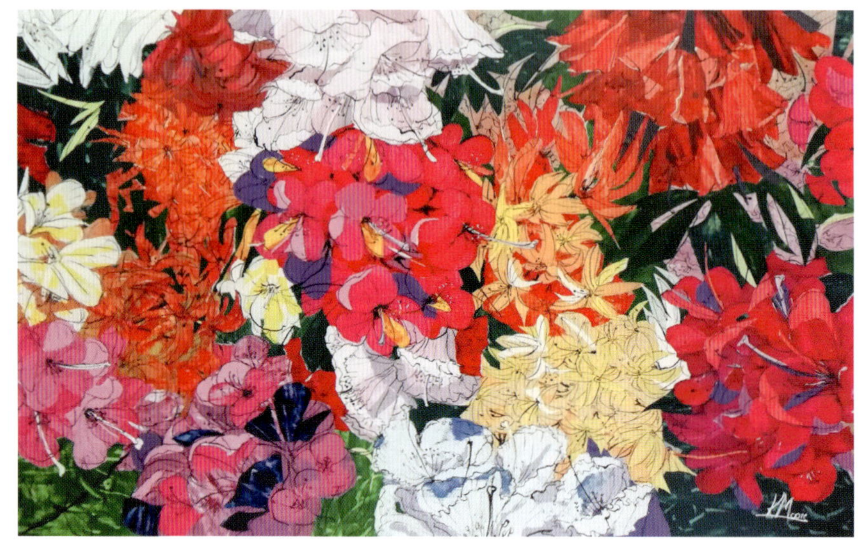

May Rhododendrons and Azaleas

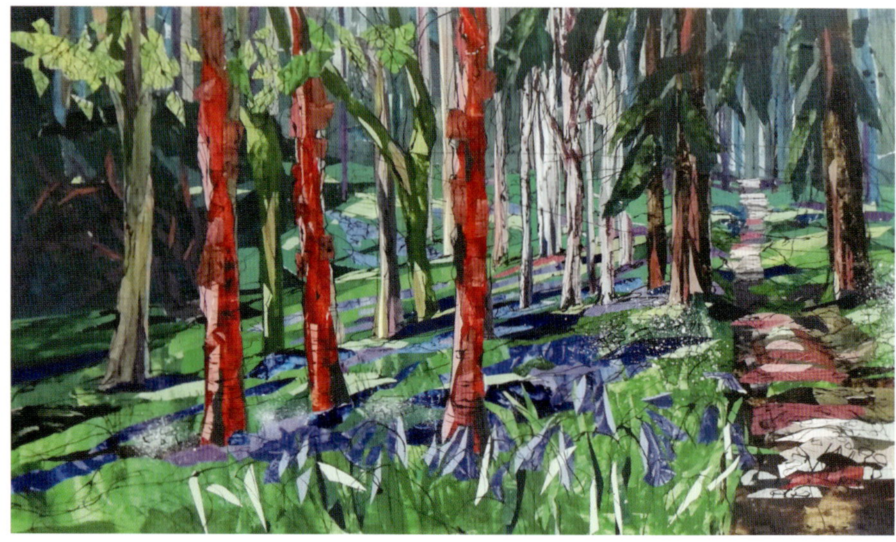

May Bluebells, Park Wood

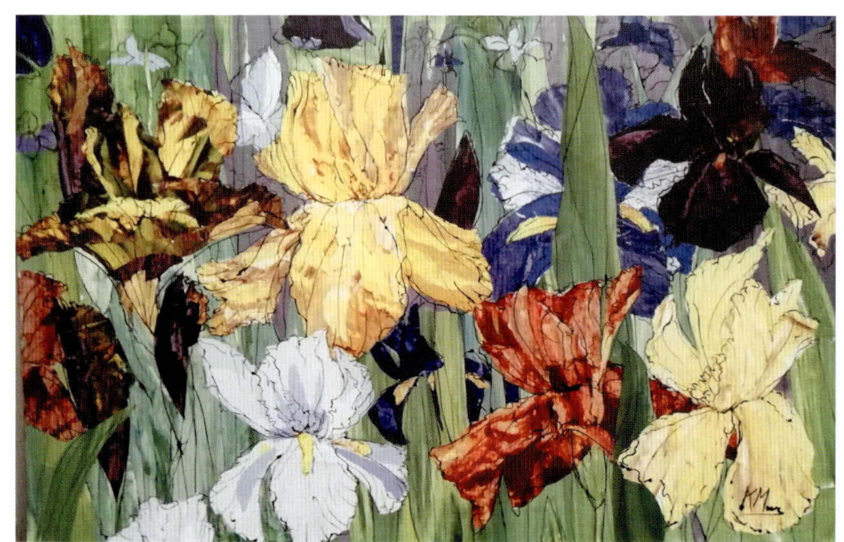

June Irises

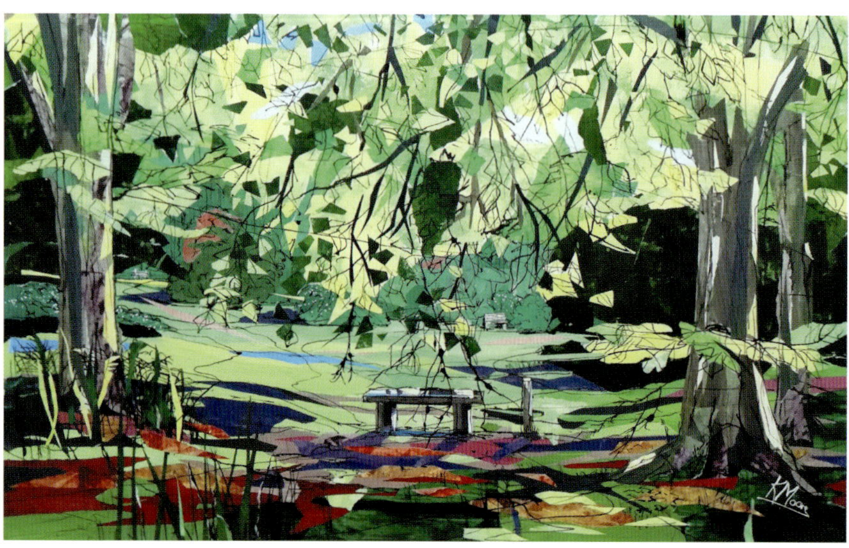

June June morning beneath beech trees

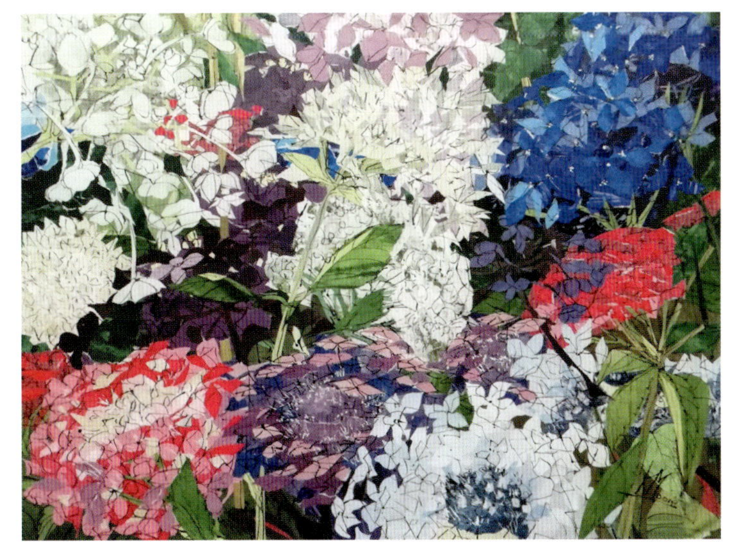

July Hydrangeas

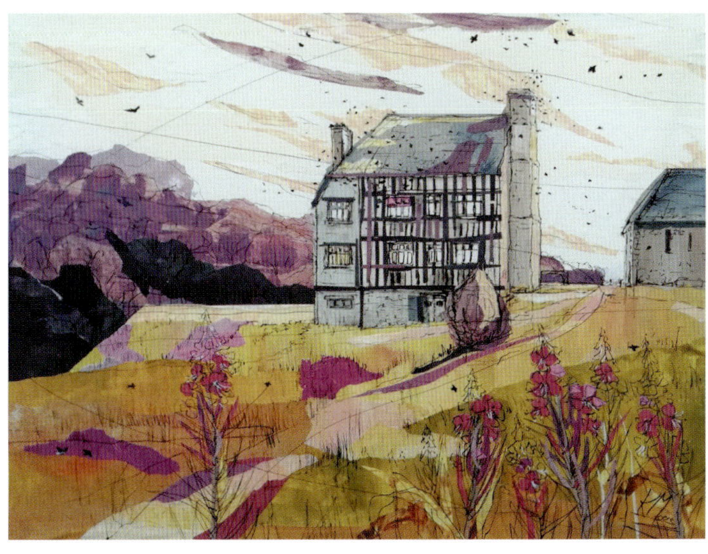

July Hergest Court with House Martins

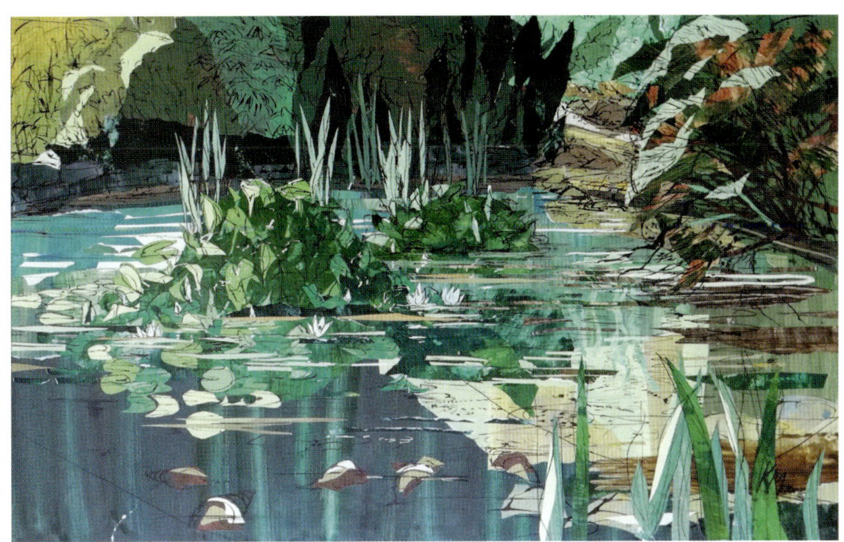

August Rockery pond

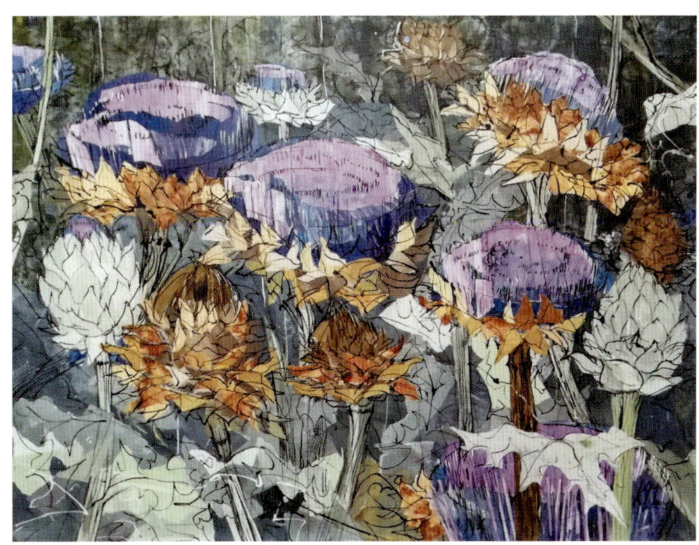

August Artichokes

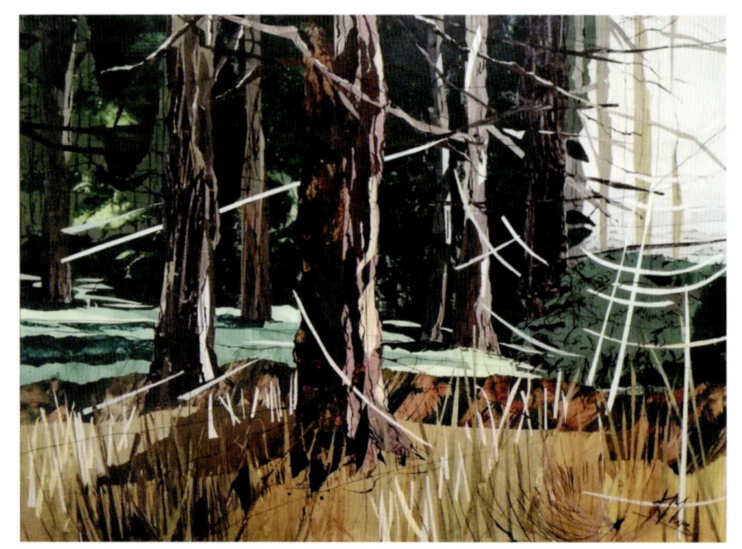

September Morning haze through the pines

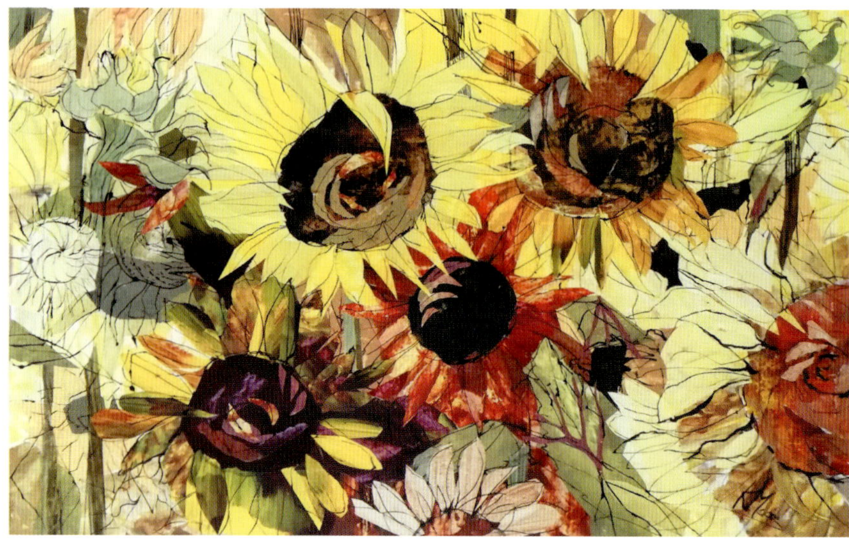

September Sunflowers

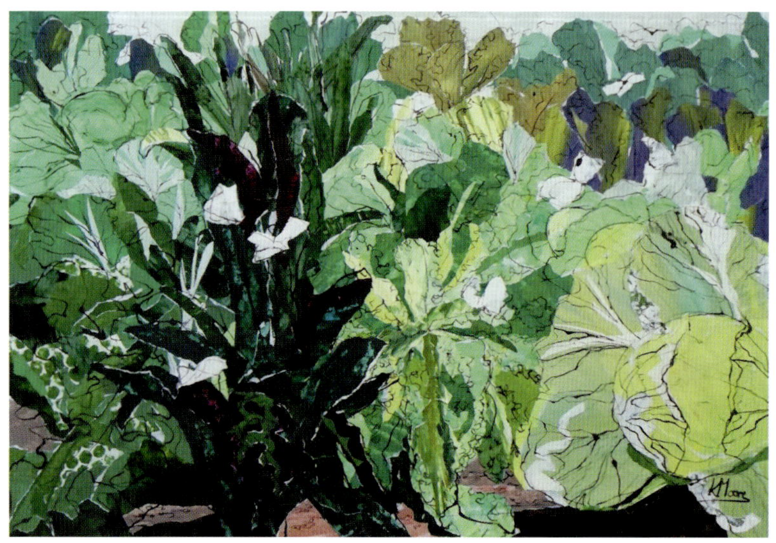

October Brassicas and Cabbage Whites

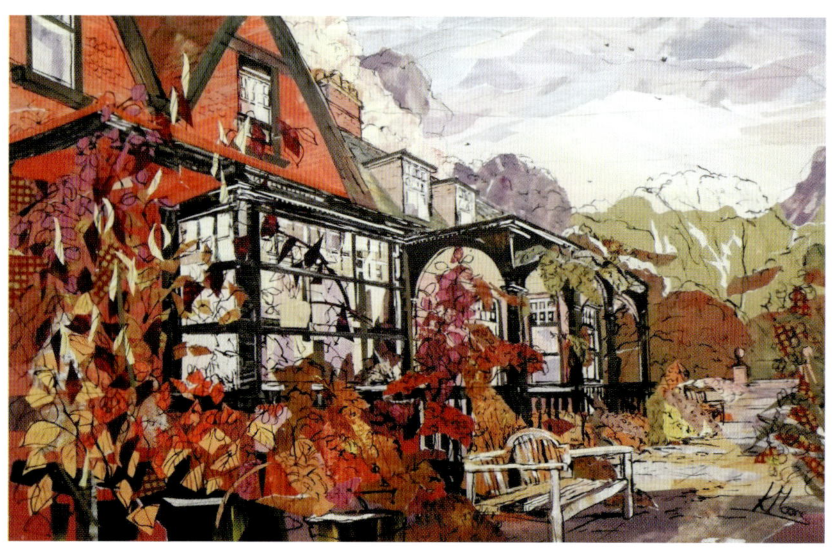

October Maples Tearoom, autumn terrace

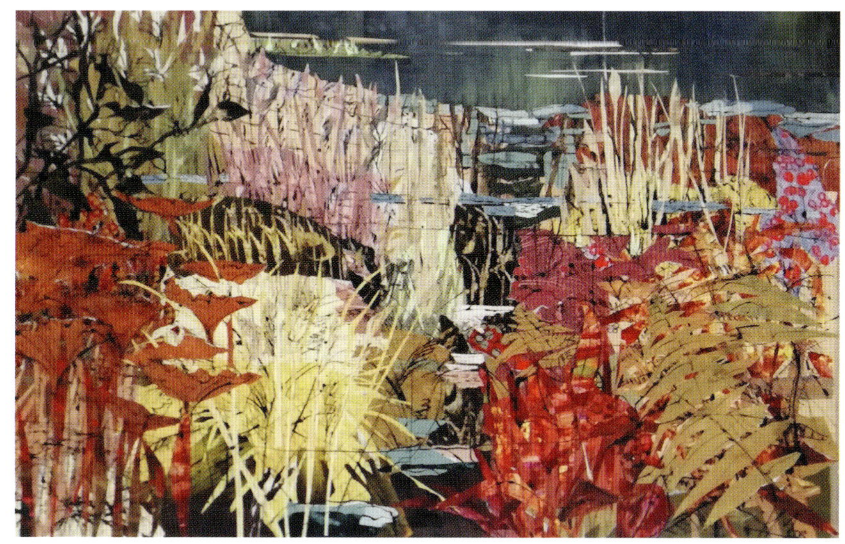

November Rockery border

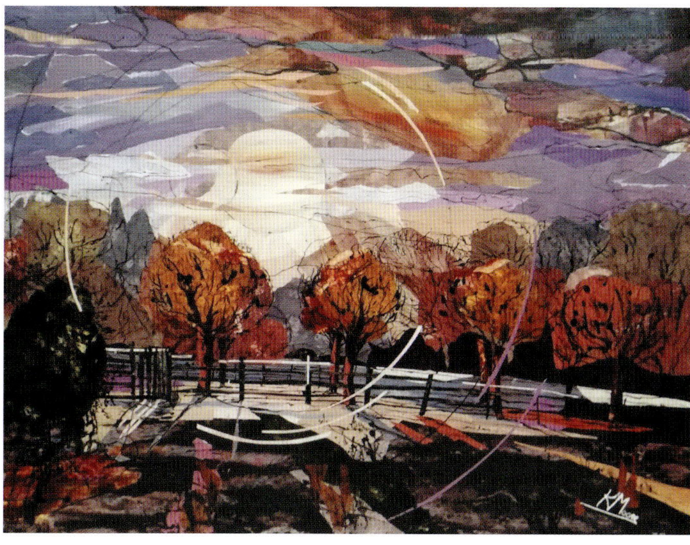

November Beaver Moon rising over Ridgebourne

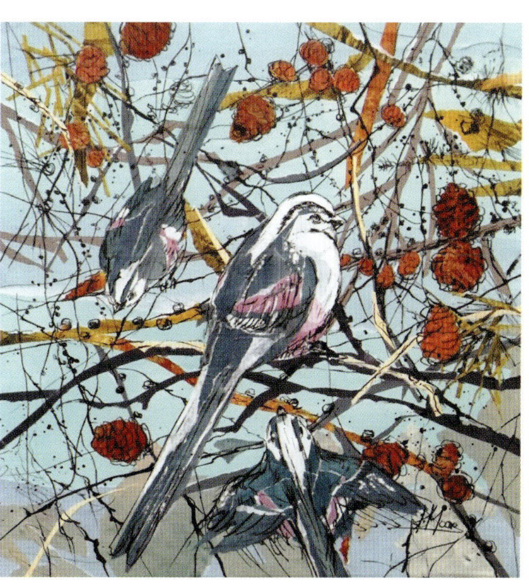

December Holly and Ivy

December Long-tailed tits in Larch

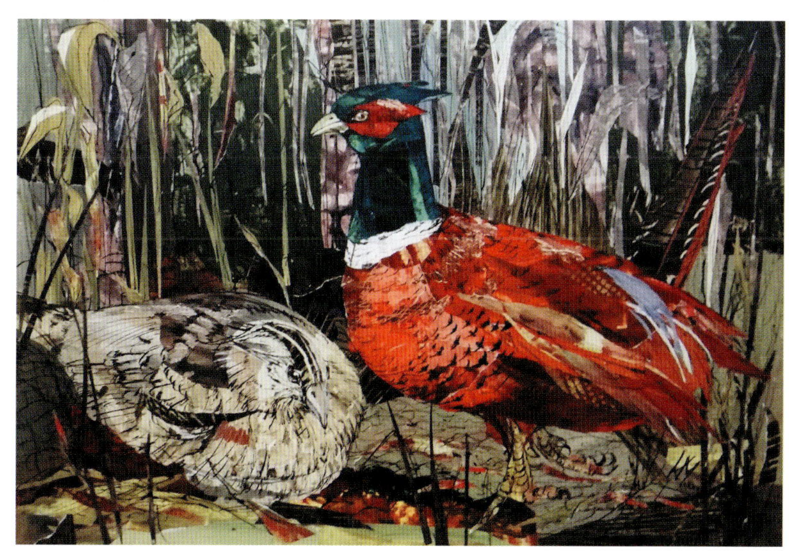

December Pheasants

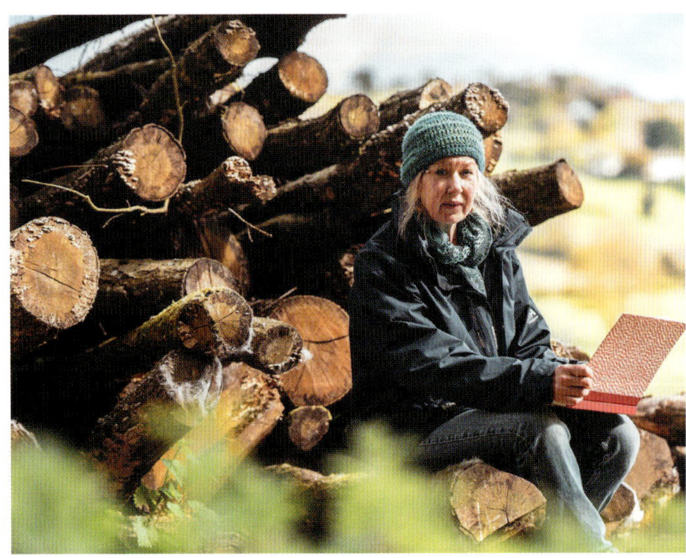

photograph © Paul Harris

KATHRYN MOORE studied Fine Art at the University of the South West of England, specialising in painting. She has worked abroad, which resulted in two major solo shows: 'Travelling Light – The Australian Experience' and 'Colour Ways – Journeys across Continents' in the UK. Kathryn now lives in Herefordshire, with the Welsh border being the predominant subject for her paintings.

www.kathrynmoore.co.uk